LIFE IN THE
FARCE LANE

LIFE IN THE FARCE LANE

or

Tragedy with its Trousers Down

The A to C (Aristophanes to Cooney)
of Farce

by

Brian Rix

With additional scenes by Jonathan Rix
and decor by David Drummond

ANDRE DEUTSCH

First published in Great Britain in 1995 by
André Deutsch Limited
106 Great Russell Street
London WC1B 3LJ

ISBN 0 233 98936 6

CIP data available for this title from
the British Library

Printed in Great Britain by
St Edmundsbury Press, Bury St Edmunds, Suffolk

WITH A LITTLE HELP
FROM MY FRIENDS

I would like to dedicate this book to the first Greek who slipped on a banana skin, the Roman who caught his toga in the wardrobe door, the dumb Italian lady who thought that *commedia dell'arte* was best eaten with a Paul Newman barbecue sauce, the Frenchman who believed that all men and women were adulterous and the Englishman – with his trousers round his ankles – who discovered that they are not . . . They helped to make this potted history of farce possible. But then, so did the following, some posthumously, some personally and some plagiarised:

POSTHUMOUSLY:

PERSONALLY:

Aristophanes	Farquhar	Ayckbourn
Menander	Fielding	Chapman
Plautus	Garrick	Cooney
Terence	Boucicault	Frayn
Molière	Pinero	Gale
Labiche	Travers	Marriott
Feydeau	Sylvaine	Morris
Udall	King	Prior
Shakespeare	Orton	Stoppard
Wycherley	Pertwee	Toksvig etc.

The greatest help, however, came from my younger son, Jonathan Rix (an award-winning author with *Some Hope*, also published by André Deutsch), who risked inhaling all those dust mites at the Garrick Club and the Theatre Museum, rooting around old books and papers, with the expert guidance of Enid Foster at the Garrick and Andrew Kirk at the Theatre Museum, in pursuit of the relevant facts and fiction. David Drummond, too, who must *exist* on a diet of dust mites in his emporium of theatrical memorabilia at 11 Cecil Court, off St Martin's

Lane, has, once again, produced a remarkable variety of historical pictures, all for your delight. Close by, in St Martin's Court, John Earl and David Cheshire of the Theatres Trust have been the joint coxswain of the lifeboat if ever I found myself not swimming but drowning.

May I thank you too, ladies and gentlemen, for attending this performance. Without you out there, we'd look pretty silly up here.

Brian Rix
1995

CONTENTS

PROLOGUE

PROLOGUES precede the piece — in mournful verse;
   As undertakers — walk before the herse;
Whose doleful march may strike the harden'd mind,
And wake its feelings — for the dead — behind.
To-night no smuggled scenes from France we show,
'Tis English — English, Sirs! — from top to toe.
Tho' coarse the colours, and the band unskill'd,
   From real life our little cloth is fill'd.

Written by Mr Garrick.
Spoken by Mr Woodward.

WHEN I THINK of all the philosophers and poets and pre-eminent personages who have pontificated about farce over the centuries, I feel a little like the eponymous Apprentice of the two-act piece by Arthur Murphy, whose work was graced by the above prologue, written by the great David Garrick himself. You will note he emphasises that the work ''Tis English — English, Sirs!' for the majority of farce writers pilfered their ideas from the French and neither Garrick himself, nor Murphy, were above such plagiarism. The habit continued until well into the late nineteenth century, and it is from that time on that I will concentrate much of this work. There are dozens of books which mull over all the various aspects of farce from Greek and Roman times (you can guess at the number by merely looking at the bibliography of the ones I've consulted – and the quantity from which I quote), but not many are written by the actor-manager concerned, who started losing his trousers for a living nearly fifty years ago, who knows what it's like to go on night after night, enduring good notices or bad notices, playing to happy laughing faces or Easter Island statues, standing room only

1

or acres of velvet and plush with ne'er a bum in sight – and who is (or was) a contemporary of a number of the masters – in other words, me. So I suspect my contribution to the canon will be more anecdotal than academic, but – I hope – nonetheless readable for that.

If Verdi and Mahler were not exactly the genesis of this book, they were at least progenitive in its publication and planning – which may seem odd, for *Stiffelio* at the Royal Opera House and Symphony No.6 in A minor at the Royal Albert Hall are unlikely bedfellows alongside farce. I will explain . . .

Until my resignation in June 1993, I was a member of the Arts Council (as well as being Chairman of both Drama and Arts and Disability) and therefore on 25 January of that same year I had been sent first night tickets for what was, in effect, the very first night of *Stiffelio* in this country. There were times when it was worth being on the Arts Council, with the added bonus of free tickets to the Opera House (£106 each for that performance) and especially if one was afforded the privilege and pleasure of seeing and hearing José Carreras in fine voice. But from my point of view, the evening was even more productive, for in the interval I ran into no less a personality than Tom Rosenthal, the Chairman and Managing Director of André Deutsch. Tom, too, was pitch perfect, and boomed across a crowded foyer to enquire if I was 'fecund and had any other books in my head' (Hodder & Stoughton had just published *Tour de Farce*). I mumbled something to the effect that I was and I had. When I told him it was an anecdotal history of farce, the deal was almost done on the spot – for Tom is nothing if not a theatre buff. It is I who am the buffo for, like all books, it might well be in the author's head, but not so easily transferred to the word-processor and it takes time to think of a beginning. Once out of the starting blocks, it's not too difficult – but inspiration and enthusiasm have to come together in perfect syncope, otherwise the screen stays blank.

So, the months passed by and I provided the usual excuses to myself for not getting on with the job: 'resignation from the Arts Council, chairing MENCAP, debating in the House of Lords' were all trotted out and there was no one to argue with me. Then, one glorious night in July at the Proms, the great soaring theme of the first movement of Mahler's Sixth echoing around the Albert Hall, I suddenly had my opening. Ludicrous really, for there was Mahler with his drama – virtually a life and death struggle – and there was I with my bit of a giggle, and the result, for better or worse, is this book. Perhaps it is understandable (well, to me, anyway), for both great music and simple farce perform the same awe-inspiring function – they uplift the spirit. The one with magnificent melody, the other with liberating laughter. In both cases you come out feeling better . . .

Towards the end of 1991 I was the guest of the New Zealand Government as 'A Living Treasure'. No, don't laugh – I was 'A Living Treasure'. Yes, I know that sounds like a joke but, in fact, the government asked about twenty of us from all round the world to visit both the North and South Islands to help celebrate the 150th anniversary of the Treaty of Waitangi, when we 'persuaded' the Maoris to become part of the British Empire. We were invited to lecture on subjects for which we had become identified. Audrey Hepburn spoke on UNICEF, whilst I contributed my thoughts and experience in the world of farce and mental handicap. Actually, the idea worked well – the only difference between us and the Living Treasures of Japan being fiscal. *They* are granted a large pension by a grateful state; *we* received much first class travel and a trip round the vineyards. Clearly, a good, but not a profitable, time was had by all.

I repeated the farcical part of the exercise early in 1992 for John Gale, who organises a British theatrical programme at the University of South Florida every February and March. Again, the lectures and workshops seemed to be popular, and the end result was my encounter with Tom Rosenthal at Covent Garden. Obviously I shall have to recount the history of farce, touching, however briefly, on Aristophanes, Plautus, Molière and the rest, but it is on British farce that I shall concentrate, beginning, naturally, with the Restoration in 1660.

As you can imagine, I have no desire to rehearse yet again my two autobiographies, *My Farce From My Elbow* and *Farce About Face*, or my tale of touring theatres and strolling players, *Tour de Farce* – although Whitehall Farce (and Garrick, too) will come into it, as will John Chapman, Ray Cooney and Michael Pertwee. However, it is clear that a number of playwrights (British, Irish and American) have written numerous farces over the past generation (or included farce techniques in their works) and a number of these authors are alive, thank God, and have been gracious enough to contribute a few welcome thoughts.

One final point. You will gather that this book will in no way be a polemic. There have been too many contributors to such

3

controversial discussions in the past. Here are a few to be going on with:

The Encyclopaedia Britannica: Farce is the form of the comic in dramatic art, the object of which is to excite laughter by ridiculous situations and incidents . . .

The Oxford Companion to the Theatre: Farce, an extreme form of comedy in which laughter is raised at the expense of probability, particularly by horse-play and bodily assault . . .

Thomas Wilkes (1759): Fit only to entertain such people as are judges neither of men nor manners . . .

Kenneth Tynan writing about Dry Rot: A play about horses, fit for donkeys . . .

And there are others, of course. Equally, there are many staunch allies of farce. Either way, I think you will find the Acts which follow illustrate the final verse of *The Apprentice*:

> Some play the upper, some the under parts,
> And most assume what's foreign to their hearts;
> Thus, Life is but a tragic-comic jest,
> And all is farce and mummery at best.

ACT I

Scene i: A Wood near Athens

As Tragedy prescribes to passion rules,
So Comedy delights to punish fools;
And while at bolder game she boldly flies,
Farce challenges the vulgar as her prize.
Some follies scarce perceptible appear
In that just glass, which shows you as you are:
But Farce still claims a magnifying right,
To raise the object larger to the fight,
And show her insect-fools in stronger light.

Prologue to *The Lottery* by Henry Fielding, Esq.
Spoken by Mr Cibber.

For once, the Greeks did *not* have a word for it. The source of 'farce' rests with the Romans – from *farcire*, 'to stuff' – and the French picked it up, originally, as a culinary delight – force-meat or stuffing for food generally. After that, 'farce' was adopted as a dramatic form in France at the end of the fifteenth century when the anonymous *Maître Pierre Pathelin* came into being, and which has gone on being produced in various guises ever since. 'Farce' as a descriptive dramatic term did not reach perfidious Albion until after the Restoration, but from 1660 it was in constant use, along with 'comedy' and 'burlesque', and often confused with both. Burlesque, by the way, has been downgraded by American films and 'burleycue' strip-tease, for it was originally immensely popular with its parodies of literary or dramatic works, together with its amusing imitations of the great and the good. Aristotle would have approved, even though the Greeks did not have a word for burlesque either, for

5

he mentioned 'the universal delight in works of imitation'. But I've been side-tracked . . .

The origin of farce in Britain is also allied to stuffing, for a farce was indeed stuffed with dialogue, verse, dance and song – and, in turn, was used as stuffing for the evening's dramatic events, with the traditional five-act drama being the centrepiece (as ordained by the neo-classic French disciples of Aristotle, who half followed his teachings and then dreamt up their own rule of the unity of time, place and action), surrounded by various fripperies which generally concluded with a short farce as an afterpiece. In due course, the curtain-raiser was often used for a farcical introduction as well, but farce, as such, was never intended to be the central core of the ever-lengthening evening's entertainment. Just like modern-day television programme controllers, theatre managers had to put on a diet of delights which would attract all manner of people, many of them coming in at half-time so that they could pay less, eat their hazelnuts (the popcorn of their time) and ensure they had a hearty laugh or two before facing the rigours of home life or the job the next day. Nothing changes . . .

Mind you, they could still enjoy a hearty laugh or two before the Restoration, but it would not have been described as a farce. Nicholas Udall's *Ralph Roister Doister* (based on a play by Plautus), as well as *Gammer Gurton's Needle*, ensured that laughter was available, but both followed the traditional dramatic form which applied to comedy – as did Shakespeare a little later, especially with *The Comedy of Errors*, also filched from Plautus. When farce did eventually appear, it was generally used to describe one ludicrous episode repeated with as many variations as possible. Comedy, being more formalised, was therefore seen as a somewhat superior creation. That superiority has continued through the ages, and was even displayed when Ray Cooney's last farce (at the time of writing) *It Runs In The Family* was originally billed as a comedy. The accurate description of its true worth only crept into the classified newspaper advertisements and displays outside the theatre when the critics raved about it as a 'farce'. Quite correctly, comedy was never mentioned again.

So what word *did* the Greeks have for it? Well, none that I can find. They had *komos*, meaning 'a revel', which is pretty close, and a *komikos*, who would appear in a *komoidia*. I don't have to translate that surely? Drama (*dramatos*) meant 'a thing done' and theatre (*theatron*) meant 'a seeing place', but audiences were not described as such until the Romans came along with *audientia*, meaning 'those who listen'. All quite straightforward really, if you can make head or tail of all those funny Greek squiggles.

Modern drama, whether serious, comedic or musical, is expected to entertain, even if the playwright's message is of serious intent. However, in Greek and Roman times – and later, too – both drama and comedy were rooted in religious rituals and we were well into the Middle Ages in this country before secular drama took over from ecclesiastical plays. That doesn't mean to say you couldn't have a laugh or two along the way. Indeed, when you think of all the opportunities afforded by those early dramatic festivals of Dionysus, the Greek god of nature, fond of the odd glass or two of Wincarnis, you can see why tragedy – ending with burlesque, plus the appearance of the libidinous and lewd Satyrs, with their ears, tails and other wobbly bits the size of a horse – was greeted with many a titter, indeed, whoops of delight, from a deliciously shocked bunch of Athenians.

Actually, the Spartans are reputed to have been messing about with burlesque at roughly the same time as their Athenian opposite numbers. Again fertility rites were involved and the revellers often wore animal or bird masks – with the inevitable phalluses. Offering a mixture of singing, dancing and scurrilous ribaldry, these masquerades beget, as it were, our interest in the next stage of Greek drama – Old Comedy.

Old Comedy (*c.*435–405BC), like those performances in Sparta, was a riotous burlesque and criticism of current personalities and movements in political life, all clearly visible today in the plays of its greatest writer, Aristophanes. Old Comedy then merged into Middle Comedy, which was still satirical, but quieter, more coherent and with a social rather than a political background. This, in turn, gave way to New Comedy, which ended in 292BC with the death of its leading exponent, Menander, who specialised in a delicate, sometimes sentimental, comedy of manners. Indeed, his work could well have foreshadowed that of Molière or Congreve.

Old Comedy exhibits a series of strictly formed scenes and, to quote the *Oxford Companion to the Theatre*, 'the chorus enters; there is a dispute between the chorus and an actor, or between two actors each supported by a semi-chorus; there is a formal "contest" (*agon*) or debate; and finally an address made by the chorus direct to the audience (the *parabasis* – "coming forward"). All this, but especially the *parabasis*, tends to be elaborately symmetrical in structure, and the contest is usually composed in metres other than the iambic trimeter of ordinary dramatic dialogue.' There were also scenes for actors alone preceding the entry of the chorus and following the *parabasis*. The *Oxford Companion* goes on: 'Old Comedy was a unique mixture of fantasy, criticism, wit, burlesque, obscenity, parody, invective, and the most exquisite lyricism. Today much of it would be obnoxious to the laws of libel, blasphemy, or indecency, and of the rest, a great deal would be rejected as too "high-brow".'

There were drama awards even in those days. The first contest for comedy was in 486BC, fifty years after the first contest for tragedy. Early 'masters', according to Aristotle, were Chionades, Magnes, Cratinus and Crates. Lampooning continued well into the fourth century – there is a story that during Aristophanes' *Clouds*, Socrates stood up so that the audience could compare him with his masked representation on stage. Crates deserves a mention, for he was the first to abandon scurrilous satire and attempt 'generalised plots'.

However, the works of Aristophanes are those which have come down through the centuries, many to be enjoyed to this very day. Their titles alone should remind you: *The Archarnians, Knights, Clouds, Wasps, Peace, Birds, Lysistrata, Thesmophoriazousae* (Women at the Festival). His last three plays, *Frogs, Ecclesiazousae* (Women in Parliament) and *Plutus* (Wealth) mark his transition to Middle Comedy. The plot grew, the chorus shrank, the parabasis went and there was more dramatic illusion. After that – New Comedy.

Strangely enough, New Comedy became the model for Roman Comedy, possibly because it used stock characters such as the testy old man and the interfering slave. Plautus certainly used the latter character to good effect.* And who were the actors during all these gay goings-on? Well, all men to begin with and there was class-distinction even in those days. Tragic actors never mixed with their lesser brethren, the *momikos* (as I've already ruefully written, nothing changes), and I'm not even sure if they were able to join the Attic version of the British Actors' Equity Association, the Craftsmen

---

* Burt Shevelove, Larry Gelbart and Stephen Sondheim also used the interfering slave when they wrote *A Funny Thing Happened On The Way To The Forum* – in turn quarried from Plautus – and featuring Zero Mostell on Broadway, with dear departed Frankie Howerd over here as Pseudolus, the slave to Hero. But just to show the classical upbringing of our film and television producers, Roman Comedy (as written by Plautus) inspired any number of productions featuring Frankie Howerd in *Up Pompeii* and similar punning titles.

of Dionysus. A much more glamorous nomenclature, don't you think? Maybe the *komikos* could sign up with the Athenian Variety Artistes' Federation, just like their opposite numbers over here, but I bet they weren't able to act as diplomatic envoys to other Greek states, like their fellow tragedian thespians. Mind you, things seem to have improved nowadays: our leading serious actor, Laurence Olivier, ended up in the House of Lords, as did one of our leading comic ones – me – so we must be a more egalitarian society. But after two-and-a-half thousand years, I should jolly well hope so.

Before we move on to more modern times, the Roman Theatre, one final word about Greece. Already mentioned on several occasions in this book is the name Aristotle. Why was this Greek philosopher and scientist so important to the theatre and why was he able to influence our theatrical thinking even up to Shavian times? After all, he did live a long time ago (384–322BC) and drama was very different in those days. Well, he wrote *Poetics*, which analysed the function of tragedy (his work on comedy was lost), together with its structural principles, and his views and strictures were carried forward further in Roman times by no less a disciple than the celebrated poet, Horace, who followed Aristotle's *Poetics* with his own version, *Ars poetica*. In this, Horace maintained that no respectable playwright could possibly construct a play of any worth that did not contain five acts and this was slavishly followed throughout the centuries. This often made it very difficult for writers of comedy, but there were only murmurs of criticism from time to time (Henry Fielding and Samuel Johnson had the odd grumble) until George Bernard Shaw announced it was all a load of old malarkey, or words to that effect, and the practice was dropped. However, as early English farce was of a shorter duration than the prescribed five acts, it was not considered to be of sufficient importance to occupy a full evening's entertainment – and once again we are back to class-distinction, which is where we came in.

When in Rome nick most of your work from the Greeks, could well have been the motto of the majority of late BC and early AD Roman playwrights who specialised in what we now call farce. Or think of all the revels which took place at harvest festivals around the Empire or the rude masked performances given by the Oscan inhabitants of Campania and take them to Rome under the title of *fabula Atellana* – in other words a fable from Atella, which was a small town on the road to Naples – and you have as many plots as you could possibly need to keep the voracious Roman citizens entertained.

9

If you failed, they simply walked out on you and turned their attention to all the rope-dancing and gladiatorial contests which were on offer and waited for you to filch another, more popular, plot, translate it into Latin and transmute it into box-office gold for, rest assured, like their modern-day counterparts, farce writers could make a great deal of money.

The most successful of these was the aforementioned Plautus, who is credited with no less than 130 plays in his time although, like Shakespeare, the authorship of some of these is disputed; but if we can't get it right four hundred years ago, what hope have we of being absolutely sure about the works of a playwright who lived in the first century BC? We don't even know when he was born or when he died with any degree of certainty. However, we do know that Plautus liked complicated plots, clearly-drawn characters, scenes of love-making, revelry, trickery and debauchery, was fond of puns, repartee and topical allusions and must be seen as the Ray Cooney of his time. Unlike Cooney, however, he also added songs when he felt the urge and was free to write about brothels in three unpronounceable plays: *Bacchides, Pseudolus* and *Truculentus*. I can't think 'Chase Me Bacchides!', 'Move Over Pseudolus' or 'Run For Your Truculentus' would look too good on a latter-day front-of-house, do you? Neither do I think a bawdy piece about a knocking-shop, which was the plot of all three plays, would match Cooney's style – although, quite recently, the Americans had a go with *The Best Little Whorehouse in Texas*; but then, to misquote Miss Mandy Rice-Davis, 'they would, wouldn't they!' Furthermore, although Cooney has been pretty consistent with his output of farces over the last thirty-odd years, Plautus's output was even greater. Mind you, plays in those days didn't run quite as long as they do now – probably because they were performed in the morning when any self-respecting Roman theatregoer was tickling his throat with a feather to get rid of last night's orgy of over-indulgence.

Only one other name of importance in the world of Roman comedy has come down to us over the centuries – Terence, full name Publius Terence Afer. We even know, roughly, the year he was born – 190BC – and the year he died, a young man still, in 159BC. To quote the *Oxford Companion to the Theatre* again: 'Throughout his plays we find an atmosphere of culture and refinement.' Six have come down to us, rejoicing in such titles as *Eunuchus* ('improving' on Menander's version of the same play), *Adelphi, Hecyra* (translated as the 'Mother-in-law' – shades of many farces to come), *Phormio,*

Andria and – wait for it – *Heautontimorumenos*, meaning, literally, the self-tormentor. As the *Oxford Companion* states: 'The contrast with Plautus is complete; there are few jokes and no buffoonery or topical allusions or irrelevancy; we find ourselves in a world which is not strikingly Greek or Roman, but independent of place and time. . . the greater freedom of women in Rome made it possible to develop the love interest.'

Terence's charm made his plays very popular until well into the Middle Ages, being taught in the schools, with *Phormio* performed by the boys at St Paul's in 1528. Furthermore, this interest continued up to the Renaissance, especially in France, with Molière basing his 1661 play, *L'École des maris* on *Adelphi* and his 1671 work, *Les Fourberies de Scapin* on *Phormio*. Aristotle, too, was extremely popular at that time and would surely have approved of Terence's works, especially the famous line: 'I am a human being and think all human affairs are my concern.'

But before we take another look at theatre in Rome with the *commedia dell'arte* or in Paris with the *Comédie-Française*, let's scoot around some other members of the human race and see what else was going on in the world of comedy.

ACT I

Scene ii: All the world's a stage

All the world's a stage,
And all the men and women merely players:
They have their exits and their entrances;
And one man in his time plays many parts . . .

As You Like It by William Shakespeare

GERMANY

Hans Sachs (1494–1576) wrote comedies that contained much broad, even crude, humour. From the late 1500s there was an influx of 'English comedians' and then, after the Thirty Years' War, an archetypal German buffoon known as Hans Wurst, Picklehering, Harlekin etc., based on the English fool, ruled the comedy stage. Even now, English farce is still very popular in Germany. A quid pro quo really, for – incredible as it might seem – it was a German farce by Von Moser, translated by Charles Hawtrey as *The Private Secretary*, which began English farce as we know it today, just over a hundred years ago, in 1884.

HOLLAND

A playwright with a name which would occupy most of the available space on a playbill was responsible for the first stirrings of farce in dear old Dutch – Gerbrand Adriaanszoon Bredero (1585–1618). I'm not surprised he died so young. Exhausted, I should think, from writing out the title pages of his works, which started as comic interludes but expanded into farces. In the next century Pieter Langendijk, a writer more akin to Molière (and influenced by him), appeared and brought some comedic zeitgeist to Zeeland, Zoom, Zwalle, Zeist, Zaandam and all Ztations north of Zohlscheid. Oh dear, old habits die hard. Funny foreigners were always good for a giggle in Whitehall farce . . .

DENMARK

I can't say that Denmark is particularly renowned for its farcical output. All right for butter and bacon, but not so productive when it comes to burlesque. However, the Danes did once provide a platform for a Norwegian latter-day Molière, one Baron Ludvig Holdberg, who wrote thirty-three comedies, the initial one being performed at the opening of the first theatre in Denmark in 1722. Apart from Molière, he was also influenced by the *commedia dell'arte* – but then, so was Molière. About one hundred years later, a certain Henrik Hertz wrote middle-class comedies and farces which were considered to be very entertaining. Nowadays, like many of the northern European countries, Denmark relies heavily on translations of modern English farces.*

NORWAY

As theatre did not really concern the Norwegians until almost the nineteenth century, it's not altogether surprising that their farce writers are not exactly thick on the ground. As already mentioned, they lost their best comedy writer, Baron Ludvig Holdberg, to the Danes a century before and then were only able to come up with one other, who concentrated on burlesque rather than farce, Johan Herman Wessel. Mind you, the Norwegians did produce Henrik Ibsen, so they can't be all that bad – just not particularly good at farce.

---

* One of our authors, John Chapman, told me that he received more royalties from Germany, alone, than he ever did from the post-London productions of his plays in the United Kingdom. There was a time when British farce was the staple diet of the Repertory movement – if you wanted to make money, that is. Now the audiences are, shall we say, more discerning, for unless it's done with great expertise, farce can be diabolical and there just aren't enough good farceurs to go round. I once went to see *Reluctant Heroes* performed by the Harry Hanson Players in Bridlington, just after we had completed its four-year run at the Whitehall Theatre. I hardly recognised it. If I hadn't known the dialogue, I wouldn't have done. Even that was shouted incorrectly for most of the evening.

SWEDEN

The Swedes did go in for drama, certainly after the Reformation. However, like their other Scandinavian cousins, farce did not come easily to them. Olaf von Dalin and Count Carl Gyllenborg produced some plays of comedic worth, but everyone pales into insignificance when compared with August Strindberg, although I can't recall any of his plots being exactly farcical. Put them in the right hands, though, and they could have been, mark my words. I mean his *Kammarspel* is described as a 'chamber play'. W-e-l-l, just imagine what you could do with that for a start. John Chapman and I once produced the banquet scene from the well-known Scottish play for a Green Room Rag, way back in the fifties. The laughs we got out of that had to be heard to be believed. Mind you, as the Thane of Cawdor, I did sit on a whoopee cushion just in time for Lennox to say 'What is't that moves your highness?' To which I replied 'Which of you have done this?' Then came a worried chorus from the assembled Lords, 'What, my good lord?' and I angrily responded 'Thou canst not say I did it', whereupon a distressed Ross – holding his nose – chimed in with 'Gentlemen, rise; his highness is not well.' You see, it's easy if you don't mind being scatological.

SPAIN

Lope de Rueda (*c.*1510–1565) was greatly impressed by Plautus and brought comedy to the people, side-stepping the church and the aristocracy in the process. In more recent times, the one-act play became very popular with its mixture of music, caricature and farce. Ricardo de la Vega and Tomas Luceno led with this form of simple entertainment, which was really going back to the curtain-raiser and afterpiece of olden days. The biggest laugh I ever had in Spain was when a Japanese Carmen was belting out Bizet in a bull-ring near Malaga, the heavens opened and all her carefully applied Andalucian make-up cascaded down her face. She looked like a mint humbug.

PORTUGAL

For a country which has a proud record in literature, Portugal is not particularly well known for its drama. Francisco de Sa de Miranda did produce some classical comedy, based on the works of Plautus and Terence and there are others who dabbled in contemporary comedy, but nothing which falls into the category of farce. You have to take a trip to Brazil to find a Portuguese-speaking nation which revels in locally written and produced farces. In fact, it is said – by those who know – that farce is top of the pops for Brazilian theatregoers.

POLAND

Like many European countries, ecclesiastical drama in Poland was the forerunner of secular plays, but from the late sixteenth century popular farces were the order of the day. They became more respectable and codified two hundred years later, when Count Alexander Fredro (1793–1876) was acknowledged as the father of Polish comedy, which delighted audiences firmly under Russian domination. Alas, the Second World War put paid to the Polish theatre entirely and farce has not been the main objective for the talented young writers who emerged from all that frightfulness.

CZECHOSLOVAKIA

I've never read one, or even seen a translation but, after the usual religious dramas, mediaeval farces led to the beginnings of modern Czech theatre early in the nineteenth century. This, in turn, led to the first playwright ever to become a President, although Poland once had a pianist, Paderewski, who attained that high office. I fear that the Czechs are now divided from the Slovaks – but I imagine they will still all enjoy Vaclav Havel's plays. Two-for-the-price-of-one takes on a new meaning, doesn't it?

RUSSIA

The Russians were somewhat late starters in theatrical terms, compared with many of their European neighbours, due mainly to the hostility of the Church and the fact that only the aristocracy were literate in any shape or form. But as they preferred to speak in French, as opposed to their native tongue, being a local Russian dramatist would hardly keep you in the style to which you had not become accustomed. You couldn't read or write anyway, so it would have been quite difficult to get your message across. As a result, French and German imports were the only offerings for many a long day, whilst local entertainment took the usual form of rough-and-ready farce and a veritable rash of performing bears. As you only had to go outside the door of your semi-detached hovel to catch one snuffling around the dustbins, there was no shortage of those. Eventually, there was no shortage of Russian playwrights either, once the creative spirit was liberated. Even Catherine II tried her hand at writing plays but I don't think Gogol, Tolstoy, Pushkin and Turgenev would care to be known as farceurs, although Chekhov certainly managed a load of laughs, from time to time. So did Michael Green with his *Art of Coarse Acting* version of a Chekhovian play. When the tap fell off the samovar, I thought I would never stop laughing. The tea kept on pouring out, too.

PERSIA

Persians did enjoy many a chuckle in the old days with their version of *commedia dell'arte*, but now they are Iranians I'm not so sure.

CHINA

The Chinese do have a form of home-grown farce, rather as our curtain-raisers used to be, and strangely enough these plays bear the closest resemblance to our own Western theatrical ways. Once Hong Kong is absorbed back into China I wonder if Derek Nimmo's hotel productions will become the rage of Peking?*

INDIA

Not much native farce, I fear, but quite a number of pirated versions of contemporary British ones are on display. When I was last there, in 1990, I saw *Run For Your Wife* advertised in Calcutta, or Bombay, I'm not quite sure which, but when I checked this with Ray Cooney, he had absolutely no idea about any of his plays being performed on the sub-continent. Mind you, it was an odd choice for an Indian production. A taxi-driver bigamously involved with two women is the plot. The taxi-driver I can understand – all those Morris Oxfords careering around the place, never mind the moped rickshaws – but bigamy? I know they've changed the rules a bit but

---

* Derek Nimmo tours West End farces around hotels in the Middle and Far East – very profitably.

16

surely 'Run For Your Wives' might have meant more out there. It would in Pakistan, that's for certain.

AMERICA

I have confined this book to the ancestry of British farce, not English-speaking farce, for if I had followed the latter course there would have to have been a vast amount of space devoted to the American version of the genre; what is more, you would have given yourself a hernia just picking up the book. Oddly enough, a General and a General's wife were the first American farce writers when Mercy Warren, the wife of General Warren, wrote *The Blockheads* as an answer to General Burgoyne's satirical farce *The Blockade of Boston*.

But it was Charles Hale Hoyt (1860–1900) who brought neighbourhood American types into his comedies and farces, and it has gone on from there ever since, with an interminable stream of situation comedies now occupying the world's television screens, wall-to-wall, almost twenty-four hours a day. Many of them are poorly-written farces about the length (and substance) of the curtain-raisers and afterpieces of old, seemingly based on Mr Hoyt's theory that recognising your 'local' characters was all that was necessary to get reflex laughs from a supine audience. Many a couch-potato would vouch for that.

Born some eighteen years after Charles Hoyt, George M Cohan left vaudeville and began to write farces and comedies before blossoming out into one of the most successful showmen of all time. From this book's point of view, *It Pays To Advertise* by Roi Cooper Megrue and Walter Hackett (the latter also wrote and presented *The Way To Treat A Woman*, the play which opened the Whitehall Theatre on 29 September 1930) is perhaps one of his more interesting productions, for he presented it at his own theatre, the 'George M Cohan' in 1914 and it was only after the First World War that it arrived in London, being the first Aldwych farce to be produced at that theatre on 1 February, 1924 (four days after I was born!). Now I know you will all be thinking I have made a mistake, but I haven't. *Tons of Money*, by Will Evans and Valentine, which preceded *It Pays To Advertise* at the Aldwych, actually was first produced at the old Shaftesbury in 1922, before transferring to the Aldwych in the October of that year. And while we are meandering down memory lane, perhaps I should record that a famous old American farce, *Nothing But The Truth*, by James Montgomery, was produced in New York at the Longacre Theatre in 1916, came to the Savoy Theatre in London two years later and was the first play I chose to present on my debut as an actor-manager on Easter Monday, 1948. But not at the glamorous Longacre or Savoy. No – my version was launched at the King's Hall, Ilkley. And if not exactly without my hat at the end of a disastrous season on 'Ilkla' Moor', I was certainly without much money.

After George M Cohan came another George, George Kaufman, with his clever farce, *The Butter and Egg Man*. Then he collaborated with Moss Hart and the words and the plays flowed out: *Once In A Lifetime, Merrily We Roll Along, You Can't Take It With You* and *The Man Who Came To Dinner* entertained audiences around the world in the thirties, on a par with George Abbott's *Three Men On A Horse* and Joseph Kesselring's *Arsenic and Old Lace*. Ben Hecht and Charles MacArthur collaborated to bring us *The Front Page*, as did Howard Lindsay and Russel Crouse when they wrote *Life With Father*. It was a glorious period of brilliant satirical writing, generally in the guise of comedy, but with many farcical overtones clearly present.

Since the Second World War, we have had one American farce (and billed as such) which has achieved great fame and fortune, first as *The Matchmaker* by Thornton Wilder (who took a leaf out of the play *Einen Jux will er sich machen* by Austrian dramatist Johann Nestroy) and then as the musical *Hello, Dolly!* with Carol Channing on stage and Barbra Streisand on film. After the American versions came Tom Stoppard's *On the Razzle* – but each and every one of these entertainments was sired by nineteenth-century playwright and critic, John Oxenford, with his original (how original is original?) play, *A Day Well Spent*.

Certainly original, inasmuch as they were largely written from personal experience, have been the brilliant comedies of Neil Simon, with one or two straying from comedy to farce, as in *Come Blow Your Horn, Plaza Suite* and *The Odd Couple*. Woody Allen, too, contributed a couple of farces to the theatre, before he concentrated on the cinema, *Play It Again, Sam* and *Don't Drink the Water*, whilst Garson Kanin brought us *Born Yesterday* – but all these plays were billed as comedies. Even across the pond, the old class-distinction remains.

It is in the world of films that America produced its greatest farces and farceurs, although two of these – well, three if you count Bob Hope – were British, Charlie Chaplin and Stan Laurel. Then there was Harold Lloyd, Buster Keaton, Ollie Hardy, Abbott and Costello, Fatty Arbuckle, Lucille Ball, Jack Benny, George Burns, Eddie Cantor, W C Fields, Mickey Rooney, Will Rogers, the Marx Brothers and, of course, the marvellous anthropomorphic cartoon farces begun by Walt Disney. (I say 'begun by' even though I saw Felix the Cat before Mickey Mouse.) The list is endless, and if I've infuriated you with its length, or because I've left someone out, I can only apologise.

Goodness me, I haven't even started on Italian or French theatre yet, and as they are essential ingredients in the ancestry of British farce I'd better deal with them right away. Please remain seated for Act I, Scene iii.

ACT I

Scene iii: A very common market in Rome and Paris

'When in Rome live as the Romans do:
when elsewhere, live as they live elsewhere.'

St Ambrose, Bishop of Milan,
offered this advice to St Augustine.

OLD AMBROSE got it about right when it came to local folk drama and festivals, for they remained pretty individual, but in terms of comedy and tragedy, Rome's influence went on for many a year – as did that of Athens.

Nevertheless, by 500AD drama in the far-flung Roman Empire was on its last legs, as was the Empire, and in constant conflict with the Christian church, whilst Juvenal's statement at the beginning of the millenium, *'Duas tantum res anxius optat, Panem et circenses'* was becoming ever more prophetic as far as the Church's attitude was concerned. Let me translate – and extrapolate – putting some of my words into Juvenal's mouth, as it were: '[The Church] limits [the Roman people's] anxious longings to two things – bread, and the games of the circus.' Those anxious longings did not translate into action though, and crumbled away with the Republic. Hardly surprising, really. After all, the early Christians were not too keen on the games of the circus, for assorted martyrs had been used as a sort of Pedigree Chum for the lions over quite a long period. Either that, or Whiskas, according to taste.

For the next thousand years, liturgical drama was the order of the day, with the usual exceptions of rustic farce, minstrels, tumblers and the like. Then came *commedia erudata*, written comedy, based on the classical works of Plautus and Terence, and *commedia dell'arte*, improvised comedy stemming, in the main, from stock masked characters and which left its future mark on the harlequinade of pantomime (once a serious rival to farce in England), on the Punch and Judy show (which we enjoyed so much in my youth on the freezing East Coast beaches) and, by a circumlocutious route through France, on farce. Incidentally, Harlequin and Punch started their theatrical lives as comic servants known as *dei zanni*, although the modern word of zany would hardly describe their antics in current comedy. *Dell'arte* is more difficult to translate but indicates that those taking part – including actresses – were, indeed, professional entertainers. Two other words I had better mention, which came from the same source and which are freely used by academics when they write about farce, are *burle*, meaning horseplay and *lazzi*, meaning stage 'business'. All the published versions of the Aldwych farces have the abbreviation 'BUS' on pretty well every page. This indicates when one of the leading actors (generally Ralph Lynn) performed some intricate manoeuvre, often with a 'prop' – trying to get to sleep under a bedroom washstand or pouring out coffee into the sugar basin or splashing somebody with a soda syphon, then milking the business for as long as the audience continued to laugh – but which is never described in any detail for the succeeding actor to copy. That is because great farceurs can perform miracles of ingenuity with inanimate objects, such expertise generally being denied lesser mortals. Certainly Ralph Lynn would have used the word 'business' but I bet he had never even heard of *lazzi*. Nevertheless, your scholarly types continue to mention it as though it were common currency in rehearsal rooms. 'Gosh, Ralph. What a wizard bit of *lazzi*' doesn't ring true somehow, does it?

As already mentioned, *commedia dell'arte* had a great deal of influence on the French, as will be seen when we come to Molière in a moment or two, and became known in Paris as *comédie-italienne*, but in Italy it influenced two actor-playwrights whose work has come down to us over the last 400-odd years – 'Ruzzante' (the stage name of Angelo Beolco) and his friendly rival, Andrea Calmo. The end came about two hundred years later, with Carlo Gozzi writing scripts which mixed farce and fairy tale. He was making one last effort to keep *commedia dell'arte* alive in the face of the new comedy writing by Carlo Goldoni, but times were changing and it is Goldoni who is now the remembered playwright, with Robert Browning's sonnet

Two Harlequin scenes from the *commedia dell'arte*.

proudly displayed on his monument in Venice:

> Goldoni good, gay, sunniest of souls,
> Glassing half Venice in that verse of thine,
> What though it just reflects the shade and shine
> Of common life, nor renders, as it rolls,
> Grandeur and gloom? Sufficient, for thy shoals
> Was Carnival . . .

Goldoni was responsible for the first *commedia dell'arte* play to be staged when the actors neither wore masks nor improvised – which has come down to us today as *The Venetian Twins*. He still died in abject poverty in 1793. Forty years later, the Venetians honoured him. A little late, I fear, for his general health and well-being.

The greatest of latter-day Italian playwrights, and the most familiar as far as we are concerned, is Luigi Pirandello. However, the wit and brilliance of his dialogue could in no way be described as farcical, although he did write a pretty broad one-act play, *La Giara*, which has been translated into New York English. It's all about a load of Sicilian olive grove workers who break the farmer's new jar, call in the repairman, who gets stuck inside the jar as he mends it; he then has a row with the farmer about payment and how he can get out of the jar and ends up being freed as the jar is kicked down the hill by its irate owner and smashes against a tree.

Sounds pretty farcical to me but certainly not in the same vein as the works of Dario Fo, the best-known farce writer in modern Italy, rivalling in his anarchic style the works of Joe Orton. *Accidental Death of an Anarchist* and *Can't Pay? Won't Pay* are probably his most famous English translations, but the title *Trumpets and Raspberries* seems to sum up his attitude to farce rather neatly – or, rather, the attitude of many characters introduced by farce writers generally, i.e. blow your own trumpet and there will be plenty of others to blow you a raspberry. It used to be called burlesque. . .

The word 'burlesque' is of Italian origin, whilst 'farce' is of French. Quite right, too, for the French gave the world the first recognisable specimen of that particular art form as far back as 1470, when the *enfants sans souci* – the kids without a care in the world is as good a translation as any – presented the anonymous *Maître Pierre Pathelin,* and all of us who have followed that theatrical trend as a way of earning a living have those long-forgotten enfants to thank for that. At the same time, another mixed form of entertainment was being practised – neither farce nor burlesque – called a *sotie* (based on the French for 'fool'), but that has long fallen by the wayside. So why was it that the French were so far advanced in the world of farce? I can only think that the liturgical drama fell into secular hands somewhat earlier than in other European countries, even though the Feast of Fools (when junior clergy swapped places with their senior brethren for a day or two of horseplay) took place in all European Christendom. The French, however, came up with the *sociétés joyeuses*, young men-about-town, who organised the odd knees-up when the clergy were being ordered to desist, and as these bands had been together for a century or two before *Maître Pierre Pathelin*, it follows that they were light years ahead of their more sedate English and European neighbours when it came to farcical ribaldry. Well, that's my theory, and I'm sticking to it.

The groups who came together in Paris to perform Mystery, Miracle and Morality plays, plus *soties*, farces and the like, formed themselves into a single entity, called themselves the 'Confraternity of the Passion' and established themselves at a theatre known as the Hôtel de Bourgogne. What is more, they guarded their right to be the only actors around with a fierce determination, occasionally letting up to permit other companies to play at fairs around the outskirts of town, although they did allow one company to go to another theatre, the Hôtel d'Argent, on payment of a royalty. I mention all this, for farce was the staple diet of the Hôtel de Bourgogne, particularly in the hands of Turlupin, Gaultier-Garguille and Gros-Guillaume, but by the time Jean-Baptiste Poquelin arrived on the scene, tragedy was the order of the day and he had to go elsewhere to amuse the Parisian theatregoer.

Jean-Baptiste who? None other than the yet-to-be-great Molière. Mind you, he had a pretty auspicious re-entry as the new man in town, for although he had failed with his first company in Paris, being imprisoned for debt and having to work in the provinces for quite a time, his reappearance some years later was at no less a venue than the Guard Room of the Old Louvre in front of the King himself, Louis XIV. In the first play performed, Molière failed to impress but then he presented a short farce of his own, *Le Docteur amoureux*, and the rest is history. The King gave Molière permission to share two theatres, first the Petit-Bourbon and then the Palais-Royal with the resident *commedia dell'arte* company under the famous Scaramouche (who was actually an Italian, Tiberio Fiorelli) and thus the story that

Molière was greatly influenced by *commedia dell'arte* came about. Actually, it is likely that his years in the provinces had a greater effect on his writing, giving him a wry, though affectionate, view of the foibles of human nature.

Incidentally, I visited one of those provincial towns fairly recently – Pézenas, near Montpelier. Molière is everywhere! The good citizens know a first-class tourist attraction when they see one: it wouldn't have surprised me to see his name plastered all over the most anachronistic business enterprises: the Molière TV, Radio & Video Shop, Colonel Molière's Pézenas Fried Chicken and the like . . . but I didn't. On the contrary, when you enquire where he performed, a Gallic wave of the hand in the general direction of a square is the only reaction you get. No one I asked could be more accurate than that – until I visited the little museum, that is, dedicated to Molière and his works. It seems that Pézenas was the seat of the Estates General of Languedoc from 1456 to 1700 and as such it enjoyed an exceptionally active social and intellectual life, with an aristocratic and prosperous audience which greatly appreciated Molière's plays at the old Hôtel Alphonse in the years 1655 and 1656, whilst he lodged at the Maison du Barbier Gély. At least I found that out for myself, for the locals continued to be airily non-committal about the whole thing. However, they do make a reasonable Vin de Pays in the name of Molière, so everyone concerned (or, rather, not concerned) can keep drinking to his memory, even if they can't remember who he was. . .

When Molière moved with his company into the Paris Petit-Bourbon he was very much the junior partner, paying rent, with the Italians keeping the two best box-office nights, Tuesdays and Sundays, for themselves and allowing their French partner the rest of the week, when he concentrated on popular farce and his version of Italian knockabout. Such was Molière's success, though, that by the time the companies moved to the Palais-Royal the boot was on the other foot, and it was the Italians who were paying the rent. Of course, there will always be disagreement as to which of Molière's plays were true farces, satires or comedies of manners, so let me just name a few of his plays, to be going on with, which should satisfy all interested parties: *Le Bourgeois gentilhomme* (with music), *L'École des femmes*, *Les Femmes savantes*, *Le Malade imaginaire*, *Le Misanthrope*, *L'Avare* and *Tartuffe*, which was banned by royal decree for five years, following an outcry from the clergy for its debunking of hypocritical puritanism. Not a bad list, you must admit, and you can see why Monsieur

Poquelin had such an influence on both French and European theatre.

There were other writers in his company, naturally, but none achieved the status of Molière and after his death in 1673 at the age of fifty-one, the troupe amalgamated with the actors from the Théâtre du Marais (another fine theatre, concentrating on tragedy) and those from the Hôtel de Bourgogne, to form what eventually became the *Comédie-Française* – the National Theatre of France. As it was also known as the *Maison de Molière*, you can see that the great man's influence continued and burgeoned, as it does to this very day.

Ignoring Racine, who treated Molière pretty shabbily by nicking his actors, including his leading lady, Mlle du Parc (who also doubled up as Racine's mistress), and because he only wrote one comedy anyway, *Les Plaideurs*, which was based on Aristophanes' *Wasps*; side-stepping Voltaire, who concentrated on drama; by-passing Marivaux, who worked on a style called *marivaudage*, and not forgetting Beaumarchais who had the knack of having his plays turned into opera (*Le Barbier de Séville* and *Le Mariage de Figaro*), we come to a shuddering Pluto-like halt before the next great farce writer, Eugène Labiche (1815–1888).

Either in solitude, or with collaborators, Labiche wrote no less than 150 plays, all of them light comedies or farces. His work elevated French farce to an art-form which has only been bettered by Feydeau, who followed him. Modern writers of French farce are but pale echoes of these two masters, with an output that falls far short of them both. *Boeing-Boeing* by Marc Camoletti goes on and on in France, but that is probably more to do with the present-day economics of the theatre, rather than anything else, whilst Alfred Jarry with *Ubu Roi*, Eugene Ionesco with *Rhinoceros*, *The Bald Prima Donna* and *Macbett* plus Jean Genet with *The Balcony* (which takes place in a brothel – shades of Plautus, yet again), really only use farce techniques, from time to time, and would not, I imagine, enjoy being described as farceurs.

Strangely enough, only a handful of Labiche's plays are known in the English-speaking world, the most famous being *Le Chapeau de paille d'Italie* (1851), presented in New York before the Second World War as *Horse Eats Hat*, and over here in London after the war with the more literal title of *The Italian Straw Hat* and described by Eric Bentley in his book *The Life of the Drama* as 'one long pretext for flight and pursuit. So is the plot of that homely English imitation of French farce, *Charley's Aunt*.' The highly regarded nineteenth-century French critic, Francisque Sarcey, once wrote about a Labiche play that 'it was adultery treated lightheartedly'. You could never say that about *Charley's Aunt* – nor any other 'traditional' British farce before the 1960s. Until then, adultery was only hinted at, never the main subject of the evening, unlike those libidinous Latins. Thank goodness other highly-regarded Labiche titles such as *Le Voyage de M Perrichon* (1860), *Le Misanthrope et l'Auvergnat* (1852) and *La Poudre aux yeux* (1861) are still in their native French and this book is not. We can remain unsullied.

So, now for the granddaddy of them all – Georges Feydeau.

Feydeau was born in Paris on 8 December 1862, the son of a stockbroker who became an author best known for one novel, *Fanny*. Strangely enough, Ernest-Aime Feydeau (for that was the father's name) rated an entry in the 1962 edition of the Encylopaedia Britannica, whereas his famous son did not. But that was thirty-odd years ago; maybe matters have been put right since then. Georges wanted to be a dramatist from the moment he first went to the theatre at an age when he was still being visited by the tooth fairy. His father encouraged him, and as a lad he wrote copiously, which he turned to good effect when he left school in 1879, forming an acting group with his friends, and specialising as a mimic and the author of many a monologue, which were very popular in those days. Actually, they still were, recited by one or two comics, even in my day. Do you remember Stanley Holloway with 'Sam, Sam, pick up tha' musket' and Billy Bennett (Almost a Gentleman) reciting his version of 'The Shooting of Dan McGrew'? I can remember two lines only, but they give you the general gist: 'Icicles hung from his eyebrows/And bicycles hung from his nose.'

Between 1882 and 1886 Feydeau wrote four one-act plays, which showed his skill with dialogue, and had some success, too, with curtain-raisers. However, it was whilst on military service, in 1883, that he wrote his first full-length play *Tailleur pour dames*, called *Fitting for Ladies* when it was translated for BBC radio by Peter Meyer in 1968, with that excellent actor and farceur, Leslie Phillips, in the lead and Andrew Sachs lending valuable support. *Tailleur pour dames* took some time to be presented in France (like its radio counterpart over here) and Feydeau had to wait until 1887 for that great occasion, when it was received with much acclaim by critics and punters alike. Not altogether surprising, for it is a skilful piece, and a synopsis of the plot (see page 32) may well convince you of that as well, apart from helping you while away the interval which follows. As Eric Bentley wrote: 'The masters of French farce in the nineteenth century used incredibly elaborate plots, and it is often said of their plays that they are "all plot".' Just trying to describe one required deep intellectual study and fathoming it out for yourselves should keep you out of the bars all night.

In the next few years Feydeau wrote four full-length plays, one short play and a musical comedy, on his own or with others, and all of them failed. He married Marianne Caroles-Duran, the daughter of a popular painter, in 1889, and was divorced, four children and twenty-six years later – but not before he had cruelly lampooned her, though, in several of his plays.

At the end of 1892 he offered two plays to the management of the Palais-Royal Théâtre who took *Monsieur Chasse*, but refused *Champignol malgré lui*, believing it to be worthless. On his way back from the Palais-Royal he bumped into the manager of the Théâtre des Nouveautés, which was facing bankruptcy. He offered his rejected play to the said manager, it was accepted and achieved even greater success than *Monsieur Chasse*, which became a pretty hot ticket, too. Needless to say, the Théâtre des Nouveautés did not go bust, and exists as a 'boulevard' theatre to this very day.

After those two successes, Feydeau went from strength to strength with *Un Fil à la patte* (1894), *L'Hôtel du Libre-Echange* (1894), *Le Dindon* (1896), *La Dame de Chez Maxim* (1899), *La Duchesse des Folies Bergeres* (1902), *La Main passe* (1904), *La Puce à l'oreille* (1907) and *Occupe-toi d'Amélie*, subsequently adapted by Noël Coward as *Look After Lulu* but not very successfully, I fear.*

Feydeau was lazy, rose late, wrote plays to pay his Stock Exchange debts, spent his evenings until the small hours at Maxims and drank mineral water out of a champagne bottle. Even so, by 1911 he was finding it harder and harder to work and in that year he wrote the first

---

* According to Tony Richardson, who directed it at the Royal Court, Vivien Leigh was a distinct drawback in the leading role: 'Rehearsals were very sad. Vivien, great star though she was, hated acting. Playing a scene, losing herself, gave her no pleasure. She was in a state of perpetual anxiety. When *Lulu* opened, it was violently attacked by the critics. Noël and Vivien fought like cat and dog.'

However, in 1967, when I presented and played in the play on television as part of my agreement with the BBC, I am happy to report there were no fights with the author, long dead, nor the adaptor, Noël Coward – yet to be knighted and six years to go before joining Georges in the celestial Garrick. My wife, Elspet, received glowing notices as the result of her performance as Lulu.

Georges Feydeau.

two acts of a play which began rehearsal, but was never completed. Two years later, only one act of another new play was rehearsed, but that wasn't finished either. In 1914 he rewrote a play with a friend which was a reasonable success, as was his last one-act piece in 1916. Then the creative flame was extinguished, for Feydeau was now in the grip of tertiary syphilis and in 1919 his sons had to put him in a home. His condition deteriorated with what was then known as GPI – general paralysis of the insane – and at times he had the symptomatic delusions of grandeur, thinking he was Napoleon III and sending out invitations to his coronation. Tragically ironic, when you think about it, for Feydeau was fond of using physical disabilities in his plays to enhance the laughter. I doubt if he would have found much to laugh at in his own pitiful condition, though, and on 5 June 1921 he died.

He wrote twenty full-length plays, fifteen one-act plays, twenty-two monologues, two musical comedies. Eleven of these fifty-nine works were in collaboration with other authors. Strangely enough, for the best-known writer of farce of all time, he did not label his works as such – plays, comedies and vaudevilles being his favourite descriptions. Not quite as odd as it sounds, for vaudevilles originated as popular songs in the Vau de Vire in Normandy during the fifteenth century, but by the eighteenth century had become plays, often in dumb-show, accompanied by parodies of the, then, top of the pops. Eventually the musical side of the entertainments became operettas, whilst vaudevilles became attached to variety and works which we would now describe as slapstick farce. Georges Feydeau chose to be remembered by that homespun description of his life's work.

In the introduction to his translations of *Three Farces by Georges Feydeau*, Peter Meyer writes: 'Feydeau once told his son, Michel, that to make people laugh you have to place your cast in a dramatic situation and then observe them from a comic angle, but they must never be allowed to say or do anything which is not strictly demanded, first by their character and secondly by the plot. On another occasion, he told one of his collaborators to cut a line because it was witty and wit must never be used unless required by the play or it would interrupt the action.'

Ben Travers would have enjoyed that story, for his first farce, *The Dippers*, was being directed by Sir Charles Hawtrey three years before Ben moved into the Aldwych with *Cuckoo in the Nest*. Sir Charles, you will remember, was the actor who adapted the archetypal modern farce *The Private Secretary*, but some thirty

30

years later had just been knighted and was now busy cutting one of Ben's favourite lines. Ben piped up: 'Sir Charles – that line – must it go? I thought it was rather a good line.' Sir Charles lowered his pencil and raised his eyes to gaze upon this young whipper-snapper of an author: 'A good line?' he boomed, 'a g-o-o-d l-i-n-e? My dear fellow, it is an excellent line. One might even go so far as to say it is a veritable masterpiece of a line. On no account lose it. Put it in another play.'

Feydeau himself admitted that his plays were 'entirely improvised, the whole and the parts. The design and the shape all fall into place while I am writing. And I have never made a first draft.' He also stressed, 'I set about looking for my characters in living reality, determined to preserve their personalities intact. After a comic exposition, I would hurl them into burlesque situations.'

In revivals over the years, those burlesque situations have been refined by classical companies, and in England there have been a number of splendid adaptations. In 1956 came *Hotel Paradiso*, Peter Glenville's version of the Feydeau/Maurice Desvallières farce, *L'Hôtel du Libre-Echange*, with Alec Guiness in the lead. Then in 1966 came *La Puce à l'oreille*, translated by John Mortimer as *A Flea in Her Ear* and starring Albert Finney, whilst *An Absolute Turkey*, with Griff Rhys Jones and Felicity Kendal, was adapted from *Le Dindon* by Nicki Frei and Peter Hall in a successful, frenetic, 1993 production at the Globe. There have been others, as well, which have resulted in Feydeau being accepted as the finest French comic dramatist since Molière. I truly believe he would have been delighted just to be called the finest French writer of vaudevilles – or even burlesques. . .

CURTAIN

INTERLUDE

The Plot For *Tailleur Pour Dames – Fitting for Ladies*
by Georges Feydeau

MY SON JONATHAN, when helping me to research this book, read Peter Meyer's translation. He comments: 'This is a beautiful piece of farce writing. There is not a single joke that does not move on the plot. There is nothing but mounting tension, and developing options. Every joke feeds another dilemma, every problem generates the next, so that in the final dénouement it is a misread problem, that has driven so much of the confusion, which provides the solution.'

So, there you are. Let's see what he means. I must warn you, though, it's like a thousand-piece jigsaw. You empty the box out on the table and everything seems completely higgledy-piggledy and impossible. Bit by bit, though, as you study the small original picture, you are able to put the puzzle together. I fear this plot is like that. It needs careful study – don't read it as the bath is filling, otherwise you'll flood the entire house. Take it steadily and all will be revealed.

ACT I
THE DOCTOR'S APARTMENT

The doctor (Moulineaux) has not spent the night at home. He went out with a prospective lover (Suzanne) but got nowhere. He arrives back in his apartment after his wife (Yvonne) has discovered he has been away. She is furious, but he tells her that, as a dutiful doctor, he has been staying with a patient who is going to die. The patient (Bassinet), apparently hale and hearty, unexpectedly turns up – and we discover his wife (Rosa) left him many years ago, and he misses her deeply. Then the doctor's mother-in-law (Mme Aigreville) arrives and takes sides with her daughter. After a tiff with her son-in-law, the doctor (Moulineaux), she rents a flat from the patient (Bassinet) who tries to tell her (and anyone else who cares to listen) that the flat used to be rented to a dressmaker. Meanwhile the doctor rents the same flat so that he can enjoy his extra-marital relations in comfort. Then his prospective lover (Suzanne) makes her, equally unexpected, entrance – but is followed into the doctor's apartment by her husband (Aubin), whom she has told to wait outside for she wishes to speak to the doctor. The husband (Aubin), however, mistakes the servant (Etienne) for the doctor and the doctor for the servant. He realises his error and goes from bad to worse by mistaking the patient (Bassinet) for the doctor (Moulineaux) – confusion reigns and all is set for a vaudevillian second Act.

ACT II
THE FORMER DRESSMAKER'S FLAT RENTED BY THE PATIENT TO BOTH THE DOCTOR AND THE MOTHER-IN-LAW

The doctor (Moulineaux) and his lover (Suzanne) are together. The lover's husband (Aubin), who is meant to be waiting outside, comes up again, and mistakes the doctor for the dressmaker, who originally occupied the flat. The doctor is now known as 'Monsieur Oh' and is further confirmed as a dressmaker, in the cuckolded husband's mind, by former clients coming up to pay off old bills. The doctor's lover's husband (Aubin) leaves, and then the doctor's mother-in-law (Mme Aigreville) turns up to take occupancy of the flat. The patient (Bassinet) arrives to check on his new tenants, and while the doctor gets his mother-in-law out of the way, by telling her his lover (Suzanne) is actually his patient and this is her flat, the real patient (Bassinet) is telling the deceived husband (Aubin), who has turned up again with *his* lover (Rosa) to have a dress fitted by 'Monsieur Oh', that the doctor's mother-in-law is the 'Queen of Iceland'. This being a Feydeau farce, the husband's lover (Rosa) turns out to be an old friend of the doctor's, but the doctor's lover (Suzanne) now discovers her husband's lover (Rosa) and storms out, followed by her husband (Aubin) who pushes *his* lover (Rosa) over to the doctor, at which point the doctor's wife (Yvonne) arrives to meet her mother, but instead finds the doctor holding his lover's husband's lover (Rosa) in his arms, and she too storms out. The doctor (Moulineaux) heads off after his wife (Yvonne), passing his lover's husband's lover (Rosa) to his landlord (Bassinet), the patient, who has just entered and who discovers to his joy that the doctor's lover's husband's lover (Rosa)

33

is the wife who left him many years before. (Only we the audience already know this – so the coincidence is not worrying, for it is perfect logic.)

ACT III
THE DOCTOR'S FLAT

The doctor's lover's husband (Aubin) enters to see the doctor. He meets the doctor (Moulineaux), who he thinks is the dressmaker 'Monsieur Oh', and the doctor gets him to wait because his wife (Yvonne) and mother-in-law (Mme Aigreville) have turned up. The doctor persuades his wife he can be completely trusted and they make up, at which point the doctor's lover's husband (Aubin) reappears to find the doctor and his wife in each other's arms, except of course he thinks he is seeing the doctor's wife in the arms of the dressmaker. At this point the patient (Bassinet), who the doctor's lover's husband (Aubin) thinks is the doctor, turns up. The husband desperately tries to warn the 'dressmaker' (the doctor) that the 'doctor' (the patient, Bassinet) has arrived, but it is no good. All hell is going to break loose. But it doesn't. To the cuckolded husband's (Aubin's) horror the 'doctor' (Bassinet) thinks the 'dressmaker' (Moulineaux) and his own wife (Yvonne) make a lovely couple. The doctor's lover (Suzanne) now arrives, and is furious with her husband (Aubin) for his infidelity, so the husband (Aubin) tries to get the 'doctor' (Bassinet) to agree to take responsibility for the lover (Rosa) that we as the audience know is his long-lost wife anyway. And it is this unknown twist that allows both husbands to explain away their lovers as wives of the other men and get away with it. Of course as the play ends the husbands are both staggering from the discovery that the patient (Bassinet) really is married to the doctor's lover's husband's lover (Rosa), at which point the curtain falls.

So far in this book I have not dwelt on the rather esoteric definition of 'mask' and 'face' – appearance and reality – for they are essential elements in all forms of drama, but in Act III of *Tailleur pour dames*, the conflict between mask and face is used to perfection when the double bluff of 'doctor' and 'dressmaker' is confused in the mind of the deceived husband, Aubin. Circumstances have led Aubin to conclude that he is watching the 'dressmaker' (in reality, the doctor, Moulineaux) kissing the doctor's wife, Yvonne, but at no point could he have stopped those circumstances which have led him to this conclusion. It is at this moment that the absurdity of people's attempts to cover up for their actions is held up to the light by Feydeau with an irony that borders on genius. Lies have become absolute reality.

And, without a word of a lie, I have described – in absolute reality – the plot. You see how the jigsaw fits together?

I do hope your bath hasn't run over.

ACT II BEGINNERS, PLEASE.

ACT II

Scene i: An auditorium

'The Roman Conquest was, however, a *Good Thing*,
since the Britons were only natives at the time.'

1066 and All That by W C Sellar and R J Yeatman

L IKE OTHER European countries pulling themselves out of the primordial dramatic slime, it was some time before the Greco-Roman influence made itself known to our woad-painted ancestors. In fact, they were covering their goose-pimples with rudimentary clothing by the time they foregathered to provide the reception committee for Julius Caesar *et al*.

So, in the fullness of time, like the plague, the Romans arrived on these shores. Before that, the earliest performances involved ritualised dancing and singing, as well as the revered storyteller, and any amount of rude and rudimentary knockabout comedy, too, of that you can be sure. Dropping your loin-cloth must have been much more revealing than its eventual successor, a pair of trousers – but certain to get a laugh, just the same. After 55BC, though, things were different; if your hutted tenement happened to be near a Roman settlement, that is.

The Romans, acting as the sort of early ENSA (Entertainments National Service), decided to build some auditoria in Britain, but their theatre was largely about controlling the masses, through popular entertainment, not about furthering the names and royalties of Plautus, Terence and the like. A visit to the theatre at St Alban's illustrates the local Roman commander's interests perfectly, for at the

36

front of the stage is a slot from which a wooden shutter was raised to hide the stage between acts. This 'curtain' was partially to increase the element of dramatic surprise, but more to do with protecting the audience from the wild animals used in the performances. St Alban's, it would seem, had the first safety curtain in Britain, but I bet only the Brits were allowed near the front of the stage. The Romans wrapped themselves in their togas to keep out the beastly damp weather and moved out of harm's way, somewhere at the back. This type of theatre has, of course, not lasted – except in circuses, and the Roman influence is mostly felt through the Code of Theodisius made in 435AD which banned Sunday performances and is still causing problems for theatre managers, Equity and the Musicians' Union to this very day, never mind the Lord's Day Observance Society and keep Sunday Special.

As the Saracen hordes moved in from the East and the barbarians from the West, box-office takings dropped off alarmingly, so that by the sixth century the Roman theatres had all closed and the dramatic form was largely left to itinerant minstrels – jongleurs – and developing church ritual. The wanderlust of the performer has been evident since recorded time, and throughout the Dark Ages scholars and bards moved about the country educating, entertaining and joining in festivities. But, back in the churches, the priests kept battling on with liturgical drama, just as many do with Passion Plays in the Parish Halls of today. Unfortunately they had to stick to a formalised, Latin script which didn't go down too well with the illiterate masses and shafts of humour were very hard to come by. Eventually, though, the performances moved out of the churches into the churchyards, then – as the crowds grew – into the market-places and the Church's monopoly on theatrical entertainment was no more. The secular interest of the man-in-the-street began to be reflected in the dramatic offerings, with much broad humour chucked in for good measure. Farce, without being called as such, had come to stay.

Mind you, there weren't too many laughs in the Miracle and Mystery plays which dominated the Middle Ages. They were, in effect, stories taken from the Bible and were organised by the Trade Guilds operating in various towns all over Britain. The performers worked from sunrise to sunset on pageants, which were two-tiered four-wheel carts, with the stage on top and the dressing-room underneath. This hot little space also doubled as hell, when the nether regions were required (with farcical overtones provided by the Devil, who was a low comedian – no pun intended), and must have been very similar to many dressing-rooms built by later managers for their weary, perspiring players, especially if those same players had been belting it out – physically and vocally – in a rumbustious farce. The early fifteenth century saw the arrival of the Morality Plays, which had as their main characters various virtues and vices – Humility, Covetousness, Ignorance and the like – battling for the soul of man and taken very much to heart by the early Tudor audiences. A lighter version was on the way, though, with the Moral Interludes, very popular in the 1500s, for they allowed a reasonable ration of entertainment, along with all that soul-searching instruction. John Heywood (*c*.1497 – 1580) is perhaps the best-known author of these, which is not altogether surprising for he was a favourite at Court, having married Sir Thomas More's niece. His most famous play (presented at Court around 1520) has the longest and unfunniest title and trailer in the business: *The Play called the foure P.P.; a newe and a very mery enterlude of a palmer, a pardoner, a potycary, a pedler* who try to outdo each other in lying. Around that time – well, 1550 to be fairly precise – Nicholas Udall wrote *Ralph Roister Doister* whilst, approximately ten years later, appeared the anonymous *Gammer Gurton's Needle*. All these plays seemed to find favour at Court, as well as before audiences of lawyers and their cronies, in universities and schools and in the houses of the aristocracy. Thus the players – rogues and vagabonds to a gentleman – were under some form of protection. Rather, I imagine, as effective and bloody as being under the protection of the Mafia Godfathers.

Godfathers or not, it was about then that the quality of work started to improve and the London playhouses – first, the Theatre, then the Curtain and the Rose, followed by the Swan, the Globe and the Fortune – began to be built. The examples of the earlier plays we know tend to mix morality and history, whilst jumping rapidly between broad slapstick and messy tragedy. It was the appearance of writers like Christopher Marlowe (specialising in tragedy), John Lyly (specialising in comedy), Thomas Kyd (specialising in full-blooded drama) and William Shakespeare (specialising in everything) which really brought about the change. The language became more powerful and the settings more meaningful; the theatre was for everyone, and names were becoming known. When the King's Men went to Barnstaple in 1605 they received the highest amount ever paid by the corporation for one show, twenty shillings. This is not altogether surprising, for not only was Shakespeare still writing for the company, but its main attraction was Richard Burbage, the first in the immortal line of leading Shakespearian actors, with the main comic roles often undertaken by William Kempe, the original Dogberry in *Much Ado About Nothing*.

Shakespeare flirted with farcical characters more than farce itself, although several of his plays could possibly have been classed as such in their early productions. There are scholars who maintain that Shakespeare's version of *The Taming of the Shrew* was a re-write of *I Suppositi* by Lodovico Ariosto, an Italian poet and author, born nearly a century before Shakespeare, who based his works on Roman comedies, and that Shakespeare's task was to tidy up the old farce for the Lord Chamberlain's Men around the end of the sixteenth century.

Then again, the Roman playwright, Plautus, was the source of Shakespeare's *The Comedy of Errors*, based (so 'tis said) on the mistaken identity themes of the *Menaechmi* and the *Amphitruo*. Of course, all plays of any durability and standing were prime targets for quarrying in those days; plagiarism and copyright were words which were not spoken 'trippingly on the tongue' and certainly did not cause playwrights many sleepless nights. Indeed, some years later during the Commonwealth, when theatre was forced underground, scenes from Shakespeare's plays were plundered just as freely and performed as drolls, and many lent themselves quite easily to such truncation, a prime example being *Bottom the Weaver*, pillaged from *A Midsummer Night's Dream* which, in turn, was 'suggested' by Chaucer's *Knight's Tale*. Later, Goldoni had a glance at his crib sheet on Plautus and Shakespeare before putting quill to paper to write *The Venetian Twins*.

Although the word 'droll' has passed into the English language as meaning amusing or odd, it had a different connotation in theatrical parlance during Cromwell's time. A droll was not a farce as such, but a crude production whose sole purpose was to elicit hearty laughter – a full chamber pot emptied on an unsuspecting head was about the level of humour. All very well, I suppose, as a piece of business, but hardly enough on its own to sustain any claim to be a dramatic work. Really, the droll was a black-out sketch – often taken from a full-length play (such as *Bottom the Weaver*) – with few actors, few props and few members of the audience, all ready to pack up at a moment's notice should the Roundhead fuzz come galloping up the drive. Not a happy way of making a living, I would have thought.

Shakespeare dallied with mistaken identity yet again in *Twelfth*

Night based, according to the Encyclopaedia Britannica, on Barnaby Rich's *History of Apolonius and Silla*. So, once more, mining for a good quality plot from somebody else's work seemed to be no practical obstruction to an ambitious author, and if ever a play had a cruel farcical sub-plot, with the planning and scheming of Malvolio's downfall by Sir Toby Belch, Sir Andrew Ague-cheek and Maria (aided and abetted by that unfunniest of clowns, Feste), *Twelfth Night* was such a work. No, Shakespeare could never be classed as a farceur. As I have already remarked, he specialised in everything, exploring all the avenues of drama available to a playwright over four hundred years ago, the majority still being explored today.

Tours abroad also began around the turn of the seventeenth century, which was one way of escaping the baleful influence of the Puritans who were making life a misery for actors. Happily, James I was very enthusiastic about the theatre and during his reign the world of drama continued much as it had for the last fifty years. Companies made reputations, actors toured, and three playwrights appeared of considerable stature – Beaumont, Fletcher and Jonson. Sir Francis Beaumont and John Fletcher wrote about fifty plays together, mainly romantic tragi-comedies. Ben Jonson, on the other hand, has been likened to Shakespeare on many occasions. The epitaph on his tombstone in Westminster Abbey reads 'O rare Ben Jonson'; rare indeed, for he was a quarrelsome, yet warm-hearted, intellectually honest man, who went to prison on several occasions for his outspokenness. Even King James couldn't resist the temptation, from time to time, of suppressing his sardonic, satirical comedies, such as *Volpone*, *The Alchemist* and his farcical *Bartholomew Fair*. But kings don't last forever: Charles I and the Civil War were just around the corner.

With the Commonwealth (1649 – 1660) came the banning of theatre, and although puppet shows, bear-baiting and a few other activities were exempt, there was little room for manouevre. The only safe venues were in the homes of nobles and in some schools, but that was all. Players like Robert Cox toured fairs and inns throughout the country, presenting waggish drolls and burlesques mixed up with rope-dancing and conjuring, in the hope of avoiding the ban. But it was a risky business, and many were arrested.

It wasn't until the Restoration in 1660 that visible life came back into the theatrical world, but unfortunately Charles II chose to issue patents to theatres, which meant that only two companies (the King's

Players and the Duke's Players) could present plays in London, whilst permits were issued to bands of strolling players, including a group supported by yet another royal bastard, the Duke of Monmouth. London was favoured once more, for it was over a century before patents were issued to the Theatres Royal in Bath and Norwich. Thus the whole nature of theatre-going was changed yet again, making it a favourite pastime for the Court, the fashionable classes, the nouveau riche and a pretty undesirable bunch of hangers-on: rakes, bullies, tarts and pimps. The actors were known as the 'servants' of the King and the Duke of York (and other nobility) but they – and the Patent Theatres in which they performed (the Theatre Royal in Bridges Street where Drury Lane now stands, and the other in Lincoln's Inn Fields) – required a new kind of play for this strange mixture of an audience and along came what we now call Restoration Comedy, together with the formalised name for knockabout, rumbustious comedy – farce. Even then there was some doubt about its actual use, and its literal derivation as a descriptive word – 'stuffing' – still applied to the evening's fillers or, sometimes, to a short humorous play of two or three acts, instead of the customary five. Indeed, playwrights, managers and printers seemed reluctant, or even confused, when it came to the word 'farce', and 'comedy' was preferred in almost all instances, although sometimes both words would find their way onto a title page and the prologue. However, in his 1902 book on Pinero (to which I shall refer later, when we reach Sir Arthur) dramatic critic, Hamilton Fyfe was in no doubt about the category which should have applied to certain of the plays: 'The difference between Comedy and Farce, then, is, I would submit, this. Farce shows us possible people doing improbable things. Thus *School for Scandal* is comedy, *She Stoops to Conquer* is farce, *The Relapse* trenches upon farce, *The Comedy of Errors* is farce, *The Country Wife* is farce, while *Love for Love*, and indeed all Congreve's plays, may justly be called comedy. Put it another way and we get almost the same result. Comedy depends more upon wit, farce more upon humour. Comedy keeps us smiling. Farce sets on us to laugh, and this is done with the greatest success when it is founded upon some incongruity which is seen at once by all the world to be an incongruity.'

Well, that's pretty trenchant stuff and allows little room for argument. So I looked up another definitive work on the ways of the theatre, the *Oxford Companion* to the same, and dug out some equally trenchant verdicts cast upon the authors and/or their plays:

41

The Rivals by Richard Brinsley Sheridan (1774),
'His first play.'
School for Scandal (1777),
'The masterpiece of English Comedy.'
The Critic; or, a Tragedy Rehearsed (1779),
'The best of the many burlesques stemming from Buckingham's *The Rehearsal.*'

The Good-Natured Man by Oliver Goldsmith (1768),
'Had a cool reception.'
She Stoops to Conquer (1773),
'Far in advance of the drama of his time.'

The Relapse; or, Virtue in Danger by Sir John Vanbrugh (1696),
'His best work.'
The Provoked Wife (1697),
'Restoration traits of coarseness, pungent wit and cynicism.'

The Country Wife by William Wycherley (1674 – 5),
'Coarse and often frankly indecent.'
The Plain Dealer (1676),
'Considered by many critics to be his finest work.'

Love for Love by William Congreve (1695),
'Greatest writer of Restoration comedy of manners.'
The Way of the World (1700),
'His best and last play.'

So, coarseness seems to indicate 'farce' as far as the *Oxford Companion* is concerned. *She Stoops to Conquer* is in limbo, although Horace Walpole thought it 'the lowest of all farces', whilst George Farquhar (1678 – 1707) is described as an 'English dramatist, usually classed among the writers of Restoration Comedy, though chronologically and spiritually he stands a little apart from them.' However, he did write the following, which seem to me to fit chronologically into the time scale of at least two of his illustrious contemporaries, Congreve and Vanbrugh: *The Constant Couple or, a Trip to the Jubilee* (1699), *The Recruiting Officer* (1706) and *The Beaux' Stratagem* (1707). I can't comment on Farquhar's spiritual isolation, but he was certainly inspired when he discovered Anne Oldfield, a superb comedy actress and the natural successor to Anne Bracegirdle, one of the first English actresses, much-loved, both as a person and as the heroine in the comedies of Congreve.

But have you noticed anything curious? Only two of these plays, *The Country Wife* and *The Plain Dealer* – both by William Wycherley

– were produced in Charles II's time, for the king died in 1685 and yet they are all consistently labelled as 'Restoration Comedy of Manners'. Wouldn't 'In the Manner of Restoration Comedy' be more apposite?

You will probably notice, too, that I have left to the last any reference to John Dryden, described by the *Oxford Companion* as 'the outstanding dramatist of the Restoration stage', for his works were inclined to be more dramatic than comedic and he was very grouchy about farce ('farce consists principally of grimaces'). Nevertheless he did write some comedies: *Sir Martin Mar-all* (1667), *Marriage à la Mode* (1672), *Amphitryon* (1690) and *Love Triumphant* (1694). Note the first two *were* in good King Charles II's Restoration days.

You will also note that Hamilton Fyfe and the *Oxford Companion to the Theatre* are somewhat ambivalent about what constitutes a farce and what does not, but you can't altogether blame them, for trying to define farce is like trying to catch feathers in a gale force wind. We all attempt to do it, but you can sound very pompous in the process. Nahum Tate in 1693 had a go in his preface to *Duke and No Duke*: 'I have not yet seen any Definition of Farce, and dare not be the first that ventures to define it. I know not by what fate it happens (in common notion) to be the most contemptible sort of drama. 'Tis thought to bring least reputation to an Author. But if the difficulty of the Task were to decide the Case, we should soon alter our Opinion.'

During this period of so-called Restoration Comedy, there were also playwrights who succeeded in writing successful farces, as such, but have never been included in the list of those aspiring to comedies of manners. Edward Ravenscroft is one, who wrote the scandalous *The London Cuckolds*, which was first performed in 1671 and kept appearing every Lord Mayor's day, until Garrick dropped it at Drury Lane in 1751. As all Ravenscroft's remaining farces leaned heavily on other sources, which he mixed and matched, they, like *The London Cuckolds*, have disappeared into the mists of time.

However, one name seems to rise to the top, although the author concerned openly mined the works of Molière and other French playwrights for his farces with aplomb and impunity. I refer to Arthur Murphy, whose plays are funny and only seem to be revived nowadays at the delightful little Orange Tree Theatre in Richmond-upon-Thames, excellently run by Sam Walters. The titles? Well, the best remembered are probably *The Way to Keep Him*, *All in the Wrong*, *The School for Guardians* and *Know Your Own Mind*.

Maybe that will jog some producer's memory and help to make up *his* or *her* mind. Just to be helpful, here are a few more to be going on with: *The Apprentice*, *The Upholsterer, or What News?*, *The Old Maid*, *No One's Enemy but his Own* and *Three Weeks After Marriage, or What We Must All Come To*. The edge of disaster, I should think, with some of those titles.

Who were the other farce playwrights of the late seventeenth and early eighteenth century? Well, perhaps the most interesting was Mrs Aphra Behn, the first Englishwoman to earn a living through writing, principally as a playwright. Theatre historian Allardyce Nicoll described her work as 'indecent, free, sometimes positively vulgar' but, then, she was only reflecting the fashion of the time. Titles will mean little nowadays for her work is rarely seen, but one piece is of especial interest, *The Emperor of the Moon*, which was produced two years after the King died, and was a pantomime-farce, based on a Parisian *commedia dell'arte* work, with Thomas Jevon as Harlequin and Anthony Leigh as Scaramouche. There were many revivals after this first production in 1687 and it was the forerunner of the harlequinades which, in turn, led to the English pantomime.

Another female author of comedies, one hundred years after Mrs Behn, was Mrs Elizabeth Inchbald, whose plays – *I'll Tell You What* (1785), *Wives As They Were, and Maids as They Are* (1797) and *To Marry or Not to Marry* (1805) – were very popular in their day but are now discarded in destiny's dustbin. Though now forgotten, Mrs Behn and Mrs Inchbald were years ahead of their time; indeed, they still are, for men continue to dominate farce writing, although Caryl Churchill and Sandi Toksvig certainly do their best to prove me wrong.

Now, the players: Tom Jevon (mentioned as Harlequin in Mrs Behn's *The Emperor of the Moon*) was himself the author of a farce, *The Devil of a Wife; or, a Comical Transformation* (1686) which was very popular over the years (turned into a play with music nearly fifty years later as *The Devil to Pay*), and he was also a farceur of considerable ability and fame, specialising in 'light-heeled' parts – meaning he was an excellent dancer, too. On the other hand, Tony Leigh, much admired by Charles II, became the other half of a comedy duo with James Nokes who, in turn, was originally a partner and foil to Edward Angel, whose untimely death robbed the theatre of a clown of real promise. Or so I am told.

James Nokes ('Nurse' Nokes as he became known) was acknowl-

Mrs Elizabeth Inchbald.

edged to be the finest farceur of his day and the first comic artist to specialise in 'drag', pre-dating all of us who have 'put on the skirts' over the years. *Charley's Aunt* would have been meat and drink to him, as would a head-on confrontation with Danny La Rue or Dame Edna Everidge.

Other comedy actors followed in 'Nurse' Nokes' bloomers a few years later: Thomas Doggett (who gave his name to the Doggett Coat and Badge to be won by Thames watermen in a race honouring the accession of George I) actually took over many of Nokes' low comedy roles; William Pinkethman (whom Colley Cibber, then one of the triumvirate with Doggett and Robert Wilks running Drury Lane, considered to be a successor to Tony Leigh) climbed into drag for a farce, *Love in a Chest*, which was produced at the Theatre Royal in 1710, fourteen years after the death of Nokes; James Spiller, Pinkethman's rival at Lincoln's Inn Fields, was in female disguise in *The Perplexed Couple*, which was produced in 1715, whilst, in the same year, comic actor, Ben Griffin, played 'herself' as 'Mother' Griffin in *Woman's Revenge*. Yet that wasn't the end of the drag scene.

Another farceur, John Harper, pranced around as 'Lady Termagant' in Charles Coffey's *The Boarding School* – and pretty ghastly he was too, according to critics of the time. Stupid old men were Benjamin Griffin's particular speciality, with one-eyed James Spiller making the most of his opportunities as a dumb English servant or a sharp French one. Physical deformity also helped John Hippisley to get laughs, for he had burned his face in a fire, which he turned to good effect as a broad West Country yokel or a drunken old man. Drunks, too, were the trade-mark of 'a superior clown of the older tradition', John Harper, whilst Dicky Norris and William Bullock put on funny clothes to get their laughs, just as many farceurs have done ever since – myself included, I fear.

I fear, too, that I have ignored the distaff side in the person of Kitty Clive – Mrs Catherine Raftor Clive, to give Kitty her full name. A comedy actress of considerable ability, she made a great success in 1731 with her hugely comic performance as Nell in *The Devil to Pay*. Her natural successor, Dorothy Jordan, was also a great success in this part years later, as she was in the breeches part of Sir Harry Wildair, a distinction she shared with Peg Woffington, the role originally being created by the actor, Robert Wilks, in Farquhar's *The Constant Couple*. Dorothy Jordan, as you may know, was to breed fourteen illegitimate children, the first to a Dublin theatre manager, three more to a certain Mr Richard Ford, and then ten little Fitz's (the name for Royal by-blows) sired by the Duke of Clarence, later King William IV. The eldest son was created the Earl of Munster and his successor – several generations later, and very much on the right side of the blanket, I hasten to add – sits in the House of Lords today, often opposite me where I am perched on the cross-benches.

Unfortunately, Kitty Clive was pretty keen on a Prince, too, for she suffered from the comedian's desire to play Hamlet. Well . . . not Hamlet exactly, but his girlfriend Ophelia, in which role she was, shall we say, miscast. She also managed to get many laughs in the wrong place as Portia in the trial scene of *The Merchant of Venice*, for she burlesqued the whole thing by impersonating well-known lawyers of the day. Garrick was *not* pleased, banned her from such parts in the future and the whole thing ended in tears.

Another row which entertained her London public was with the 'low' comedian, Ned Shuter – described at the time as being one of the 'few comic actors who have had such command over the muscles of his face' – when Mrs Clive wrote a furious letter to the press about his behaviour in regard to her benefit performance: 'He exhorts the public not to go to my benefit, because I was to have a French farce, wrote by a poor, wretched author . . . I hope I may be indulged, though a woman, to say I have always despised the French Politics, but I never yet heard we was at war with their wit; it should not be imputed to her, as a crime, to have a translation produced, when one part in three of all the comedies now acting are taken from the French, besides those of modern authors that have sneaked into the theatres without confessing from where they came.'

You must admit that, though her command of syntax and spelling is somewhat at fault, there is no denying the truth of her indictment. Ned Shuter proceeded to get his own back by printing the personal letter she had written to him at the same time. Literate London playgoers had a field day: 'I Much Desire you would Do Me the Favour to let me know if you was the author of a letter in *The Daily Gazeteer* relating to his New Piece I had for my benefet; as it was intended to hurt my Benefet, and serve yours everybody will naturely conclude you was the author if you are not ashamed of being so I suppose you will own it: if you really was not concerned in wrightin it I shall be very glad: for I should be extreamly shock'd that an actor should be guilty of so base an action; I dont often take the liberty of wrighting to the Publick but am Now under a Nessity of Doing it, therefore Desier your answer.'

She got it. Shuter, to clear himself, actually swore an affidavit before a magistrate that he was innocent. But nobody believed him . . .

My apologies. Dwelling on scandals, instead of sticking to chronology, I've leapt years ahead from one famed group of farceurs to their successors, with the exception of Cave Underhill, who spanned the generation gap with consummate ease, considering boobies and lumpish louts were his speciality, for he played 'gumps' for many years from the Restoration to past the turn of the century. A contemporary of his was Jo Haines, who also made a living out of playing buffoons. He was one of the first English Harlequins and started his career as a dancing master, as did John Lacy, another king's favourite of that period and also the author of four farces, one of which is as good as any to illustrate the plots which were acceptable in those days: *Old Troop, or Monsieur Raggou* written in 1665, but revived for many years after that.

Raggou is part of a troop of soldiers charged with plundering in the field, and is also the scapegoat for them all on a paternity charge – as the troop decide to put the blame on their devious French cook – Raggou. The early scenes set up life in the field. In Act II Raggou makes his landlady give him her last large cheese, because he claims that she has given away a pistol, which he stole, to the enemy. He then sells her back the cheese, repossesses it, sells it to a neighbour, and while the landlady and the neighbour fight for the cheese, he escapes. In Act III Raggou dresses like another scoundrel called Flea-Flint, and Flea-Flint dresses like Raggou. The rest of Raggou's company try and get rid of him by planting a treasonable letter in his pocket. Raggou runs off, buys a puppet company, then sells the show to Flea-Flint which means Flea-Flint is captured in his place. In the next act Raggou pretends to be a statue to escape capture and is painted by a workman. Raggou drives the painter away by throwing things at him every time he's not looking. Then the joiner arrives to build the statue that the painter has already painted, the joiner thinks someone else has taken his work, he walks off and Raggou steals his tools and escapes. The painter and joiner return arguing about the statue to find it has gone. Raggou then disguises himself as an old woman, but is found out and ends up having to marry the woman who accused the entire troop of being the father of her child.

Apart from illustrating the level of credibility which was demanded by an audience in Restoration times, *Old Troop* also illustrates other much-used farce devices. First, the chase, which provides suspense, without distracting the attention, and means the audience cannot examine too closely the logic of the piece; it also allows for disguise, repetition, physical action and noise. Mrs Behn used pursuit and evasion in a lot of her farces. Second, the use of funny props, for in *Old Troop* there is a ludicrous joust between two men on hobby-horses and a 'bear' which the puritanical Captain of the troop meets en route to a Bristol fair and which generates much laughter at his expense.

I must confess that exactly three hundred years later the funny prop animal and a serving officer were still being used to engender much laughter in Ray Cooney's *Chase Me Comrade*.

At least the word 'farce' was now on the books, becoming more and more in common usage during the early part of the eighteenth century with the advent of the afterpiece. Playbills advertised 'entertainments of singing and dancing' which were elements contained in the farce structure of the time. I write 'of the time' but, come to think of it, musical farce was an extremely popular form of entertainment until the recent past – except it was always called musical comedy. Sir Seymour Hicks, Dame Cicely Courtneidge, Jack Hulbert, Jack Buchanan, Bobby Howes, Leslie Henson, Lupino Lane and on and on, kept my parents' generation rolling about in the aisles for many happy, laughing, melodious years.

I believe that the increasing popularity of short farces, particularly the newly-developed afterpiece, was perhaps the most significant dramatic event of the eighteenth century. That and the opening of more theatres, plus the comedies of Mrs Susannah Centlivre (intrigue), Colley Cibber (sentiment), Sir Richard Steele (virtue), Oliver Goldsmith (wit), Richard Brinsley Sheridan (manners) and George Coleman the elder (*The Clandestine Marriage*). The afterpiece was of social significance, too, as only the non-working population could get along for the opening of an evening's entertainment – somewhere between five and six o'clock in the late afternoon – whilst the middle-class, slaving away over a hot quill pen in many a coffee house, or supervising the servants slaving away over a hot chafing-dish in many a des. res., could only get along sometime later in the performance. Even though they gained entrance at a reduced price, they wanted value for money, not the scraps and left-overs from the main five-act drama, and thus the afterpiece was devised. For a short time, in the 1720s, pantomime looked as though it might rival, or even supersede, farce in the public's affection as the afterpiece, but John Gay's satirical musical burlesque *The Beggar's Opera* soon put paid to that and farces, admittedly with the odd spot of singing and dancing, became the order of the day, although pantomime continued as a very popular form of entertainment. Now there was a difference, though, for these farces were properly constructed plays, sometimes cut-down versions of longer comedies but, as often as not, specially written for a particular theatre or a particular actor. As we have seen, Arthur Murphy contributed his quota, as did Henry Fielding, George Coleman and Samuel Foote, whilst the great David Garrick (1717 – 1779) was not only prepared to appear in the comic afterpiece, but also to write them. *Miss in her Teens* (1747) and *Bon Ton; or, High Life Above Stairs* (1775) were his two most successful attempts, but he was keen on adapting plays as well, and his re-writing of Wycherley's *The Country Wife* as *The Country Girl* must have shown more imagination than the change of title, for it was very popular.

Garrick's huge influence for the good in the theatre is well known and equally well chronicled. Item: How his triumphant first season at Goodman's Fields Theatre in 1741 had a tremendous effect on the self-satisfied Patent Theatres. Item: How he took part in the management of Drury Lane from 1747 and spent most of his career there. Item: How he loathed touring and preferred to spend his holidays at the great houses of his aristocratic friends. Item: How his vanity, snobbishness and quick temper brought him many enemies. Item: How his indecision as to whether or not he should be a tragedian or a comedian brought the greatest possible pleasure to his public, and how his interest in farce, and his delight in showing off his comedic talents after his *King Lear* or *Richard III*, brought the beginnings of respectability to an art-form which is still considered by some critics, even today, to be beneath their intellectual level. Perhaps rather surprisingly, some deign to be members of the Garrick Club, which was *not* founded by Garrick himself – or, if it was, he would have been 114 years old at the time . . .

Farces were equally popular in the provinces and strolling companies would tour a selection of plays, including farces, from London. There were local productions as well, of course. In 1680 there was one collection of three traditional farces doing the rounds under the generic title *The Muse of Newmarket*. All the plays contained bits of farcical business, were full of pratfalls and distinguished by their unbelievable coarseness.

Bedroom farce, too, was well represented. For instance, in 1710 a play was printed in Gosport called *A Trip to Portsmouth* by a certain Essex Walker. It may have started as a satire, but it soon leaves well alone and gets on with the serious business of slapstick bedroom farce. Anyone who had seen *The London Cuckolds* might just have noticed a touch of plagiarism, but then, Pompey was not readily accessible from London's West End.

In the fairs there were drolls and compressions of favourite plays or scenes, and then adaptations of French farces from the early 1700s. There was plenty of money to be made, and out came the great and the good (in comic terms) to make it. So, in 1703, we have Pinkethman with Bullock and Simpson, and in a rival booth Doggett teamed up with Parker. There were battles with authorities but the fairs seemed to keep coming back as strongly as ever. Admittedly, Bartholomew Fair (the real thing, not Jonson's version) was limited in 1708 to three days, but twenty years later there were still at least two major fairs in August and September offering farces as part of their entertainment. The fairs acted as a training ground for actors as well, but by the

1750s their heyday was over. Yet rogues and vagabonds still found a way of scraping a living. One such was Anthony Aston.

A wild, irresponsible Irishman, Anthony Aston was at Drury Lane from 1721 – 22, but was not able to get much work in the two patent houses, so he set up and played in illegal theatres around London and in the fairs. In 1717 we find *Tony Aston's Medley from Bath* at a Fleet Street Tavern, being made up from bits and pieces of various farces. But to get around the law against charging for admission, Tony was nothing if not inventive: 'Mr Aston performs to divert his friends gratis, and hath toothpickers to sell at 1s. each.' His career could accurately be described as being somewhat up and down, for he could often be found in the Dog Tavern near Billingsgate, at the Globe and Bull-Head in Fleet Street, or somewhere like the Three-Tun Tavern in the Borough. He had trouble with his creditors, and probably with the government censors as well, for his extremely rude impersonations. In 1740 Fielding wrote in *The Champion*: ' 'tis expected that he [Ashton] will be call'd upon to rehearse his said faces at the Dramatical Excise office, that such as are judged obnoxious, may be superseded, and a regular permit be taken out for the rest.'

Anthony Aston had one great claim to fame, though. He was the first professional actor to appear in the New World, at such diverse places as 'New York, East and West Jersey, Maryland, Virginia (on both sides Cheesapeek), North and South Carolina, South Florida, the Bahamas, Jamaica and Hispaniola', giving a sort of variety entertainment, like his *Medley from Bath*. How on earth he made all those journeys beats me, but they show the determination which drove the man and made him such a competitor, helping to force the Patent Houses into establishing the afterpiece.

In my last book, *Tour de Farce*, I described the happenings towards the end of the eighteenth century which helped the provincial actor and lessened the battles of people like Anthony Aston. I think many of the points I made in that earlier publication are worth examining again, for they apply to the history of farce as much as to the history of touring.

In 1788, about forty years after the death of Anthony Aston, an Act was passed which gave the Justices the power to licence plays for sixty days at a time. This provided a stability for actors which they had never previously enjoyed, as well as allowing full-length productions outside the Patent Houses and ensuring that Stock Companies – those based mainly in one town – could develop their repertoire and their theatres. Many were already established on this basis but up to that time their activities were illegal. The Act also made it easier for the big names to go on tour in the summer season, moving from town to town, making brief appearances at local theatres, often with the Stock Companies, and giving the provinces the chance to keep up with the London scene.

Most Stock Companies had twelve main players and added to these utility players and occasional extras, when required. There was a pecking order in the company, starting off with the Star performer, who would travel from company to company, followed by the leading man and ending with the walking lady at number twelve. The low comedian (in other words, the farceur) was number eight, sandwiched between the light comedian and the villain, and this lowly position gives a clear indication as to why farce is so often denigrated by those with loftier brows than mine. Even the great Edmund Kean suffered in his early days because of his height, which convinced provincial managers that he was the perfect Harlequin. Indeed, he was, but wanted to be the perfect leading man instead. In 1807, however, he re-joined Samuel Jerrold on his South East circuit based around Sheerness, for he had been offered the lead – Alexander the Great. The opening night came, Kean entered, and immediately a shout went up from one of the boxes: 'Alexander the Great, indeed! It should be Alexander the Little.'

Mind you, actors in those days were used to being catcalled by members of the audience. It's only in fairly recent times that a cathedral-like hush is enjoyed in a theatre. Before that, ribald advice was offered to the various characters, arguments would break out around the auditorium, all manner of missiles would be thrown from the gallery into the pit, as well as at the actors, and generally theatre-goers behaved like latter-day football fans. There were just less of them, that's all.

In spite of a certain air of respectability bestowed by the Act of 1788, the Great British Public still thought that the morals of theatre-goers and, especially, the performers left much to be desired. In their view, actresses were only one step above whores, actors were permanently inebriated and fornication was freely enjoyed by all. Perhaps that was one of the factors leading to a sharp decline in audiences around the middle of the nineteenth century, but the quality of the shows also declined, with melodramas and burlettas being presented all too often, thus driving away any theatre-goer interested in more serious drama. The prim and proper Victorians wanted morally virtuous productions with bigger and better sets, and it was some time before their wishes were granted. Eventually, though, they had their way, resulting in the proliferation of respected and respectable touring actor-managers, with the Music Hall developing to cater for the tastes of the groundlings. Not unlike television today: drama being squeezed more and more into soaps, with game shows and chat shows providing a cheap alternative, quite good enough, it seems, for the average punter. I wonder how long it will be before television audiences decline in the face of such cynical opportunism?

Throughout all these theatrical sea-changes, however, farces continued to be popular. But they were certainly cleaned up in the process, even though they were habitually 'borrowed' from the French. So let's look at the nineteenth century in Act II, Scene ii, shall we? But not before we have one last backward glance at the eighteenth century – 1782 to be precise, when they published Garrick's farces, and others, three years after the great man's death. The title pages to his two most famous afterpieces looked as overleaf. Rather fmall letterpreff, wouldn't you fay? Efpecially if you're fhort-fighted . . .

David Garrick

BON TON;

OR,

HIGH LIFE ABOVE STAIRS.

IN TWO ACTS.

By DAVID GARRICK, Esq.

DRAMATIS PERSONÆ.

MEN.

	Drury-Lane.	Edinburgh 1783.
Lord Minikin,	Mr. Dodd.	Mr. Ward.
Sir John Trotley,	Mr. King.	Mr. Johnson.
Colonel Troy,	Mr. Brereton.	Mr. Woods.
Jessamy,	Mr. La-Mash.	Mr. La-Mash.
Davy,	Mr. Parsons.	Mr. Moss.
Mignon,	Mr. Burton.	

WOMEN.

Lady Minikin,	Mrs. King.	Mrs Walcot.
Miss Tittup,	Mrs. Abington.	Mrs. Sparks.
Gymp,	Miss Platt.	Mrs. Mills.

MISS IN HER TEENS:

OR, THE

MEDLEY OF LOVERS

IN TWO ACTS.

BY DAVID GARRICK, Esq.

DRAMATIS PERSONÆ.

MEN.

	Drury-Lane.	Edinburgh, 1782.
' Sir Simon Lovelt.'		
Captain Loveit,	Mr. Havard.	Mr. Simpson.
Fribble, -	Mr. Garrick.	Mr. Hallion.
Flash, -	Mr. Woodward.	Mr. Ward.
Puff, -	Mr. Yates.	Mr. Johnson.
Jasper, -	Mr. Blakes.	Mr. Banks.

WOMEN.

Miss Biddy,	Mrs. Green.	Mrs. Sparks.
' Aunt.'		
Tag, -	Mrs. Clive.	Mrs. Charteris.

ACT II

Scene ii: Somewhere in Brazil

'I'm Charley's Aunt from Brazil, where the nuts come from.'

Brandon Thomas

IT TOOK most of the nineteenth century – the end of George III's reign, all of George IV's and William IV's, plus the first fifty-five glorious years of Queen Victoria's – before *Charley's Aunt* blew in from Brazil (well, Bury St Edmunds, actually), lifted up her bombazine skirts and showed her bloomers to a London audience on 21 December 1892 at the Royalty Theatre. Before then, there had only been Pinero's Court productions to keep the British farcical flag flying, other than translations from a foreign tongue – generally French – or some pretty mundane work of a native hue. Even the description 'farce' was Victorianised as 'petite comedie', 'comedietta' or that ghastly hybrid, 'farcical comedy', which persisted well into this century.

J R Planché (1796 – 1880) was perhaps amongst the best-known playwrights at that time, specialising in burlesques, extravaganzas (similar to burlesques, but without the satire, simply based on myths or fantasies) and pantomimes, although he did have a stab at melodramas and comedies, too. In his latter years he became interested in heraldry and was created Rouge Croix Pursuivant of Arms at the College of Heralds, as well as fighting for the reform of the laws governing theatrical copyright. What is more, he won the battle. Yet how many of his works are remembered today? Very few, I fear, except at the remarkable little Player's Theatre in Villiers Street, London. There his burlesques are revived regularly at Christmas, along with H J Byron's pantomimes, offering us a brief glimpse of how the Victorians enjoyed their Yuletide entertainments.

Would you enjoy the two hundred, or more, plays of Frederick Reynolds (1764 – 1841)? I doubt it. Equally H J Byron's *Our Boys*, which achieved an unheard-of run of 1,362 performances at the Vaudeville Theatre, from 16 January 1875 to 18 April 1879, is completely forgotten, as is John Baldwin Buckstone's *Married Life* (1834), one of the very first three-act farces. In this there are highly emotional scenes when a husband is suspected of adultery, although he is really protecting the honour of a young girl. Set against this pair of 'serious' characters are four more couples who are all at odds with themselves and extreme caricatures, who confide in the audience, are caught in snowballing misunderstandings which follow one another with absurd speed, the whole being overburdened with a surfeit of comic business. I can't say I fancy that particular storyline as a sure-fire box-office hit today, but it was in 1834, as was its successor *Single Life*. I wonder if that hinted at promiscuity? I think not, for the Lord Chamberlain and the local magistrates would never countenance anything that was critical of love and marriage, whilst the mention of sexual relations, in any form, was completely and utterly taboo. That is why the consumption of food was an integral part of Victorian farce, allowing a healthy appetite for grub to substitute for an equally healthy appetite for sex. Even Pinero had to resort to these coded messages in *The Magistrate*, with lines spoken by a courting couple who are unaware of each other's presence in the same hotel room. Here is an example, with Charlotte, the young lady, speaking first: 'The odour of cooking here, to a hungry woman, is maddening', whilst her suitor, Captain Vale, perched on a balcony in the pouring rain, responds: 'I'm wet to the skin and frightfully hungry!'

I am certain that no one in the Lord Chamberlain's office, stuffed-shirts to a man, would recognise that as having sexual overtones and probably Pinero himself would have denied all knowledge of it, but the substitution of one hunger for another occurs in too many English Victorian plays for it not to seem more than a coincidence. Meanwhile, the Filthy French just got on with it. Cuckolding was more popular than cooking and for the French to admit *that* shows they had their priorities right, even then. In farce, I hasten to add. I am not casting any aspersions.

Buckstone, quite apart from his writing, also had the advantage of being a very popular low comedian and a successful actor-manager at the Haymarket Theatre – hence the club in his name in my day.

When I first went to the Whitehall in 1950, many a young West End actor used to end up eating his or her after-show supper in the Buckstone club, opposite the Haymarket Theatre's stage door.* He lived from 1802 to 1879, and ever since he died his ghost is said to haunt the theatre. Still trying to get laughs, I suppose; or maybe he's just hungry.

A playwright in the mould of Tom Robertson, who concentrated on realistic, contemporary dramas, was one James Albery, who – some might say – fell from grace by adapting a successful farce 'from the French', *Pink Dominos*, which began life at the Criterion Theatre in 1877 where his wife, Mary Moore, was playing the leading parts. This was only the beginning of a successful dynasty, for Albery died in 1889 and his widow re-married Charles (later Sir Charles) Wyndham, who was a fine light comedian, as well as a 'serious' actor, and together they continued at the Criterion, eventually building and managing the New (now the Albery) Theatre and Wyndhams. James Albery had sired a son, Bronson, before he went to meet the Great Farceur in the sky, and this scion of a theatrical stock joined forces with his step-brother, Howard, and jointly they ran the three theatres with great success. Howard died in 1947, but Sir Bronson (as he now was) continued with the help of his son, Donald. Eventually, Donald, too, had the royal tap on the shoulder, but he sold out the enterprise, leaving *his* son, Ian, as managing director of the new company. Alas, in these days of mergers and take-overs, the inheritance was somewhat bedevilled and Ian is no longer in charge. After James's *Pink Dominos* the family were not particularly well-up in the world of farce, although Donald and I did present *Diplomatic Baggage* by John Chapman at Wyndhams in 1967. It was not a roaring success and neither was *Instant Marriage*, a musical farce which we produced at the same time at the Piccadilly Theatre, so Donald rather lost heart after that. A pity, for there is really no triumphant climax to this story, but I thought it worth the telling.

Probably the most successful actor of his era, in farce, not tragedy, was John Liston (*c*.1776 – 1846). In appearance, I suppose he was a cross between Leslie Henson and Leo Franklyn, both superb farceurs

---

*It was run by the indefatigable Gerald Campion, who achieved fame and fortune later playing Billy Bunter on television. But he was always in the food game and ran many a club and restaurant and hotel before retiring to France to enjoy the culinary delights of Provence. I think theatrical delights there are in somewhat shorter supply.

in the recent past. Henson with his frog-like eyes and Franklyn with his solemn, craggy face could get laughs by just appearing, with the right expression turned full-face to the audience. Liston was the same. He only had to step on-stage and the hilarity began, whilst the grotesque characters he portrayed – Paul Pry, Lubin Log, Tristram Sappy, to mention but three – delighted audiences and ensured full houses as a matter of course. Such was his popularity that he received a salary far higher than any tragedian of the period, for he was an actor prized above all others by managers; he could ensure bums on seats and, in his day, had an awful lot standing, as well.

Liston began two other practises which we like to think are unique in this day and age. His likeness was marketed, in pottery and prints and, like a radio comic of old or a television comic of

John Liston as Figaro.

John Liston as Endless.

today, he invented the catch-phrase. Paul Pry's 'hope I don't intrude' became as well known as 'nice to see yer, to see yer, nice', 'come on down' or 'can I do yer now, sir?' What is more, he perfected the trick subsequently used to great effect by Jack Benny, that of fixing the audience with a basilisk stare and sighing inwardly at the gross injustices of fate.

Another comic around at the same time as Liston was Joe Munden (1758 – 1832), who also had a face which was his fortune, according to his contemporary critic Charles Lamb: 'Out of some invisible wardrobe he dips for faces . . . In the grand grotesque of farce, Munden stands out as single and unaccompanied as Hogarth.' Then there was Frederick Robson (1821 – 1864), seen by many as Edmund Kean's successor and, like him, capable of comic as well as tragic acting. Clearly, he knew how to make an audience laugh, for here is the *Morning Chronicle* notice of his appearance at the Olympic

Theatre (where he stayed for many years), playing the part of Jem Bags, a pathetic street musician, in a farce called *The Wandering Minstrel*. This sad, bedraggled figure must have been recognisable to the majority of the audience, but no pity was shown, as you can see:

What a roar of merriment greeted the appearance of the woe-begone little figure of Robson, who, in smashed hat, shambling on in muddy shoes that could hardly be held together by bits of string finished on the flageolet the last notes of no air in particular, as after looking up beseechingly at the windows of the street, disappointed of coppers, he wandered down to the flote [sic] where with an intensely comic look of abject misery, he silently surveyed the already convulsed audience.

Health, or rather lack of it through the demon drink, finally slayed poor old Robson. Towards the end, his hacking cough was so bad it could be heard more clearly than his words but, in spite of these problems, for a time he was the joint manager of the Olympic Theatre, which had been re-built after a disastrous fire.

Before then it had been in the hands of Madame Vestris, an actress and a manager, who married Charles James Mathews (son of eccentric comedian Charles Mathews) and together they had a mixture of success and failure, both there and at Covent Garden and the Lyceum. Charles' greatest success, though, was probably as Dazzle in Dion Boucicault's *London Assurance*, which I must admit was a huge hit long before Pinero came on the scene. Mark you, many critics think *London Assurance* is an attempt to copy the style of Vanbrugh and Farquhar, with a pretty laboured comic contrivance of a father failing to recognise his own son who is staying in the same house under an assumed name. Its most outrageous characters, Lady Gay Spanker (Mrs Nesbitt) and the impudent Dazzle (Charles Mathews), are incidental to the main story, but the play's long life can only be attributed to a complete lack of sophistication on the part of a Victorian audience. Remember, though, that audiences had changed greatly from the previous century. I hesitate to use the words in today's egalitarian society, but the upper- and middle-class had begun to go elsewhere for their entertainment, prices dropped and the lower-middle class and working-class now became the theatregoers who supported farce and melodrama – and remembering their lack of education, can you wonder at the simplicity of the storylines?

How about this one to be going on with? It is an example

Madame Vestris and Charles Mathews.

of a Victorian plot, giving the farce lead to a woman. As the woman concerned was none other than Mary Anne Keeley (1806 – 1899), famous for her appearances in 'pathetic, appealing parts' and her popular husband, Robert Keeley (1793 – 1869), was playing opposite her and as the production was at the Haymarket, you might have expected something a little more sophisticated, but I suppose the titles give it away: *Lola Montez; or, a Countess for an Hour*, changed to *Pas de Fascination; or, Catching a Governor*; changed, by the way, because there *was* a Lola Montez, who was having a bit of a ding-dong with the King of Bavaria, and politically the original title was not considered to be, well, politic. The author of this farrago was a certain J Stirling Coyne. The story goes thus: a poor maid is at home, when a dancer appears being chased by the police. The maid agrees to take the dancer's place so that the dancer can escape, and manages to pass herself off as the dancer to the point that she is arrested and brought up before the bored Governor. She manages to cheer him up, though, with her dancing and so he decides to make her a Countess. However, the maid's sweetheart is the State Barber who recognises her in her disguise and the Governor enters whilst they are in each other's arms. It looks like trouble's afoot, but at that moment a messenger announces the real dancer has been caught. So now the Governor has to pay off the maid on her wedding day so she will renounce her title, which is now clearly inappropriate.

And that's it. If you can see many laughs in that, you're a better man than I am. I mean, what a load of codswallop. But the audiences loved it – melodrama and farce – all in an uneasy moral mess. I trust Mr Coyne was paid off in his own coin – fool's gold would seem appropriate.

What other perils beset the playwright writing in those late Georgian or early Victorian days? The licensing laws, for one. In London, the two old theatres at Drury Lane and Covent Garden were still the only ones able to stage legitimate drama, apart from those licensed in the provinces. All the other theatres had to get around the law by putting on plays (generally known as burlettas) which had to include five or six songs, whatever the storyline. Even Shakespeare's work was not exempt from this strait-jacket and you could enjoy the absurd spectacle of King Lear or Richard III suddenly bursting into a ballad. I think 'She Was Only a Bird in a Gilded Cage' would have been a suitable requiem for the old king to belt out over Cordelia, don't you? But with Thomas Bowdler still providing happy endings for Shakespeare's tragedies, it was probably acceptable to the average theatre-goer of that time. They were besotted with melodrama, anyway, for the size of the theatres, plus the extraordinary moral climate which pervaded the nineteenth century made this form of entertainment the most popular of all. Even farce was second best. Can you wonder, then, that a common theme running through plays at that time was the moral superiority of rural life, with its simple, virtuous people compared to the arrogant, fashionable villains who lived in those elegant London squares or occupied some huge ancestral pile.

Eventually though, in 1843, the Act for Regulating the Theatres came into being, which ended the Patent Theatres' monopoly, and this allowed more artistic freedom but as the censor, in the form of the Lord Chamberlain, lasted until 1968, this did not free everyone at one bound, as it were. Indeed, as late as 1952 I had a farce banned by the Lord Chamberlain. It was *Tell the Marines* by Roland and Michael Pertwee (father and son) and centred around a piddling little island which was the subject of a dispute between the, then, Soviet Union and Britain. The troops contrive to avoid any confrontation until the brass-hats arrive, when they stage-manage a battle, being careful to aim over each other's heads. Michael and I were summoned to St James's Palace and told by the censor and a gentleman from the Foreign Office that under no circumstances could we show Russia and Britain in such a warlike role, and the play must not go any further. It didn't. Well, it did, but the re-writing ruined it, the ironical joke was lost and the Official Secrets Act swallowed the remains. It must have been harder in Victoria's reign, though.

Many farces aimed to parody melodrama, mocking their speech styles, situations and emotional drive. In *Box and Cox* (1847), a hugely successful farce by John Maddison Morton based on a couple of French farces, two long-lost brothers are engaged to the same awful woman. The melodramatic build up of scenes is also used to build up the tension which is then turned on its head in a comic anti-climax:

COX: What shall part us?
BOX: What shall tear us asunder?
COX: Box!
BOX: (About to embrace – Box stops, seizes Cox's hand, and looks eagerly in his face.) You'll excuse the apparent insanity of the remark, but the more I gaze on your features, the more I'm convinced that you're my long-lost brother.

COX: The very observation I was going to make to you!

BOX: Ah – tell me – in mercy tell me – have you such a thing as a strawberry mark on your left arm?

COX: No!

BOX: Then it is he!

          (They rush into each other's arms.)

As you can see, the strong emotions of melodrama fit the rough comedy of the day very well and, since melodrama and farce share the need for coincidence and revelation, the two forms can easily cross over. Of course, in farce the sentimental does not need to be rounded off so fully, and virtuous behaviour can become the cause or exacerbation of a character's problems but, being Victorian, they have to be a tinge careful, for they cannot mock morals too pointedly. The Lord Chamberlain or the City Fathers would be watching, as would the tut-tutting audience.

Thus, sentimental Victorian farce was tied to the domesticity of other Victorian drama, and so the mad world of farce – where snowballing disorder is faced with desperate seriousness, forcing the protagonists to plumb the depths of their ingenuity – was not presented as in the works of Labiche and Feydeau, where the world is harsh and anarchy is almost the only rule. Whereas Labiche and Feydeau were able to be cruelly mocking, the Victorian writers were constrained by the over-arching necessity to be prim and proper at all costs, thus providing an altogether gentler jollity.

George Rowell, in his book *The Victorian Theatre 1792 – 1914*, has some further thoughts on this subject: 'In nineteenth-century England the audience shaped both the theatre and the drama played within it; for patronage, the only card with which a manager may sometimes outbid public taste, was at its lowest ebb at Victoria's accession.'

All that I have read of the Victorian era confirms George Rowell's view. But although storylines had to be self-opinionated, self-righteous and self-satisfied, performances were anything other than self-conscious. With the enormous increase in the London population between 1811 and 1851 theatres proliferated all over the capital and the buildings themselves, including the stage area, became so vast that actors, whether comic or tragic, were forced to broaden their performances to such an extent that all credibility went flying out through the stage lantern and the stage door. This pernicious habit persisted well into the twentieth century; indeed, there are one or two early recordings of performances which indicate that tearing a passion to tatters was endemic, even amongst the most illustrious of actor-managers.

A modern-day audience would watch such posturings with open-mouthed incredulity, but audiences in those days demanded both overblown performances and over-length bills to keep them happy. Spectacle, too, was an essential ingredient of an evening's entertainment, and when the London Hippodrome was built for Moss Empires, designed by Frank Matcham and opening in 1900, it was intended to give London a circus in the stalls area, plus other vast spectacles in a huge 100,000 gallon water tank in front of the stage. Strange how the wheel has come full circle. A century later we find ourselves fighting to get seats to watch a helicopter hovering over the stage, or the stage itself journeying round us, or any other spectacular effect a designer can devise. The Victorians did know a thing or two, after all. 'Before your very eyes' still has a fascination no film can equal.

Joe Munden, John Liston and Frederick Robson were all beset by the problems of space when achieving their comic effects, as was William Dowton, who was described by that renowned critic William Hazlitt as 'a genuine and excellent comedian', particularly good (according to early-nineteenth-century lights) as Falstaff and Sir Anthony Absolute. On the other hand, two actor-managers, Benjamin Webster and the aforementioned John Baldwin Buckstone, maintained a comedy tradition at the Haymarket Theatre, relying on their comic personalities to achieve their laughs, rather than bawling out funny lines or pulling funny faces, but it must have been a struggle.

Writers of English comedy, too, suffered, being mainly engaged to cobble together curtain-raisers or afterpieces to satisfy the demands of the actors or the managers. Mind you, nothing seems to change much. In his Huw Wheldon Memorial Lecture on BBC2 at the beginning of 1995, renowned author, Andrew Davies, remarked that 'TV shows that seemed fresh and bright and sparky when we first saw them are flogged relentlessly until the last dodgy plot possibility flops exhausted on the living-room carpet to bleed to death . . . you cannot order up [works of genius] like rolls of carpet.' Nearly two hundred years earlier, in 1803 to be precise, James Kenney wrote such a piece, *Raising the Wind*. Not a work of genius, but a roll of carpet which went on for years and years. First to perform the comic lead of Jeremy Diddler was W T Lewis, but years later Charles Mathews and Henry Irving both continued the success of the play and the part, with many a wink and a nudge and a swagger in a piece which had, according to George Rowell, 'neither plot, dialogue, nor subsidiary characters [of] any substance.'

I think it only fair to note that when Kenney published *Raising the Wind* he paid the following graceful tribute to his leading actor: 'To Mr Lewis I am particularly indebted, not only for the very great share he contributed to the performance but also for some very friendly suggestions at the rehearsals; which, I have no doubt, proved of considerable advantage.' If they are being truthful, there is no farce writer alive who would not agree with those sentiments. Indeed, many have generously done so already, even though such co-operation has still led to indifferent notices. Nothing, though, could equal Lord Macaulay's jaundiced view of Kenney's work. He describes him as 'a writer of the class which in our time is at the very bottom of the literary scale. He is a dramatist and most of the farces and three-act plays which have succeeded during the last eight or ten years are, I am told, from his pen. Heaven knows that, if they are the farces and plays which I have seen, they do him but little honour. However, this man is one of our great comic writers. He has the merit, such as it is, of hitting the very bad taste of our modern audiences better than any other person who has stooped to that degrading work.'

You could describe that, along with Mr Rowell's views, as a double-whammy.

Mr Rowell also reminds us that 'minor theatres fostered in burlesque the only true spontaneous form of Victorian comedy.' However, he does not mention the Penny Gaffs, which then flourished in the inner-cities and where farces were being 'performed' up to six times a night. The Gaffs went under many names – Penny Dookey's, Geggies or Bursts in Glasgow, Dives in Liverpool. The writer for these places had to produce plays night after night; great favourites were one-act farces in which slapstick and the mocking of officialdom, particularly coppers, were very popular with adolescent audiences. The hacks received about ten shillings for each script, and the pressure on the actors is demonstrated when you think that Robert Loraine (later in Shaw's *Man and Superman*) appeared in fourteen new plays a week at the Liverpool Dive where he started working, and in four months did 140 plays and 370 parts. Often the hapless author simply gave the actors the scenario and their stock characters during the day and that night the actors busked it.

Victorian burlesques, burlettas and extravaganzas, too, seemed to rely heavily on the old 'low comedy' for their laughs. There was a strong streak of farce essential to their success, even though it could not be said that they had any of the structure of what had come to be seen as farce.

A playwright whose name has not been left in dusty books to moulder on some theatrical shelf is Sir William Schwenk Gilbert (1836 – 1911) – the other half of Gilbert and Sullivan, whose comic operas are still performed with unceasing regularity by amateur companies of Savoyards up and down the country, as well as by the resuscitated D'Oyly Carte Company, and others. Yet he, too, began his writing with a burlesque – encouraged by the man who changed the face of English theatre with his so-called 'cup-and-saucer drama' (realistic plots, dialogue and stage settings), T W Robertson – and went on with dramatic sketches, pseudo-classical romances and farces. One of these, *Engaged*, is totally forgotten today, and yet it was on the ludicrous logic of this play that Oscar Wilde based his *The Importance of Being Earnest* some eighteen years later in 1895. But the latter was billed as a 'trivial comedy for serious people', remember, not a farce.

It is clear that the development of farce as a full-length play can be seen as a take-over of the French tradition, led by Labiche, Feydeau and others. Originally their works were simply translated or their style half-heartedly copied, removing all sexual innuendo and substituting a castrated lampoon in its place so as not to disturb Victorian susceptibilities. Guilty of this white-washing work was the great W S Gilbert, but long before his beatification as the other half of Arthur Sullivan. He must have learnt something, nevertheless, and his sarcastic humour, which he was to aim at all the Great and the Good, was fired, no doubt, in the furnace of farcical failure. We remember the ironical words of Gilbert's libretti, not his plays, and no doubt *Trial by Jury* (1875), through to *The Gondoliers* (1889), will be performed as long as there is a village hall or a theatre, with live people on the stage entertaining us with their productions of Gilbert and Sullivan's comic operas. All of which leaves the way clear for the man who changed the face of British farce – Sir Arthur Wing Pinero.

Well, not quite. He was pipped at the post with a highly-successful farce by another author, who went on to be knighted as well, but more for his light comedy acting than for his writing, Sir Charles Hawtrey. When Hawtrey was at Cambridge in 1883 he adapted a play by the German writer Gustav Von Moser, *The Private Secretary* and brought it to the Prince's Theatre the following year with another knight-to-be, H Beerbohm Tree, playing the put-upon Reverend Robert Spalding. It was not madly popular. Hawtrey believed in it, though, and felt Tree was not the ideal casting, so revived it in the same year at the Globe Theatre, with W S Penley in the part, and from then on it enjoyed almost as great a success as *Charley's Aunt* would do sometime later. Which is not altogether surprising, for W S Penley was to be the original 'Babs' – Lord Fancourt Babberly – and if any actor could hold a farce together it was that one-time boy chorister at Westminster Abbey, only by now his voice had broken.

There was one slight hiccup with this second production, though. When it transferred to the Globe, a pirated version was being presented in the north of England, called *The Secretary*. Hawtrey immediately applied for an injunction and the judge who heard the case was Vice-Chancellor Bacon, who was over ninety years of age. The hearing began just before lunch, with Hawtrey's counsel, Mr Hamilton, all ready to plead at length:

> 'If your Lordship pleases, I have to apply on behalf of my client, Mr Hawtrey, proprietor of the Globe Theatre, in the matter of a play now running there called *The Private Secretary* . . .'
>
> 'Oh yes! Yes, I know. Ha! Ha! A very funny play. I saw it a couple of nights ago. Mr Penley – Ha! Ha! Ha!'
>
> Mr Hamilton then mentioned the pirated version.
>
> Vice-Chancellor Bacon was outraged: 'Disgraceful! Utterly disgraceful!'
>
> Mr Hamilton then asked for the injunction.
>
> 'Most certainly, Mr Hamilton, most certainly. Take your injunction.'

Exit Vice-Chancellor Bacon, still chuckling at his memories of Mr Penley's performance, but in time for his lunch.

However, if you think that *The Private Secretary* was only an English adaptation of a German creation (which it was), then Pinero is clearly the father of all the farce writers who followed – Travers, Sylvaine, King, Chapman, Cooney, Pertwee, Stoppard, Orton, Frayn, the lot – right up to the present day. We must explore the lineage.

Arthur Wing Pinero (1855 – 1934) was an Englishman through and through, even though he had a Portugese name, which had been anglicised from 'Pin-heiro' many generations earlier. Like so many of us, he was an amateur actor as a child and loved it. At nineteen he went to the Theatre Royal in Edinburgh as a utility

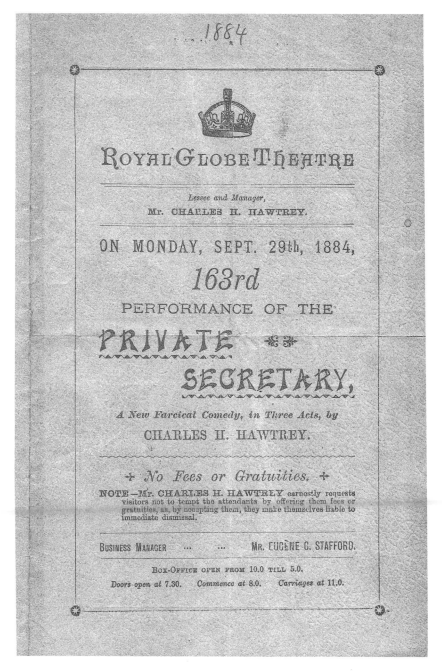

1884

ROYAL GLOBE THEATRE

Lessee and Manager,
Mr. CHARLES H. HAWTREY.

ON MONDAY, SEPT. 29th, 1884,

163rd

PERFORMANCE OF THE

PRIVATE ❊

SECRETARY,

A New Farcical Comedy, in Three Acts, by
CHARLES H. HAWTREY.

✚ *No Fees or Gratuities.* ✚

NOTE—Mr. CHARLES H. HAWTREY earnestly requests
visitors not to tempt the attendants by offering them fees or
gratuities, as, by accepting them, they make themselves liable to
immediate dismissal.

BUSINESS MANAGER ... ... MR. EUGENE C. STAFFORD.

BOX-OFFICE OPEN FROM 10.0 TILL 5.0.
Doors open at 7.30.   Commence at 8.0.   Carriages at 11.0.

Above and over page: Two programme covers demonstrating the long run of Sir
Charles Hawtrey's *The Private Secretary.*

ROYAL GLOBE THEATRE,

LESSEE AND MANAGER,
MR. CHARLES H. HAWTREY

Licensed by the Lord Chamberlain to
CHARLES H. HAWTREY, ESQ., 24, CHESTER TERRACE, S.W.

MATINEE.

ON WEDNESDAY, JAN. 27th, 1886.

700th

PERFORMANCE OF

THE
PRIVATE
SECRETARY,

A NEW FARCICAL COMEDY, IN THREE ACTS,
BY

CHAS. H. HAWTREY.

NO FEES OR GRATUITIES.

NOTE.—Mr. CHAS. H. HAWTREY earnestly requests
Visitors not to tempt the Attendants by offering them Fees or
Gratuities, as, by accepting them, they make themselves liable
to immediate dismissal.

Business Manager - *Mr. E. F. BRADLEY.*

BOX-OFFICE OPEN FROM 10 TILL 6.30

Doors open at 2.30. Commence at 3. Carriages at 5.

player, having failed to complete his law studies so that he could join his father as a London solicitor. Soon after he arrived in the Athens of the North, the theatre burned down and he went to Liverpool to play in *Miss Gwilt*, a drama by Wilkie Collins, adapted from his novel *Armadale*. Mr Collins came to see the show to make

Sir Arthur Wing Pinero.

notes for the London version of the play, misread Pinero's name for that of an actor who impressed him, and thus Pinero was invited down to London to appear and before the end of that year, 1876, he had been engaged as a member of Henry Irving's company at the Lyceum. He was a painstaking actor who was only given small parts to play, though Ellen Terry thought he was good as 'the silly ass type'.

Irving was renowned for cutting all but his own scenes and lines and once, at a rehearsal, he caught sight of Pinero sitting on the edge of a piece of scenery propped upright in the wings. Irving remonstrated: 'Get up, my boy, get up. You will cut yourself.' 'Oh, that will be all right, Mr Irving,' Pinero replied ruefully, 'we're accustomed to having our parts cut in this theatre.'

In 1877 Pinero had his first two farces produced, although neither bore any relationship to the life and manners of the time, unlike his later ones at the Court. His first was *Two Hundred a Year*, which was performed at a benefit for a fellow actor, F H Macklin. Then he asked Irving if he could write a curtain-raiser for the Lyceum. Nothing happened until one day the great man said to him, somewhat diffidently, 'If you would like to write me a little piece for-er-next season I will give you-er-fifty pounds for it.'

So, for £50 a time (we presume) he wrote three pieces for Irving, the first being *Two Can Play At That Game* (1877), *Daisy's Escape* (1879) which proved to Irving that he 'would be sure to take-er-a good position as a dramatic author,' and followed this with *Bygones* (1880). In the same year came *The Money-Spinner* at the St James's Theatre, with William and Madge Kendal (later Dame Madge) and John Hare (later Sir John) in the cast. Prior to that he had *Hester's Mystery* on at the Folly (afterwards Toole's) Theatre. Work was beginning to come in thick and fast and, after a short time at the Haymarket with the Bancrofts, in 1882 he made his last appearance as an actor in *The Rivals*. He was now a fully-fledged playwright: *Imprudence* (Folley's, 1881), *The Squire* (St James's, 1881), *Girls and Boys* (Toole's, 1882), *The Rector* (Court, 1883), *Lords and Commons* (Haymarket, 1883), *The Rocket* (Gaiety, 1883), *Low Water* (Globe, 1884), *The Ironmaster* (St James's, 1884) and *In Chancery* (Gaiety, 1884). All were written before the great day, 21 March 1885, when *The Magistrate* was first produced and Pinero's Court farces had begun their run into theatrical history.

GLOBE THEATRE

NEWCASTLE ST.   STRAND

Licensed by the Lord Chamberlain to Mr FRANCIS C. FAIRLIE
Actual and Responsible Manager, Newcastle Street, Strand.

ENGAGEMENT OF
MISS
ADA CAVENDISH

Who will appear Every Evening in the New Drama, in 5 Acts,
entitled

MISS GWILT

BY

WILKIE COLLINS.

Concluding every evening with

Cryptoconchoidsyphonostomata

IN WHICH

MR CHARLES COLLETTE

WILL APPEAR.

Programme of Wilkie Collins' production, *Miss Gwilt*.

Actually, only the first three Court farces (*The Magistrate* [March 1885], *The Schoolmistress* [March 1886] and *Dandy Dick* [January 1887]) were at the original Royal Court Theatre, which was demolished in July 1887. The present Royal Court re-opened some fourteen months later with 'a farcical-comedy' (such a description of a play could only be judged nowadays as indicating the author was trying to hedge his bets) called *Mamma!* by Sydney Grundy, preceded by *Hermine*, a play in one act by Charles Thomas. Pinero's first production at the new theatre was a comedy, not a farce, *The Weaker Sex*, but in April 1890 came the first of his last two Court farces (and, subsequently, the least popular), *The Cabinet Minister* and *The Amazons* in March 1893. In between these productions, Pinero was churning out a number of other plays, too, which went on at different theatres in London, including *Sweet Lavender* and *The Profligate*, followed by *The Second Mrs Tanqueray*, *The Notorious Mrs Ebbsmith*, *Trelawny of the 'Wells'*, *The Gay Lord Quex*, and *His House in Order*. You can see why he was the foremost playwright of his day and one of my great pleasures is using the Gents loo at the Garrick Club and looking at a Sir Alfred Munnings cartoon of the great man, then Sir Arthur, in celebration of one of his birthdays and surrounded by the titles of all his plays. It makes a very impressive list as you adjust your dress.

If you remember, I quoted earlier the difference between comedy and farce as laid down by dramatic critic, author and journalist, Hamilton Fyfe. He must have been only fifteen when he saw his first Pinero farce, but his subsequent criticism of this – and others – in a book he wrote about Pinero in 1902, is based on contemporary views about the plays and therefore I offer no apology for quoting Fyfe again. The last production I saw was some years ago, anyway, with Nigel Hawthorne as Mr Posket in the Royal National Theatre presentation of *The Magistrate*. Michael Coveney, then the theatre critic on the *Financial Times*, was reminded of what many consider to be the definitive performance of Mr Posket – that of Alistair Sim – and spent most of his notice remembering it: 'I recall a strain of surreal panic forever associated in my mind with Alistair Sim in the main role . . . all but sliding into the wallpaper, back to the audience, searching for a crack in the wall.' Both of us are too young, however, to have seen the original magistrate, Arthur Cecil.

Ladies and Gentlemen, someone who did, Mr Hamilton Fyfe: 'Of the first three farces *Dandy Dick* is, I should say, the best,

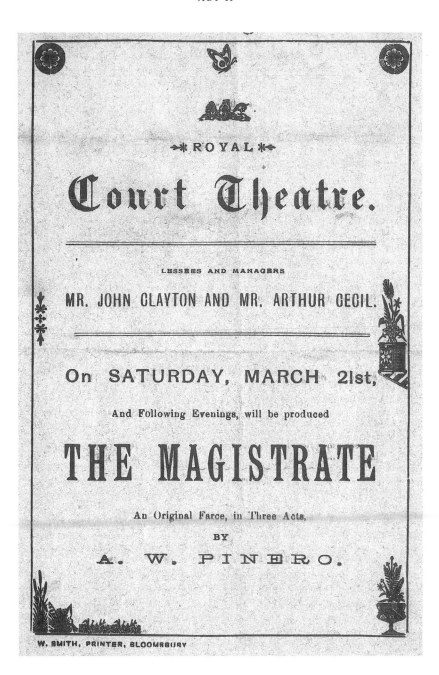

Above and over page: Programme of Pinero's farce *The Magistrate*.

PROGRAMME.

THIS EVENING, at Half-past Eight o'clock,

THE MAGISTRATE

An Original Farce, in Three Acts,

By A. W. PINERO.

Mr Posket	} Magistrates, of Mul- {	Mr ARTHUR CECIL
Mr Bullamy	} berry St. Police Court {	Mr FRED CAPE
Colonel Lukyn (from Bengal—Retired)		Mr JOHN CLAYTON
Captain Horace Vale (Shropshire Fusiliers)		Mr F. KERR
Cis Farringdon (Mrs Posket's son, by her first marriage)		Mr H. EVERSFIELD
Achille Blond (Proprietor of the Hôtel des Princes)		Mr CHEVALIER
Isidore ... (a Waiter) ...		Mr DEANE
Mr Wormington (Chief Clerk at Mulberry Street)		Mr GILBERT TRENT
Inspector Messiter	} Metropolitan Police {	Mr ALBERT SIMS
Sergeant Lugg		Mr LUGG
Constable Harris		Mr GEORGE
Wyke ... (Servant at Mr Posket's)		Mr BURNLEY
Agatha Posket (late Farringdon, née Verrinder)		Mrs JOHN WOOD
Charlotte (her Sister)		Miss MARION TERRY
Beatie Tomlinson (a Young Lady, reduced to teaching Music)		Miss NORREYS
Popham		Miss LA COSTE

ACT I.

THE FAMILY SKELETON.

AT MR. POSKET'S, BLOOMSBURY.

ACT II.

IT LEAVES ITS CUPBOARD.

ROOM IN THE HOTEL DES PRINCES, MEEK STREET.

ACT III.

IT CRUMBLES.

Scene First—THE MAGISTRATE'S ROOM, MULBERRY ST.
Scene Second—AT MR. POSKET'S AGAIN.

The Curtain will be lowered for a few moments between Scenes 1 and 2.

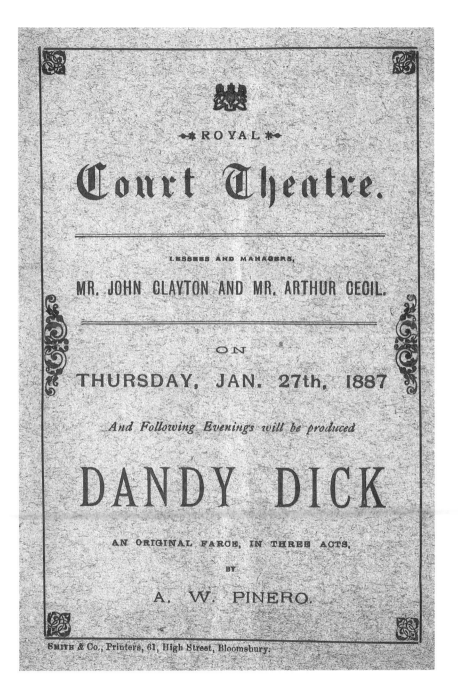

Above and over page: Programme of Pinero's farce *Dandy Dick*.

�֍ PROGRAMME. �֍

THIS EVENING, AT 8.30 PUNCTUALLY,

DANDY DICK

An Original Farce, in Three Acts, by

A. W. PINERO.

The Very Rev. Augustin Jedd, D.D.   Mr JOHN CLAYTON
(Dean of St. Marvell's)

Sir Tristram Mardon, Bart.   Mr EDMUND MAURICE

Major Tarver ⎱ —th Hussars, quartered ⎰   Mr F. KERR
⎰ at Durnstone, near ⎱
Mr Darbey ⎰   St. Marvell's   ⎱ Mr H. EVERSFIELD

Blore   ...   ...   Mr ARTHUR CECIL
(Butler at the Deanery)

Noah Topping   ...   ...   Mr W. H. DENNY
(Constable at St. Marvell's)

Hatcham   ..   ..   Mr W. LUGG
(Sir Tristram's Groom)

Georgiana Tidman ...   ...   Mrs JOHN WOOD
(a Widow, the Dean's Sister)

Salome ⎱   ⎰ Miss MARIE LEWES
⎰ The Dean's Daughters ⎱
Sheba ⎰   ⎱ Miss NORREYS

Hannah Topping   ...   Miss LAURA LINDEN
(formerly in service at the Deanery)

Act I. At The Deanery, St. Marvell's -   -   Morning

Act II. The Same Place - - - - - - Evening

Act III. Sc. 1. 'The Strong Box,' St. Marvell's ⎱ The
Sc. 2. The Deanery again ⎰ Next Day

The Curtain will be lowered for a few minutes between the Two Scenes.

NEW SCENERY BY MR. T. W. HALL.

considered all round. The character is more developed and riper, and the situations grow naturally out of the idiosyncrasies of the dramatis personae. *The Magistrate* is perhaps more mirth-provoking, but the fun is more forced than in *Dandy Dick*. There are signs here and there of a determination to get a laugh at any cost, and when you come to think it over, the idea of the young man nearly twenty passing as a schoolboy of fourteen is not very delicately worked out . . .'

You can see how it *is* worked out, by the sisters Agatha and Charlotte anyway, if you care to read the scene between them in the Interlude which follows (see p. 84). For the moment, back to Hamilton Fyfe: '*The Schoolmistress* is wilder farce than either *The Magistrate* or *Dandy Dick*, but the wit of the dialogue and the neatness of the characterisation remove it far away from anything like the rough-and-tumble variety of comic drama . . . When you think of *The Magistrate*, your memory goes back to situations – to the raid on the gambling establishment or the confronting of the unlucky Mr Posket on the bench with his wife and sister-in-law in the dock.'

When Hamilton Fyfe writes 'gambling establishment' I think he means the 'Hôtel des Princes'. Note the French name, with a French proprietor, Monsieur Achille Blond and the French waiter, Isidore. Underlining these French farce points even further, Pinero adhered to the Feydeau principle that all characters who stand to lose most by being brought together in compromising circumstances, *are* brought together to ensure maximum embarrassment and confusion. Thus everyone arrives at the hotel – husbands, wives, boyfriends – with the law there, as well. Piling Pelion on Ossa, Pinero uses the old farcical trick of darkness in this scene – shades of Harlequin and Molière (and, subsequently, Peter Shaffer) – which will no doubt continue to be trotted out as long as farceurs and pantomimists inhabit this earth.

Fyfe is not so enthusiastic about *The Cabinet Minister*:

Another triumph for Mrs John Wood, another popular success, but not another comic masterpiece like its predecessor . . . a play that can always be counted to amuse, but it goes no further than that. Vastly better in every way is *The Amazons*.

To sum up in a few words, the qualities that give these farces their special merit are the substantial reality of the character-drawing – not of the central figures alone, but many of the subordinate characters as well; the natural manner in which the plots and situations arise out of the idiosyncracies of the people; the easy humour and wit of the dialogue

. . . they will scarcely live, then, as Congreve's and Sheridan's plays live. But they will not be willingly let die, at any rate by this generation.

Needless to say, they weren't. And, apart from *The Amazons*, they still pop up from time to time several generations later.

Hamilton Fyfe may have been a Pinero enthusiast, and therefore one with a close understanding of farce. However, the genre, as ever, and particularly Pinero, did have a severe critic at that time, in the shape of GBS – George Bernard Shaw. Indeed he attacked one of Pinero's plays, *The Hobby Horse*, as a 'provincial farce . . . distorted and debased to suit the childishness and vulgarity of the theatre of 1886.' He also had a go at nineteenth-century farce in general: 'We have had it again, and again under various titles: Act I, John Smith's home; Act II, the rowdy restaurant or casino at which John Smith, in the course of his clandestine spree, meets all the members of his household, including the schoolboy and the parlourmaid; Act III, his house the next morning with inevitable aftermath of the complications of the night before; who has any theatrical experience, does not know it by heart?'

A thinly veiled attack on the *The Magistrate*, wouldn't you say? And not too thinly-veiled at that . . .

Hamilton Fyfe reacted with a critique of Shaw's plays: 'Of course there are farces which depend upon wit rather than humour; such are the plays of Mr Bernard Shaw . . . these would be comedies if the characters were possible people. Mr Shaw's wit is so spontaneous that he almost persuades us his characters are real. But really they are only so many Mr Bernard Shaws in disguise . . . Shaw, in his impatience with the genre, is here inclined to underestimate the extent to which even conventional or stale plot devices can be freshly and imaginatively handled; and indeed, his own *You Never Can Tell* (1899) is a case in point.'

Later, Hamilton Fyfe added Shaw's *Misalliance* (1910) and *Too True to be Good* (1932) to GBS's cerebral creations.

Just before the most famous farce of all time opened, another author who, like Pinero, wrote farce as a springboard to literary legend, produced his first success, *Walker, London*. His name? J M Barrie, author of *Peter Pan*, later created a Baronet and in receipt of the Order of Merit. But on 25 February 1892, he was jolly grateful that John Laurence Toole decided to present his farce at the one-time Charing Cross Theatre. It was later re-named after its owner, Toole's

Theatre, for Toole was at his most popular in farce but gout curtailed his career a mere three years later. A close run thing but, unlike so much of Sir James's later work, *Walker, London* is as forgotten as Toole's Theatre, which was pulled down when its owner, quite literally, could no longer bear to tread the boards.

John Lawrence Toole

Forgetful, too, was Toole himself. A young actor, who popped in and out of farce, burlesque, musical comedy, music-hall and review with equal facility for many years after his West End appearance in *Walker, London*, was Seymour (later Sir Seymour) Hicks – then aged twenty-one. He recalls that the play 'was produced eventually in the face of many difficulties, not the least of which was that Mr Toole did not know his part, and indeed was still imperfect when the piece was withdrawn after 600 performances.' Sir Seymour's own memory was a little rusty on that occasion, for the play actually ran for 511 performances – but who's counting . . .?

The most serious rival to Pinero's supremacy as a farce writer turned out to be no rival at all when it came to output, for he only needed to write just one success, *Charley's Aunt*. Brandon Thomas was the lucky author and, apart from that single play, have you ever heard

GLOBE THEATRE.

Lessee ... ... Mr. W. S. PENLEY.

Every Evening at 9 o'clock,
The Farcical Comedy, entitled

CHARLEY'S AUNT

By BRANDON THOMAS.

Stephen Spettigue	(Solicitor, Oxford) ...	...	Mr. SYDNEY PAXTON
Col. Sir Francis Chesney, Bart. ...	(late Indian Service)	...	Mr. WALTER EVERARD
Jack Chesney			Mr. H. REEVES SMITH
Charley Wykeham	... Undergraduates, St. Olde's College, Oxford) ...		Mr. HARRY FARMER
Lord Fancourt Babberley			Mr. W. S. PENLEY
Brassett	(College Scout) ...	...	Mr. CECIL H. THORNBURY
Donna Lucia D'Alvadorez ...	... (from Brazil) ...	...	... Miss ADA BRANSON
Amy Spettigue	... (Spettigue's Niece)	...	... Miss EMMIE MERRICK
Kitty Verdun	... (his Ward) ..	...	Miss RHODA KILDARE
Ela Delahay	(an Orphan)	...	Miss KATE GRAVES

Time.—The Present.	Commemoration Week.	Oxford.

Act I.—Jack Chesney's Rooms in College.
" When pious frauds . . . . are dispensations."—*Hudibras*.

Act II.—Garden outside Jack's Rooms.   **Act III.—Drawing Room at Spettigue's House.**
" While there's tea, there's hope "—*Pinero*.   " Dinner lubricates business."—*Boswell*.
(The Piece produced under the direction of the Author).

Preceded at 8 o'clock by a Play in One Act, entitled

"THE JOURNEY'S END,"

By HORACE W. C. NEWTE.

Allan Blair	...	Mr. SYDNEY PAXTON
Edwin Clements	...	Mr. H. REEVES SMITH
Theophilus Briggs...	...	Mr. CECIL H. THORNBURY
Eleanor		Miss ANNIE L. AUMONIER
Ethel	... Blair's Daughters ...	Miss MABEL LANE

Scene ... Blair's Estancia in the Andes; Chili.   TIME—THE PRESENT.
The New Scenery specially painted by Mr. BRUCE SMITH.

Business Manager	...	Mr. FRANCIS GOSNAY
Treasurer	...	Mr. W. A. TINNEY
Musical Director... ... ... Mr. FRANZ GROENINGS	Stage Manager	Mr. WILTON HERIOT

Wigs by Fox. Dresses by Messrs. MARSHALL & SNELGROVE. Furniture &c., by OETZMANN & Co., Piano by KIRKMAN & Co.

Engravings and Etchings by Messrs. DOWDESWELL & DOWDESWELL, 160, New Bond Street.

Photographs of Mr. W. S. PENLEY & COMPANY, by T. C. Turner & Co., 10, Barnsbury Park, N.

Matinee Every Saturday at 3.

PRICES OF ADMISSION.—Private Boxes, £1 1s. and £3 3s.; Stalls, 10s. 6d.; Dress Circle, 6s.; Upper Circle, 4s.;
Pit, 2s.; Gallery, 1s.

Box Office open 10 to 5, under the direction of Mr. H. W. ANDERSON, and during the Performance.
Doors open at 7.30. Carriages 11. Seats can be secured by Telegram and at all Libraries.

Opera Glasses on hire 1s. 6d., can be had of the Attendants. ICES, TEA AND COFFEE.
All ICES sold at this Theatre are supplied by The AUTOMATIC AND HORTON ICES, Limited, Queen's Road, Bayswater.

Programme from the first production of Brandon Thomas' *Charley's Aunt*.

of him in any other context? Probably the answer will be 'no', but he was an actor, a manager and a composer, too. Mark you, such was the success of his one and only smash-hit, it provided a huge income to all concerned long after his death in 1914 at the age of fifty-seven and his other talents were simply not needed.

Charley's Aunt began its never-ending run at the Theatre Royal, Bury St Edmunds on Leap Year's Day, 29 February 1892, with W S Penley playing the part of 'Babs'. We met him last in *The Private Secretary*, you will recall. Of course, he was far too old for the part of Lord Fancourt Babberly, being forty at the time, but he wasn't the oldest by a long chalk. Jack Benny, for instance, was forty-seven when he made the film. Ten months after Bury St Edmunds, *Charley's Aunt* came to the Royalty Theatre in London, where it remained for 1,466 performances, enjoying a further forty productions all round the world at the same time, and since then it has been revived almost fifty times in the West End alone. For years there was an annual Christmas production – just like Barrie's *Peter Pan* – with a leading comic always prepared to have a go, and in 1992 a centenary tour was mounted, starting life again at Bury St Edmunds, which was very successful. It has been filmed several times, once, as mentioned, with the unlikely Jack Benny, not only making a mockery of the young undergraduate theme but also scarcely qualifying as a typical, silly-ass English aristocrat, and still it was a hit, as was an Arthur Askey version as *Charley's Big-Hearted Aunt*. George Abbott and Frank Loesser turned it into a musical, *Where's Charley?*, which ran for 779 performances at the St James' Theatre on Broadway, managing a further 380 performances at the Palace Theatre in Shaftesbury Avenue. It is virtually indestructible, and will survive quite happily, I am sure, into the twenty-first century, shaking off any occasional unpleasant notices such as that received by a Christmas 1994 production at the Royal Exchange, Manchester, with the *Times* headline: '*Charley's Aunt* – she's not even a close relative.'

I remember its last West End outing well, in 1981, because my wife, Elspet, was playing Charley's real aunt, Donna Lucia. The production began life at the Lyric Theatre, Hammersmith, with Griff Rhys Jones as 'Babs' (and almost the right age, too), and then transferred to the Aldwych. Within days Griff had succumbed to the dreaded mumps, so his sparring partner, Mel Smith, took over. Both were excellent in entirely different ways. Eventually Griff recovered, returned, and the production went merrily on its way. Yes, an incredible piece. As the annual advert used to say: '*Charley's Aunt* – still running.' And she still does to this very day. But one thing always niggles . . .

Do you know how Brandon Thomas billed his phenomenon? Yes, you're right. A FARCICAL COMEDY. How low can you get.

QUICK CURTAIN

INTERLUDE

The Magistrate

Court Theatre, *March* 1885

Mr Posket	Mr Arthur Cecil
Mr Bullamy	Mr Fred Cape
Colonel Lukyn	Mr John Clayton
Captain Horace Vale	Mr F Kerr
Cis Farringdon	Mr H Eversfield
Achille Blond	Mr Albert Chevalier
Isidore	Mr Deane
Mr Wormington	Mr Gilbert Trent
Inspector Messiter	Mr Albert Sims
Sergeant Lugg	Mr Lugg
Constable Harris	Mr Burnley
Wyke	Mr Fayre
Agatha Posket	Mrs John Wood
Charlotte	Miss Marion Terry
Beatie Tomlinson	Miss Norreys
Popham	Miss La Coste

Now follows some typical Pinero dialogue when, in Act I, Agatha Posket explains to her sister, Charlotte, how Cis is younger than he seems:

> AGATHA. Now, we can tell each other our miseries undisturbed. Will you begin?
> CHARLOTTE. Well, at last I am engaged to Captain Horace Vale.
> AGATHA. Oh, Charley! I'm so glad.
> CHARLOTTE. Yes, so is he, he says. He proposed to me at the Hunt Ball – in the passage – Tuesday week.
> AGATHA. What did he say?

84

CHARLOTTE. He said, "By Jove, I love you awfully."

AGATHA. Well, and what did you say?

CHARLOTTE. Oh, I said, "Well, if you're going to be as eloquent as all that, by Jove, I can't stand out." So we settled it in the passage. He bars flirting till after we're married. That's my misery. What's yours, Aggy?

AGATHA. Something awful.

CHARLOTTE. Cheer up, Aggy! What is it?

AGATHA. Well, Charley, you know, I lost my poor dear first husband at a very delicate age.

CHARLOTTE. Well, you were five-and-thirty, dear.

AGATHA. Yes, that's what I mean. Five-and-thirty is a very delicate age to find yourself single. You're neither one thing nor the other. You're not exactly a two-year-old, and you don't care to pull a hansom. However, I soon met Mr Posket at Spa – bless him!

CHARLOTTE. And you nominated yourself for the Matrimonial Stakes. Mr Farringdon's The Widow, by Bereavement, out of Mourning, ten pounds extra.

AGATHA. Yes, Charley, and in less than a month I went triumphantly over the course. But, Charley dear, I didn't carry the fair weight for age – and that's my trouble.

CHARLOTTE. Oh, dear!

AGATHA. Undervaluing Æneas's love, in a moment of, I hope, not unjustifiable vanity, I took five years from my total, which made me thirty-one on my wedding morning.

CHARLOTTE. Well, my dear, many a misguided woman has done that before you.

AGATHA. Yes, Charley, but don't you see the consequences? It has thrown everything out. As I am now thirty-one instead of thirty-six, as I ought to be, it stands to reason that I couldn't have been married twenty years ago, which I was. So I have had to fib in proportion.

CHARLOTTE. I see – making your first marriage occur only fifteen years ago.

AGATHA. Exactly.

CHARLOTTE. Well, then, dear, why worry yourself further?

AGATHA. Why, dear, don't you see? If I am only thirty-one now, my boy couldn't have been born nineteen years ago, and, if he could, he oughtn't to have been, because, on my own showing, I wasn't married till four years later. Now you see the result!

CHARLOTTE. Which is that that fine strapping young gentleman over there is only fourteen.

AGATHA. Precisely. Isn't it awkward? And his moustache is becoming more and more obvious every day.

CHARLOTTE. What does the boy himself believe?

AGATHA. He believes his mother, of course, as a boy should. As a prudent woman I always kept him in ignorance of his age in case of necessity. But it is terribly hard on the poor child, because his aims, instincts and ambitions are all so horribly in advance of his condition. His food, his books, his amusements are out of keeping with his palate, his brain and his disposition; and with all this suffering, his wretched mother has the remorseful consciousness of having shortened her offspring's life.

CHARLOTTE. Oh, come, you haven't quite done that.

AGATHA. Yes, I have, because, if he lives to be a hundred, he must be buried at ninety-five.

And the complications continue . . .

ACT III BEGINNERS, PLEASE.

ACT III

Scene i: Definitely in the West End

A Lloyd's 'name', down in the City,
Lost millions, which was a pity,
When told of his folly
He said 'I'm no wallie –
I haven't a bean, so tough titty.'

Anonymous, 1993.

Aᴺᴰ ɪ ʙᴇᴛ that doggerel has been around, in various versions, since the crash of 1929 and Black Wednesday in 1992. Only 'a stockbroker' would have have taken the place of 'a Lloyd's name' on the first two occasions.

Be that as it may, it's a pretty clumsy way of introducing the names of the two farce writers who dominated the West End stage 'twixt Pinero and Brandon Thomas at the end of the nineteenth century and Ben Travers some thirty-odd years later. But both of them were Wallys, or Walters, to be more precise: Walter Ellis and Walter Hackett. There was a third Walter, Walter Greenwood, but he came later and was renowned for his drama *Love on the Dole* (which he adapted with Ronald Gow from his novel of the same name), rather than his North-country farces – *Ma's Bit o' Brass*, *The Cure For Love* and *Saturday Night at the Crown*.

Let's take a look at Walter Ellis first. His greatest hit was *A Little Bit of Fluff*, which was presented at the Criterion Theatre on 27 October 1915, where it ran for 1,241 performances. It was revived on two other occasions in the West End, both productions being at the Ambassadors Theatre, one in 1923 and the other for a brief run before the *Sweet and Low* Reviews in 1943, but the troops on leave in the 1914 – 18 war gave it almost as great a reception as that which they accorded Oscar Asche's musical, *Chu-Chin-Chow*, which ran for 2,238 performances at His Majesty's Theatre, from 31 August 1916 – then the longest West End run ever.

A newspaper cutting at the time seems to capture the essence of the public's attitude to the Great War, especially before the full horror of the Western Front had been borne in upon them. You can see how easy it must have been for young ladies to feel qualified to hand out white feathers to those not in uniform. Oh dear, oh dear.

Companions in Arms

One of the most interesting features of the first night performance of *A Little Bit of Fluff*, at the Criterion Theatre, was the presence in the stalls of many members of the 9th London Regiment. They all came to see their companion in arms, Ernest Thesiger, play the highly-amusing character of Bertram Tully.

Both Wounded

I noticed among them Bertram Forsyth, playwright and actor, who came with Mr Russell-Jones. Mr Forsyth and Mr Thesiger, who enlisted in the Queen Victoria Rifles were wounded early in the war. They have, I believe, both been discharged.

In spite of his wounds, Ernest Thesiger lived to the age of eighty-one, still working away and famous for his embroidery, rather than his performance as Bertram Tully. He even wrote a book called *Adventures in Embroidery* and I remember hearing that he loved long train calls, for he could settle in a corner, quietly tatting away. A funny lot, actors.

What kind of notices were given to *A Little Bit of Fluff*? Well, pretty good, as far as I can see. B N Findon, the editor of *Play Pictorial* wrote:

A farce that has a plausible motive with comic situations that have a basis of reasonable probability, and which can keep going with no weakening of the action in the last act is a masterpiece of its kind, and that is what may be said of Mr Walter D Ellis' *A Little Bit of Fluff*. The success of a farce can be quickiy gauged, for unless it is productive of abundant laughter, it has failed in its purpose. Hilarious laughter was never more in evidence in the playhouse than it is at the present time at the Criterion, if the two performances I have seen represent the others. [*Two* performances! Critics, please note!]

We are interested from the very beginning, when John Ayers makes a matutinal entry to the connubial flat in dress clothes. [How many farces

Mr CHARLES HAWTREY
as
Bernard (Bunny) Darrell.

Sir Charles Hawtrey.

Programme from a recent production of Pinero's *The Magistrate*.

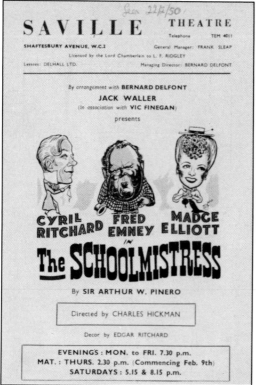

Programme from a production of Pinero's *The Schoolmistress*.

Productions of Walter Ellis' *A Little Bit of Fluff*.

GRIFF RHYS JONES

IN

CHARLEY'S AUNT

BY
BRANDON
THOMAS

WITH
ELSPET
GRAY

ADAM
BLACKWOOD

ANITA
DOBSON

EVA
GRIFFITH

TERENCE
LONGDON

BRIONY
McROBERTS

MARK
PAYTON

JOHN
RINGHAM

AND

DAVID
ROSS

DIRECTED BY
PETER
JAMES
AND
PETER
WILSON

DESIGNED BY
MARTIN
SUTHERLAND

LIGHTING BY
DAVE
HORN

ALDWYCH THEATRE
ALDWYCH, LONDON WC2

01-836 6404, 01-379 6233
CREDIT CARDS 01-836 0641

TWELVE WEEKS ONLY

'WONDERFULLY
FUNNY PERFORMANCE'
IRVING WARDLE, THE TIMES

'A VERY FUNNY MAN'
MICHAEL BILLINGTON, THE GUARDIAN

Various productions of Brandon Thomas'
Charley's Aunt.

Opposite page: Norman Wisdom in the
musical version of *Charley's Aunt*,
Where's Charley?

Jack Buchanan.

Lupino Lane.

Leslie Henson and Sydney Howard.

Cicely Courtneidge.

Seymour Hicks.

Ralph Lynn and Tom Walls.

have used that opening scene in one form or another? Except they might be more easily understood than Mr Findon's somewhat arcane and archaic English.] The angry wife comes to the charge without delay. Where had he passed the night? John mentions one or two friends to prove the story of his nocturnal misadventure, but Pamela Ayres has him in a cleft stick. She had wired to some half dozen of his friends, and each had answered that John had slept at his place.

The complications pile one upon another in true farcical style with Ernest Thesiger's performance as Bertram Tully described thus: 'Bertram is a namby-pamby sort of person without an atom of guile in his composition, and his absurd efforts to assist John in his difficulty adds enormously to the innocent merriment of the play.'

'Innocent merriment'! A far cry from Feydeau and Labiche, but until the Lord Chamberlain's exit in 1968, English farce writers were only permitted to hint, in the vaguest terms, at any sexual activity between consenting heterosexuals. As soon as the baleful influence emanating from St James's Palace was removed it became possible for the Joe Ortons of this world to flourish, whilst farces like *Not Now Darling*, by Ray Cooney and John Chapman and *Don't Just Lie There, Say Something!* by Michael Pertwee, with assorted contributions from me, could edge uneasily towards the greater freedom of a world where you could climb into bed with your mistress, as long as you were tipped out of it before any actual bonking took place. You *could* do that too, I suppose, but you would have lost your family audience, I fear – and a farce is physically exhausting enough for the principal actors anyway, without them being called upon to display any undue simulated extra-marital activity.

A Little Bit of Fluff made a great deal of money for everyone. Three touring companies went around the country from one year to the next, whilst three films were made of the piece – two silent pictures and one 'talkie'. In addition, the 'colonial' rights added considerably to the revenue, so Anthony Ellis and Herbert Jay, who presented it, plus the author, Walter Ellis, were well satisfied. Indeed, they set a pattern for the exploitation of farces which changed little until the 1960s, when the film rights of such plays were no longer snapped up. However, by then I had embraced television as a successful medium for screening farces but, alas, that method is no longer popular with the television moguls. I'm not so sure about the viewing audience, but since when did telly controllers care about them?

Walter Ellis wrote many other plays, with rather obvious titles (as though farce titles have ever been otherwise) such as: *Night Duty*, *What Woman Wants*, *Glass Houses*, *Bedtime Story*, *Good Men Sleep At Home* and – the title perpetuating the myth about promiscuous performers – *Actresses Will Happen* which, in fact, was only about a suburban household where mother and daughter are both so film-struck they cannot open their mouths without giving a performance. One more title for your delectation, and one more Walter Ellis farce which was a great success, *Almost a Honeymoon*. This ran for over two years (894 performances) at the Apollo Theatre, moving there on 24 March 1930, from the Garrick Theatre, where it had opened a couple of months before, on 9 February, with notices which really showed the constraints under which playwrights laboured (and critics too – notice the anonymity, initials only, but almost certainly Horace Horsnell, himself the author of a 'farcical comedy' with Herbert Farjeon, *Advertising April*):

ALMOST A HONEYMOON
By Walter Ellis

I visited this farce on Thursday afternoon, expecting – what does one not expect from a farce so named, and on a Thursday afternoon? The grimness of my anticipations, however, was in no way responsible for the agreeable surprise it gave me. The audience was genially and generously laced with clergymen, as if some moral issue were to be tried; and my programme contained a printed slip, asking: (1) Whether I considered the play a clean English farce, and (2) whether I disapproved of its bedroom scene. I consider it a clean English farce, and would answer the second question in the manner most complimentary to Miss Renee Kelly and Mr Gerald Pring, who, occupying the two beds in the bedroom scene, amused me as much as they amused my clerical neighbours. There wasn't a blush between us. The plot would not puzzle even a judge of the High Courts; it would probably divert him; and it is played by a capital company, including miss Grace Lane and Mr Lamont Dickson, with just that mixture of high spirits and intimacy that makes so many pure playgoers look forward to Thursday afternoons.

H H

Perhaps prurient would be more accurate than pure, but let's give them the benefit of the doubt.

Now, Walter Hackett. I should mention *It Pays to Advertise* first (which Hackett wrote with Roi Cooper Megrue), for it was originally produced at the George M Cohan Theatre in New York on 8 September 1914 but, probably due to the Great War, was not seen in London for a further ten years, when it was the second play of the thirteen farces presented at the Aldwych Theatre, and which I will discuss a little later. By then Walter Hackett was a firm fixture on this side of the Atlantic, having been born in California and bringing his Pennsylvanian bride over to England for a three-week honeymoon in the same year *It Pays To Advertise* opened in New York, hoping to sell one of his plays to pay for the trip. He didn't, but he stayed on this side of the Atlantic with his newly-wedded wife and eventually they presented an average of one play a year in tne West End, with Hackett writing the piece and his bride, Marion Lorne, in the lead. Together they were responsible for twenty-one productions, many of them farces or comedy-thrillers and, furthermore, they opened the Whitehall Theatre in 1930 – my London home some twenty years later – with a transfer from the Duke of York's Theatre, *The Way to Treat a Woman*. They went on to present *Good Losers* (written in collaboration with Michael Arlen), *Take a Chance*, *The Gay Adventure*, *Road House* and *Afterwards*. In 1934 they left the Whitehall and took over the management of the Apollo Theatre, where they stayed for three more years, before leasing the Vaudeville Theatre. Walter Hackett died in 1944, aged sixty-seven, his wife went back to America and became a highly-successful television star from 1964 – 68 as Aunt Clara in *Bewitched*. Her last film appearance was in 1967 as Miss De Witt, with Dustin Hoffman, in *The Graduate*. Remember?

Walter Hackett's first big success in this country, though, was in 1921 with *Ambrose Applejohn's Adventure*, which ran at the Criterion Theatre for 455 performances, transferring to the Savoy Theatre for a further 148. This was the play which saw the final performances of a great light comedian, Sir Charles Hawtrey. I hesitate to call him a farceur, even though he adapted the original 'modern' farce, *The Private Secretary*, for he has received many conflicting descriptions as an actor. Ben Travers described him in *Vale of Laughter*: 'He held all the gifts of comedy in the palm of his hand and manipulated them gracefully and fondly like a master conjurer.' Keble Howard in *The Sketch*: 'He was knighted in 1922; the honour was conferred on him as the best living representative of the art of comedy.' George Rowell in *The Victorian Theatre*: 'The idea that a man was "fast" added salt to Victorian gossip and provided Charles Hawtrey with the theme for a long series of successful farces, wholly acceptable to his fashionable public.'

Finally, an anonymous critic described him as 'the best stage liar of his time' and went on to remember him for his swan-song in Walter Hackett's play, *Ambrose Applejohn's Adventure*: 'It is fitting that his last big success should have been one bringing out the ridiculous incongruity between romantic adventure and the actor's incurably anti-romantic temperament . . . This was characteristic; and when his posthumous memoirs came out, edited by Mr Somerset Maugham and finished by him, it appeared that the actor had a far keener zest for the turf than for the stage. It struck Mr Maugham as singular that a man should excel in an art which took second place in his life to racing. But that also was somehow characteristic of the temperament which Hawtrey projected on the stage.'

Four other comic actors of recent memory had a well-known liking for the turf, too: Tom Walls, Robert Morley and Wilfred Hyde White, with Fabia Drake keeping up the distaff contribution to the bookies, so this passion seems to be of little hindrance when it comes to making people laugh. Indeed, both Hawtrey and Walls were actor-managers and sometimes it's impossible to gauge which is the bigger gamble – putting your shirt on a play or a gee-gee. You just know the result a damn sight quicker with one than the other, that's all, but it generally ends in tears either way. Unless you win the Derby, that is – like Tom Walls.

Now, a little name dropping to finish off Sir Charles Hawtrey's potted biography. I was a guest at the Prime Minister's country seat, Chequers, one New Year's Day and, along with many others, enjoying coffee in the long library after lunch. I wandered up to the far end of the room, past Napoleon's desk, and looked at the stained-glass windows which are full of various coats-of-arms. There I noticed the name Hawtrey and John Major (who was our host) pointed out that the actor's family had owned the original house for a couple of centuries. No wonder he was able to play landed gents with such consummate ease . . .

Before we take the next sequential step to the Aldwych farces, I think I should spend a short time with musical comedies, which had farcical storylines and were very popular from the late-nineteenth century until the 1960s. Indeed, they had a good pedigree for, until Pinero, the majority of English farces had musical interludes woven into them, although the songs were not so essential to the story as in their twentieth-century counterparts. I fear that for the next few pages there will be a number of occasions when you might think you are reading a Samuel French or Warner Chappell catalogue, for titles, writers, librettists and composers will be appearing in profusion. That is simply because I wish this book to be historically correct and, at the same time, I think it only right and proper that those who did the original donkey work of composition are given due credit. All too often they are forgotten in the general genuflexion granted to great actors, even Shakespeare, and sometimes his work is credited to Francis Bacon, Philip Massinger, Christopher Marlowe, the sixth Earl of Derby and the seventeenth Earl of Oxford. Quite a list there for starters.

I've already made a passing reference to the great musical-comedy stars, Sir Seymour Hicks, Dame Cicely Courtneidge, Jack Hulbert, Jack Buchanan, Bobby Howes, Lupino Lane and Leslie Henson. There were others, of course, including the superb, stately Sydney Howard and the monumental Vera Pearce, whilst those who came

Sydney Howard.

from a music-hall background included George Formby with his ukelele and his films, Arthur Askey with his 'broadcasting', his pantomimes, his musicals, his farces and *his* films and Will Hay with his genius which even *survived* his films. All added immeasurably to the gaiety of nations – well, this nation, anyway – and their names on a playbill were certainly guaranteed to give any production more than an even chance at the box-office.

Each and everyone of them sometimes appeared in non-musical comedies or farces too; some went into management or, occasionally, put pen to paper, especially Seymour Hicks (1871 – 1949) who claimed to have written no less than sixty-six plays. I'm not sure how many are still available or how many reflected other author's works. In the States, Hicks was renowned for his 'borrowing' of material, especially songs and jokes, so much so that performers used to apologise to the audience on certain nights, saying they wouldn't be presenting all their act, as 'Seymour Hicks is out front'. He brought his first great success over from New York, *A Night Out*,

Seymour Hicks.

94

in 1896, which he adapted from the work of Charles Klein who, in turn, had adapted it from the French. Hicks was the same age as me when I presented *Reluctant Heroes* in the West End, just twenty-six years old, but his 'home' was the Vaudeville Theatre, whereas mine was a few hundred yards away at the Whitehall. Also, his production ran for 531 performances, but mine added eleven hundred more to that total. Nevertheless, his overall profit in real terms was probably greater than mine, for he made over £32,000. I made more, but two world wars had sadly depleted the value of the pound. One other similarity: Seymour Hicks appeared in many plays with his wife, Ellaline Terris; I appeared in many with mine, Elspet Gray, especially in the television farces from the Whitehall and Garrick Theatres. It's a marvellous recipe for a happy marriage. All your arguments can take place in the rehearsal room. By the time you get home, you're too exhausted to continue the struggle or you can't remember what all the fuss was about!

I shall bracket another married couple Dame Cicely Courtneidge (1893 – 1980) and Jack Hulbert (1892 – 1978) together, for they were as inextricably linked in British audiences' minds as roast beef and Yorkshire pudding. Cis was the daughter of impresario, Robert Courtneidge, and worked for her father from the age of eight. Then Jack was employed by Robert direct from the Cambridge Footlights, married Cis in 1913, but was soon serving on the Western Front in the First World War. Cis was what is known as 'available for work', tried her hand at music-hall, got many a laugh and realised she was a comedienne. Jack was demobbed, went back to the 'legitimate' theatre but he and Cis hated being apart, so in 1923 they launched themselves at the Little Theatre in *The Little Revue Starts at Nine* (by Harold Simpson, Reginald Arkell, Douglas Furber, with music by Herman Finck). This led to a bigger theatre, and a bigger show with *By-the-Way* (by Ronald Jeans, Harold Simpson, with music by Vivian Ellis and lyrics by Graham John) at the Apollo Theatre in 1925, and they were on *their* way. Henceforward, it was a succession of revues and musicals, including *The House that Jack Built* (by Ronald Jeans, Douglas Furber, with music by Ivor Novello and lyrics by Donovan Parsons, plus additional numbers by Vivian Ellis and Arthur Schwartz), *Folly To Be Wise* (by Dion Titheradge, with music by Vivian Ellis), *Hide and Seek* (by Guy Bolton, Fred Thompson, Douglas Furber, with music by Vivian Ellis, Lerner, Goodhart and Hoffman), *Under Your Hat* (by

Jack Hulbert.

Archie Menzies, Arthur Macrae, Jack Hulbert, with music and lyrics by Vivian Ellis), *Full Swing* (by the same writers as for *Under Your Hat*, but music by George Posford, Harry Parr Davies and Robert Probst), *Something in the Air* (again by the same writers, but music by Manning Sherwin), *Under the Counter* (only one writer, Arthur Macrae and one composer, Manning Sherwin), *Her Excellency* (by Archie Menzies, Max Kestner, with music by Manning Sherwin and Harry Parr-Davies), and *Gay's The Word* (an ironic title in today's politically correct language when you recall its two writers were Ivor Novello and Alan Melville). Cis and Jack appeared together – and separately – in a number of films, as they did in a few 'straight' plays. My last memory of them as a couple was at Heathrow Airport, patiently waiting to board the 'plane to Canada, where Cis was to perform in the Ray Cooney, John Chapman farce *Move Over Mrs Markham* along with Honor Blackman, Terry Alexander and my wife, Elspet. Jack, well into his eighties and fresh out of hospital, went along for

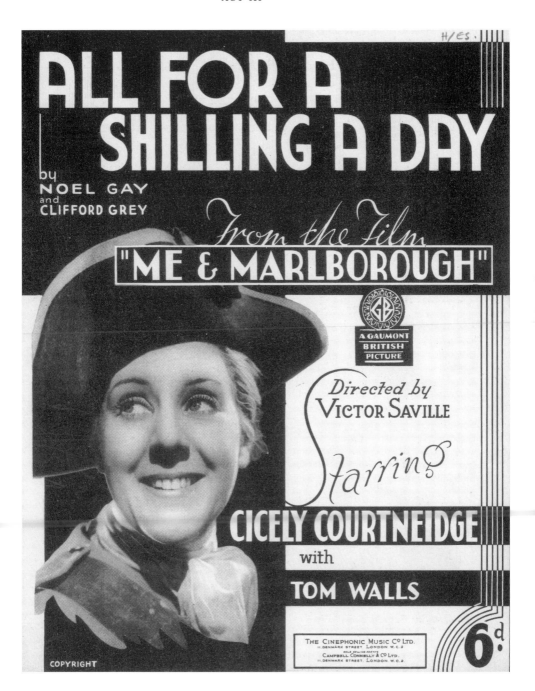

Cicely Courtneidge.

Cicely Courtneidge, Alfred Lester and Jack Hulbert in a production entitled *The Pearl Girl*.

the ride. A somewhat anti-climactic end to the careers of two great comedy artists, who had entertained millions over the years. But then, I suppose that's the way it goes. Not only in the theatre, come to think of it. Even the House of Lords is known as 'God's Waiting Room' . . .

If you mention the name of Jack Buchanan (1891 – 1957) there will still be some who remember that scratchy old 78 of him singing *Goodnight Vienna*, but that was only one film amongst many in which he appeared, generally as a song-and-dance man in stories which veered towards farce rather than romance. *Yes Mr Brown* (from the German *Ein Bißchen Liebe*, by Paul Frank and Ludwig Hershfield), *That's a Good Girl* (from the musical comedy by Douglas Furber, music by Philip Charig and Joseph Meyer), with his favourite leading lady, Elsie Randolph, *Brewster's Millions*, (from the farce by G B McCutcheon, Winchell Smith and Byron Ongley), *When Knights Were Bold* (from the farce by Charles Marlowe) and *This'll Make You Whistle* (from the musical show by Guy Bolton and Fred Thompson, with music and lyrics by Sigler, Goodhart and Hoffman) were great successes in the thirties, the latter being a huge hit in 1937, on screen and on stage in London both at the same time. Some fifteen years later, *Reluctant Heroes* achieved a similar double, with the play still happily filling the Whitehall, whilst the film was playing to packed houses in the West End and in the suburbs. You couldn't do that nowadays. Later Buchanan films included *The Middle Watch*, a naval farce by Ian Hay and Stephen King-Hall, and one in Hollywood with Fred Astaire, directed by Vincente Minnelli, *The Band Wagon*. On stage he appeared in numerous plays, revues and musicals, ending just before his death with a Vernon Sylvaine farce, *As Long As They're Happy* at the Garrick Theatre, of which he was then the lessee. When I went there in 1967, Jack's manager, John Hallett, was still around as the Managing Director of the theatre, occupying magnificent offices which had once been splendid 'chambers' for the actor-managers who ran the Garrick in its early years – John Hare (from 1889 to 1896) and Arthur Bourchier, with his wife Violet Vanbrugh (from 1900 to 1915). Actually, John Hare was lucky to get into the building at all, even though the theatre was built for him by W S Gilbert as, when it was half-finished, water flooded the foundations from an old underground river known to the Romans, but not, apparently, to Gilbert's architects. The dramatist is said to have remarked that he 'did not know whether to go on with the building or let the fishing rights'. Luckily, he chose the former course and many an entertaining evening has been enjoyed there by actors and audience, alike.

Bobby Howes (1895 – 1972) began his West End career with Cis Courtneidge and Jack Hulbert in *The Little Revue Starts at Nine*, went on to *The Second Little Revue* and then became a firm fixture in London for the next thirty years. Just a few titles tell the tale: *Mr Cinders* (by Clifford Grey and Greatrex Newman, with music by Vivian Ellis and Richard Myers) in which he was described as 'Chaplinesque', *Tell Her the Truth* (based on *Nothing But the Truth* by James Montgomery, adapted by R P Weston and Bert Lee, with music by Jack Waller and Joseph Tunbridge), *Yes, Madam?* (by the same group responsible for *Tell Her the Truth*, with K R G Browne added to the authors), *Please, Teacher* (same lot again), *Hide and Seek* (with Cis and Jack), *All Clear* (devised by Harold French; one name only – that makes a pleasant change), and *Paint Your Wagon*. Unhappily, his successes did not continue into his old age, although he battled on, generally on tour, as his career slowly slid downhill, whilst that of his daughter, Sally Ann Howes, began to climb. The cross-over point came during the run of *Paint Your Wagon*, for Sally Ann achieved an enormous success in that Alan Jay Lerner, Frederick Loewe musical, putting her father's performance somewhat

Bobby Howes.

in the shade. In his day, though, Bobby Howes was one of musical comedy's fixtures and fittings, along with his friends, Binnie Hale, Peter Haddon, Wylie Watson, Bertha Belmore and Vera Pearce. The contrasting size and personality of Vera Pearce and Bobby Howes – she large and aggressive, he small and modest – were much enjoyed by my parents' generation.

Lupino Lane (1892 – 1959) was a member of the famous Lupino family of dancers and acrobats, whose theatrical connections stretched back over two centuries. Lupino himself first walked on the stage at the age of four, during a benefit performance for Vesta Tilley at the Prince of Wales's Theatre, Birmingham. He was only nine when he performed at the London Pavilion, and from then on it was a succession of appearances at all the great Stoll Moss variety theatres in this country, in the principal cities of the United States and Canada, and over the Channel in Paris. Revues, musicals, films, all followed predictably, one after the other, but it is for his appearance as Bill Snibson, first in *Twenty to One* and then in *Me and My Girl*, that he is best known and remembered. *Twenty to One* was a musical farce by L Arthur Rose and Frank Eyton, with music by Billy Mayerl, in which was created the immortal, chirpy Cockney, presented first at the London Coliseum and subsequently at the Victoria Palace by Sir Oswald Stoll and Lupino Lane himself. Realising he had hit the jackpot with this loveable character, Lupino carried on playing the same part in his next smash-hit presentation, *Me and My Girl*, again written by L Arthur Rose, but this time with Douglas Furber and the music composed by Noel Gay. It opened at the Victoria Palace on 16 December 1937 and has been produced almost continuously ever since, with a succession of actors as Bill Snibson, many progressing to stardom from this well-worn role and that oh-so-familiar song and dance, 'The Lambeth Walk'. We were doing that extraordinary 'Oi!' and backward flick of the thumb in my young days in the late 1930s. I bet there will be somebody doing it in the 2030s, too. Pity I won't be around to see it.

Nowadays Lambeth Walk is really rather dreary – just a group of modern houses, flats and maisonettes. Not even a tiny statue to Lupino Lane. I bet one would have been erected by now to Garrick or Irving, though. Comics never get the same attention. Odd, really. I'd have thought laughter was one of the most precious commodities around. Life in any lane – farce, slow or Lupino – would be very dull without it.

101

I have kept Leslie Henson (1891 – 1957) until the end, for he was the last of the 'twixt war 'greats' who popped into my dressing-room at the Whitehall during the run of *Dry Rot*, shortly before he died. He had come to see the show, but had other things on his mind; frankly – work. I'm not for one moment suggesting he was skint – simply that he couldn't persuade any manager to employ him, and this perplexed and distressed him greatly. Indeed, in his obituary in the *Daily Mail*, Cecil Wilson wrote: 'Leslie Henson, who died yesterday after a heart attack at his home in Harrow Weald, Middlesex, aged sixty-six, will be remembered, ironically, as the comedian London forgot. The goggle-eyed, fog-voiced little clown with the public-school accent . . . was the musical comedy riot of his day. But his day was before the war.'

It was at the old Gaiety Theatre, in 1915, that Henson shot to fame overnight, in true theatrical style, as the understudy who took over the leading role in *To-night's the Night* (by Fred Thompson, with music by Paul Rubens). He featured in one triumph after another, mainly at the old Winter Garden and Gaiety Theatres, in such smash-hits as *Kissing Time* (a musical play, from the French, by Guy Bolton and P G Wodehouse, with music by Ivan Caryll), *A Night Out* (another musical play from the French, adapted by George Grossmith and Arthur Miller, with music by Willie Redstone) and *Funny Face* (by Fred Thompson and Paul Girard Smith, with music by George Gershwin). In 1930 he dropped the music from a couple of Austin Melford farces *It's a Boy*, followed by *It's A Girl*, both at the Strand Theatre. Then it was back to musical comedy at the Strand, with *Nice Goings On* (by Douglas Furber, with music by Arthur Schwartz) and, in 1937, one of his greatest successes, *Going Greek* (by Guy Bolton, Fred Thompson and Douglas Furber, with lyrics and music by Lerner, Goodhart and Hoffman). After that, it was one final musical at the Gaiety before the Second World War, *Running Riot*, a musical show by Douglas Furber, from a plot by Guy Bolton and Firth Shephard, with music and lyrics by Vivian Ellis. The show closed at the outbreak of war, as did the Gaiety, never to re-open. Leslie Henson battled on, though, entertaining the troops in many a war zone, playing again in the West End and, after the war, teaming up once more with Austin Melford in *Bob's Your Uncle* (with music by Noel Gay), his last really big success, which ran for 363 performances at the Saville. Then it was revivals, take-overs and tours – pretty ignominious really for a man who had been acclaimed by no less a critic than W A Darlington of the *Daily Telegraph* as 'the funniest comedian of them all' and 'a genius'. His name lives on, though, through his son, Nicky Henson, himself pretty adept at getting laughs.

In addition to his career as an actor, Leslie Henson was also a successful manager, co-presenting many a hit, but for the purposes of this story I will mention but three: *Tons of Money* (1922), *It Pays to Advertise* (1924) and *A Cuckoo in the Nest* (1925); in other words, the first three Aldwych Farces, which Leslie produced along with Tom Walls. After that, Leslie dropped out, and Tom presented the remaining ten plays without his erstwhile partner. I wonder if Leslie regretted that? Probably not, for Tom Walls must have been a very autocratic manager and, after all, he was in the plays; Leslie was not. Mind you, Tom Walls had a rather cavalier attitude to his audiences too, missing (according to Ben Travers) at least a third of all the performances because he was late at the races, or enjoying the company of his friends at the club, or because of any other excuse he could dream up at a moment's notice, picking up the 'phone and telling the stage-manager to put on his understudy. Ben swore there were theatre-goers who saw every Aldwych farce, but never saw Tom Walls! I imagine such an unprofessional attitude irked his co-manager, Leslie Henson. It certainly irked his co-star, Ralph Lynn.

Nowadays, as a result of the blandishments of the Arts Council, or local authorities taking over theatres, theatrical companies have to be professional in a somewhat different way. Business plans are called for, in the short-term, the medium-term and the long-term; performance indicators are studied, sponsorship is sought and corporate hospitality evenings are negotiated as part of the deal – when the actors have to wend their weary way to post-performance suppers, don their nodding and smiling faces and grovel their gratitude for the financial crumbs of comfort on offer. All this is light years away from the Court Farces, the Aldwych Farces and the Whitehall Farces. The only performance indicators that interested us were bums on seats, 'angels' risked their petty cash on a bit of a gamble, whilst the only business plans we ever discussed were generally hatched over a good lunch or dinner at the Ivy, the Caprice, the Trocadero or the Café de Paris, with a great deal of booze oiling the wheels of fortune as the meal went along. Tom Walls would have had an apoplectic fit if he'd been asked to take part in any such latter-day strategic shennanigans,

whilst Pinero would have hastened to the Garrick Club in total disbelief, to drown his sorrows in a glass of excellent club port and I
would have arranged another television excerpt, which guaranteed
capacity houses for months ahead. Indeed, I suspect that none of
the three farce seasons which have gone into theatrical history, the
Court, the Aldwych or the Whitehall, were ever planned ahead in
any detail. The managers, the writers and the actors realised that
there was a popular gap to fill and went about filling it. Certainly,
the genesis of the Aldwych farces couldn't be more haphazard, if it
tried. To begin with, the first one, *Tons of Money*, began at the old
Shaftesbury Theatre, anyway, and had taken years to find its way
into such a legitimate setting, before wending its way up the Strand
to its final and fateful destination, the Aldwych.

According to W Buchanan-Taylor, who was the publicity agent
for the show, *Tons of Money* was the amalgam of two plays, which
had already met with some success in both theatre and music-hall.
They were *Three of a Kind* and *Tom, Dick and Harry*, featuring
three men who looked exactly alike and who were regularly mistaken
for each other. Shades of *One For The Pot* (Cooney/Hilton) some
forty years later, when I played *four* identical brothers. *A Flea in
Her Ear* (Feydeau), *Box and Cox* (Maddison Morton), *Ring Round
the Moon* (Anouilh), *The Venetian Twins* (Goldoni) and *The Comedy
of Errors* (Shakespeare) plus *Menaechmi* and the *Amphitruo* (Plautus)
milked the same idea, too. Well, it's a jolly good one as a basis for
that most useful of farcical ploys, mistaken identity. Personally, I
always thought *Tons of Money* showed its heritage, and this was
confirmed when I saw a costly Royal National Theatre production of
the piece in 1986, which I found to be singularly unamusing after the
beginning of Act II. I was disappointed, too, with the much-praised
Michael Bogdanov production of *The Venetian Twins* for the Royal
Shakespeare Company's presentation at the Barbican in 1994. The
switching of the twins took such a long time, the magic was lost.
Surely the basis of mistaken identity relies on the audience being
fooled as much as the characters on stage. Perhaps Goldoni needed
longer for his actors to effect the changes back in 1747.

Tons of Money was originally written by a *Daily Mirror* journalist,
Archibald Thomas Petchley, who used the pen-name 'Valentine' for
his theatrical work, and polished by music-hall comic Will Evans, who
had made a great deal of money with a variety of knockabout sketches
on the halls and in silent films. It was ten years before the combined

talents of these two writers fulfilled the promise of the title of their work, for *Tons of Money* was finished in about 1912 and it was only in 1922 that it was first presented at the Opera House, Southport, en route to the old Shaftesbury Theatre (which was bombed during the Second World War and is now a fire station opposite the side of the Palace Theatre) where it opened on 13 April, transferring to the Aldwych on 30 October in the same year, 1922. It was Leslie Henson who had first recognised the potential of the play, when it was drawn to his notice by J Bannister Howard, a Manchester theatre manager. Henson had recently formed a company with Tom Walls, who was a fellow musical-comedy performer, and they decided to have a go.

Henson and Walls then made an extraordinary decision to open the play on the Thursday night before Good Friday, a notoriously bad night in the theatre anyway but an additional problem in those days for there would be no Good Friday performance and, therefore, no second night when all the provincial press came in to revue the play. Their decision, though, turned out to be remarkably prescient, for there were no papers either on the Good Friday, which gave press representative W Buchanan-Taylor time to work on the *Daily Mail*, appealing to the inherent jingoism, in those days, of the paper's critic and editorial policy by extolling the British virtues and background of the piece.

On the Saturday, the *Daily Mail* came out with a banner headline, 'British Triumph' and ran up-beat stories about the show for over a week. Other papers followed suit – 1986 critics in no way reflected their '20s predecessors – and what might have been a disaster was turned into a triumph, indeed, by clever publicity, and the fact that a brilliant new farce team was on display getting a load of laughs. The team? Tom Walls himself (in a small part in the last act, which enabled him to appear in the first two acts of another production at the same time, dashing backwards and forwards to the Lyric in Shaftesbury Avenue every night of the week, for months on end!), Ralph Lynn, Mary Brough, Robertson Hare, Gordon James and Yvonne Arnaud. Winifred Shotter came later, in 1926, when she played Rhoda Marley in *Rookery Nook*, as did Ethel Coleridge, playing Gertrude Twine ('Bunny' Hare was that 'swine of a Twine' – Harold). Both Walls and Lynn came from a musical-comedy and music-hall background, Hare had been a touring actor, playing small parts, for over ten years, whilst Mary Brough had spent many years in classical and contemporary drama. Gordon James was actually Ralph

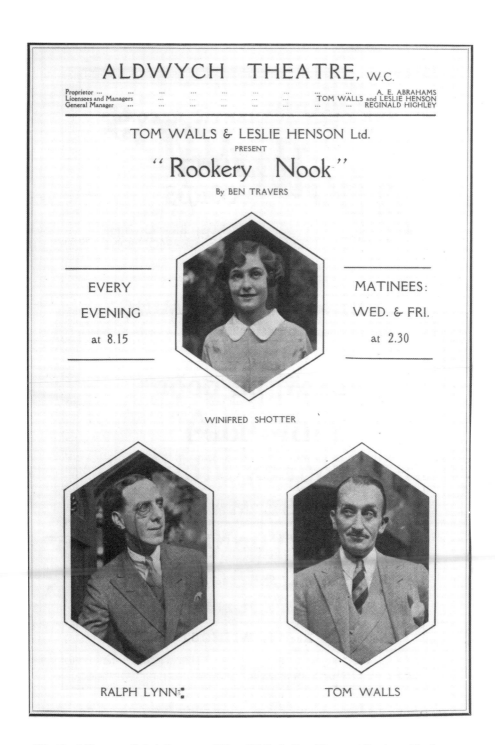

Winifred Shotter, Ralph Lynn and Tom Walls in Ben Travers' *Rookery Nook*.

Lynn's brother, Sydney, but worth his place in spite of any hints about nepotism. As for Yvonne Arnaud (once a youthful French piano-playing prodigy, who then became the West End's archetypal, saucy, theatrical coquette, beginning with *The Quaker Girl* at the Lyric Theatre in 1912), she gurgled her delicious French accent through *Tons of Money* and then returned to the Aldwych in 1925 to play Marguerite Hickett in Ben Travers' first play there, *Cuckoo in the Nest*. After that, Winifred Shotter became the thinking man's crumpet, whilst Ethel Coleridge propped up all the boring women in Travers' farces. She became a close friend of Mrs Travers, which must have provided her with some compensation for her loyalty to the Aldwych team in such dull parts . . .

Tons of Money ran for a total of 737 performances, an amazing run for those days, and was succeeded by Walter Hackett's *It Pays to Advertise* which, in turn, ran for 598 performances. Rather like me at the Whitehall some thirty years later, Tom Walls realised that he was on to a good thing, if only he could keep the plays going and the laughs coming. That was when he met Ben Travers.

In the first part of his autobiography, *Vale of Laughter*, Ben describes himself as 'Ben Thumb', which gives you some idea as to his size. With his red hair (fading by the time I met him) and his clipped Carthusian accent, he always made me think of a somewhat peppery admiral (rather like Admiral Juddy in *Rookery Nook*), but that fleeting impression was soon dismissed when you realised what a delightful man was Ben, with an infectious laugh, a ready wit, a charm with the ladies which assured their ready support for his old age when he was well into his nineties, a love of cricket, coupled with an encyclopaedic knowledge of the game which far outshone anyone (or anything) I knew and, above all, an ability to listen to suggestions in regard to his plays with absolutely no antagonism whatsoever. Mind you, he admitted that all through his life he was extremely sensitive to criticism 'but to none more keenly than self-criticism. The self-criticism which has caused to be destroyed – unproffered – about seventy per cent of all I have ever written.' Even so, by the time I met him in the mid-fifties, he might have been expected to turn down any suggestions made to alter his famous Aldwych farces; but no, I presented his 'famous five' on BBC television – *Cuckoo in the Nest*, *Rookery Nook*, *Thark*, *Plunder* and *A Cup of Kindness*, and he cut and adapted them all to fit into our ninety-minute slot with speed, good humour and expertise. Furthermore, I had the temerity to suggest to him that the ending of *Thark* was pretty weak, so why didn't he re-write it to make it more logical? I was expecting a Juddy-like riposte, but Ben simply scratched his head, gave it a moment's thought and said 'you're absolutely right' and went away and re-wrote it! As dear old Tommy Cooper would have said, 'just like that'. I was amazed, but very grateful for such friendly co-operation. Incidentally, when Peter James came to direct Griff Rhys Jones in a successful revival of *Thark* a year or two ago (it was due to transfer from the Lyric, Hammersmith to the Savoy Theatre, but unhappily the Savoy burnt down) I was asked if I had a copy of the amended version for them to consider but, unfortunately, I did not. As our television transmissions used to be 'live' in the fifties and early sixties there was no record of it on video or film either, so Ben's second thoughts never made it into the theatre.

Ben was originally intended to go into the family wholesale grocery business of Messrs Joseph Travers & Sons Ltd., which had especial interests in the Far East, and indeed did spend a short time in Singapore and Malacca, where – somewhat to his surprise – he discovered a small public library with a complete set of the plays of Sir Arthur Wing Pinero. Being a theatre-goer and actor-manqué, with a great love of the business, he fell upon the works with 'the rapturous excitement of Ben Gunn lighting upon the treasures of Captain Flint'. Travers continues: 'They were not merely plays to read. Each one of them was a guide-book to the technique of stagecraft . . . I discovered for myself the real secret of Pinero's mastery, namely his attention in every line and in every scene to the importance of climax.' It was then he determined to become a dramatist. But there was a long way to go . . .

The First World War, for one thing. Ben enlisted in the Royal Naval Air Service, having left the family business sometime earlier to work for several years in the publishing house of the Bodley Head, and became an extremely competent flying instructor, teaching such unlikely recruits as Ivor Novello (who failed) and Henry Kendall (who passed, winning the Air Force Cross) and becoming the first pilot to drop a torpedo from a land-based aircraft. For this, and other exploits he, too, was awarded the Air Force Cross. Ivor Novello had to be content with the royalties from 'Keep the Home Fires Burning'.

After his demob, Ben was further fired in his enthusiasm to become a dramatist by Sir Henry Irving's son, H B Irving (himself a well-known and highly-respected actor), and wrote his first farce, *The Dippers*, but soon lost faith in it as a play and re-wrote it as a novel. Nevertheless he followed the guidelines he had learned from reading Pinero – making the characters recognisable types of human beings. Indeed, Hank and Pauline Dipper were based on the real-life ballroom dancers, Vernon and Irene Castle. 'The funniness must be in the situations and circumstances in which these human beings find themselves, and these are only funny because the characters are so recognisably human.' Absolutely spot on – and remember the human race has all manner of varying types, from the prim

---

TUESDAY, AUGUST 22nd, and Every Evening at 8.40

Matinees—Tuesdays and Saturdays at 2.30

By arrangement with MISS MARY MOORE

THOS. C. DAGNALL

PRESENTS

"THE DIPPERS."

A FARCICAL COMEDY IN THREE ACTS, BY BEN TRAVERS.

CHARACTERS

In the Order of their Appearance

The Porter ...	... ...	W. WILSON BLAKE
The Old Woman	... ...	HERMIONE GINGOLD
Theodore ...	... (Her Grandchild) ...	DOROTHY DEBENHAM
Henry Talboyes	... ...	... CYRIL MAUDE
Chauffeur ...	... (From Mellingham Hall) ...	ARTHUR HAMBLING
Lord Mellingham	... ...	HENRY WENMAN
Miss Carter ...	...(His Secretary) ...	AILSA GRAHAME
Wattle ...	... (A Butler) ...	GEORGE BELLAMY
Peter ...	... (Lord Mellingham's Nephew) ...	ALGERNON WEST
Minnie ...	... (A Maid) ...	CHRISTINE RAYNER
Stella ...	... (A Guest at Mellingham Hall) ...	VIOLET GRAHAM
Helen ...	(Lord Mellingham's Niece and Stella's Friend)	WINIFRED McCARTHY
Pauline Dipper	... (Of " The Dipper Dancing Duo ") ...	BINNIE HALE
William ...	... ... (A Footman) ...	ARTHUR HAMBLING
Alma Norton ...	(A Guest at Mellingham Hall) ...	DOROTHY DEBENHAM
Leader of the Coon Band	... ...	ERNEST TRIMMINGHAM
Hank P. Dipper	... ...	JACK RAINE

ACT I. Scene I. ... ... The Railway Station at Mellingham
The Curtain will be lowered after Scene I. for a few moments to denote the lapse of time.

      Scene II. ... ... Stella Tavistock's Private Apartment at Mellingham Hall

ACT II. ... ... The Armorial Hall, Mellingham Hall

ACT III. ... ... The Same

Time—THE PRESENT.

The Entire Action of the play takes place during an evening in the late Autumn.

Miss Binnie Hale's and Miss Violet Graham's dresses by PÉRON, LTD., 184, Regent Street.
All other dresses by Miss MARIE LINDEN, South Molton Street.

The Play produced by SIR CHARLES HAWTREY.

The song " Dusky Nipper," sung by Miss Binnie Hale, and played during the evening, has been specially composed by Mr. IVOR NOVELLO, and is published by ASCHERBERG, HOPWOOD & CREW.

Manager ..	.. ..	} (For Thos. C. Dagnall) {	.. .. WM. PATRICK
Stage Manager ..	..		.. .. WILSON BLAKE
Business Manager ..		(For Miss Mary Moore)	.. FRANCIS J. DUGUID

Selected Programme of Music played under the direction of **George Cathie.**

Ladies are earnestly requested to remove hats, bonnets, or any kind of head dress. This request being made for the benefit of the audience. the Management trust that it will appeal to everyone, and that ladies will assist in having it carried out.

Box Office open 10 to 10.   Telephone Nos.—Gerrard 3844, Regent 3365.

NEAREST TUBE STATION—PICCADILLY CIRCUS.

Programme from Ben Travers' farce *The Dippers*.
Note – it was billed as a farcical comedy!

and proper, through the lewd and libidinous, to the eccentric and egocentric, every one a possible target for the farce writer.

The Dippers was published by the Bodley Head, as were Ben's next four novels, on terms which he describes as 'a contract that ought to be placed, as an historic document, on public exhibit in some appropriate berth, preferably the Black Museum at Scotland Yard.' But God moves in mysterious ways, and God in this case was H B Irving, who sent the original farce script to a leading play-agent, Golding Bright who, in turn, sent the script to Sir Charles Hawtrey who, also in turn, accepted it. Ben was overwhelmed and overjoyed. His first farce, written for Charles Hawtrey, accepted by Charles Hawtrey. 'I swung the bath-towel round my shoulders with a sweep of triumph and embraced my wife. At length – at long length – I released her. And then I turned and shook hands with Pinero.' Metaphorically speaking, of course. Pinero was not in the bathroom.

But, in true theatrical tradition, there were disappointments ahead. Eventually, Hawtrey decided to go into his last success before his death, *Ambrose Applejohn's Adventure*, but agreed to direct Ben's play with Cyril Maude in the leading part. It did not do well on its pre-London tour, play-doctors were called in, one of whom took over the play's re-direction and it opened to a luke-warm reception at the Criterion Theatre on 22 August 1922, where it ran for 173 performances. Ben, though, was now a playwright and a novelist. Not bad for a wholesale grocer.

A Cuckoo in the Nest and *Rookery Nook* followed next in novel form, and a 'competent light comedian' (Travers' words, not mine) Lawrence Grossmith asked Ben to adapt *Cuckoo* for the stage. Grossmith then approached Sir Gerald du Maurier to direct the piece, who accepted. However, there seemed to be no possibility of getting a West End theatre in the immediate future, so Lawrence Grossmith went to work on Leslie Henson and Tom Walls who were looking for a farce to succeed *It Pays to Advertise*. Sir Gerald was informed and gave his blessing to any proposed future for the play, and quietly withdrew from the scene. Lawrence Grossmith, on the other hand, received two per cent of the play's takings at the Aldwych for his preliminary introduction but, to be fair, he does appear to have shown it to the right people at the right time, whereas Golding Bright, Travers' agent, just seems to have sat back in benevolent anticipation of the commission ahead. 'Twas ever thus . . .

At first, Travers was horrified by the proposed deal for the

Aldwych. He appears to have taken a very sniffy attitude to his leading actors, Walls and Lynn:

> Tom Walls? I had seen him sometimes in past years as an unfunny and too red-nosed comedian playing small parts in musical shows . . . When I think of the glorious study Tom Walls made of Major George Bone (in *Cuckoo*) it makes me fear I must have been rather a prig about the values of my characters.
>
> The other and more conspicuous Aldwych comedian, an individual named Ralph Lynn . . . specialised in types who were the direct descendents of the Edwardian 'nut' and he had a monocled fatuity about him which had gained him a moderate reputation as a funny man, until he had suddenly, one night in 1922, sailed up to join the stars.

Ben found that Ralph, like all good farceurs, believed that the character he was playing at the time shouldn't try to be funny, but must be motivated by an honest and serious conviction. Even when he was an old man, with a croaking, barely audible voice, Ralph maintained his integrity, and I had the privilege of seeing him several times during, and after, the Second World War. One of those plays, a single – and singular – success called *Is Your Honeymoon Really Necessary?*, by E V Tidmarsh, necessitated him playing a virile 35-year-old man who is stymied when his first wife turns up on his wedding night to his second wife, claiming his divorce was invalid and he has committed bigamy. Ralph was already in his mid-sixties when the play commenced its 980-performance run at the Duke of York's Theatre in 1944, his voice was virtually inaudible, but such was the perfection of his timing and his dexterity with props (known as BUS – business – in the Aldwych scripts – remember? Nobody can ever recall what the BUS was!) that he convulsed his audiences night after night for nearly three years. I know. I was a member of one of them at a bad matinée, but I still found myself falling about at his characterisation and technique. I also found myself remembering it with a certain degree of envy when I eventually played the part on BBC television some fifteen years later – but at least I was the right age.

Ralph went on playing farce until well into his seventies, but almost invariably as the young silly-ass about town. Two of those plays were later works by Ben Travers, *Outrageous Fortune* in 1947 and *Wild Horses* in 1952. I saw the latter. It was rather sad, really. Back in his heyday, though, both he and Ben were unbeatable. Well, until

17 April 1961 that is, when we at the Whitehall passed the Aldwych Farce record. We held a dinner to celebrate. The invitation went like this:

TWO FARCICAL MARATHONS

1922 – 1933   1950 – 1961

I have great pleasure in inviting you to a Dinner at the
Pastoria Hotel, St Martin's Street, Leicester Square
on Sunday, April 16th 1961

On the following day the Whitehall Farce Team stumble past the
Aldwych team's record of ten years seven months and four days of
continuous laughter-making in one theatre. Somewhat puffed and
dishevelled, the Whitehall athletes are still running on, but are
pausing on this Sunday to take a little refreshment with some of
their illustrious predecessors. I do hope that you can join us.

The RSVP was rather neat, I think: 'Informal dress – but trousers will be worn.'

Ralph Lynn.

It was a great do. All the dishes on the menu were headed by the title of one of our farces. I was particularly fond of:

ASPERGE à la 'DIRTY WORK'
(Asparagus Tips swimming in butter)

but they were all like that. Ben and Ralph made speeches. Both were very funny. Ralph's was a masterpiece, for he must have made it on numerous occasions over many years, but it was carefully adapted to fit the bill. He used the old gag of pulling out his notes which turned out to be his laundry list, but even that *ancien regime* was turned into a gem in his expert hands.

The programme and the invitation are framed on the wall of my study, very close to the word processor as I type, for the messages and the signatures scrawled on them mean a great deal to me. All the, then, regulars at the Whitehall are there – Leo Franklyn, Larry Noble, Wally Patch, Basil Lord and author John Chapman – as are all the remaining regulars from the Aldwych – Ralph Lynn, Robertson Hare, Winifred Shotter and author, Ben Travers. Ben's scribble reads as follows: 'A great and enjoyable occasion. I rejoice in the success of FARCE in this, its second generation – the most difficult form of play to write, to produce and to act. Of course the Whitehall differs from the Aldwych – this is shown by the fact that the Whitehall has used very little (under 50% I should say) of the Aldwych material! God Bless – and thanks for a lovely party.'

Also on the programme were the list of plays given at the two theatres up to that time. The Aldwych ran as follows:

	Opened	Performances
Tons of Money	October 30th 1922	737
It Pays to Advertise	February 1st 1924	598
Cuckoo in the Nest	July 22nd 1925	376
Rookery Nook	June 30th 1926	409
Thark	July 4th 1927	401
Plunder	June 26th 1928	344
A Cup of Kindness	May 7th 1929	291
A Night Like This	February 18th 1930	267
Marry the Girl	November 24th 1930	195
Turkey Time	May 26th 1931	263
Dirty Work	March 7th 1932	195
Fifty-Fifty	September 5th 1932	161
A Bit of a Test	January 30th 1933	144

The Whitehall was then listed, somewhat smugly, as follows:

Reluctant Heroes	September 12th 1950	1610
Dry Rot	August 31st 1954	1475
Simple Spymen	March 19th 1958	1283
		and still running

Of the thirteen Aldwych farces, nine were written by Ben Travers. The exceptions were the first two: *Tons of Money* (Will Evans and Valentine) and *It Pays to Advertise* (Roi Cooper Megrue and Walter Hackett), whilst *Marry the Girl* (George Arthurs and Arthur Miller) and *Fifty-Fifty* (H F Maltby, adapted from the French) came towards the end of the run. The reason the two latter plays were not by Ben Travers is quite simple. His agent, Golding Bright, held up the film rights of *Plunder* to conclude a deal with Gilbert Miller for a Broadway production of the play. The deal fell through, but Tom Walls was furious at not being able to get on with his own film production of the piece (he did not appear at the Aldwych after *Dirty Work* in order to concentrate on film-making) and commissioned two other plays – *Marry the Girl* and *Fifty-Fifty* – by different authors, and put them on with Ben merely an interested onlooker. By that time, though, Ben was making a great deal of money, with the touring and repertory rights of his plays, quite apart from the fact that the majority of them were being filmed by Tom Walls and the original company, so financially he was very secure. Nevertheless, he read the notices for *Marry the Girl* with a certain degree of self-satisfaction, for they compared the play unfavourably with his works. Actually, there was a certain amount of self-delusion in Ben's self-satisfaction, for after *A Cup of Kindness* the standard of his own writing fell away and really never quite recovered, although his last West End play, *The Bed Before Yesterday*, which was produced in 1975 when Ben was aged eighty-nine, received a rapturous press. I'm not sure how much of that reaction was caused by sentiment and also I never discovered at what age Ben had originally written the play, but he was long past his sell-by date when it was revived, with some success, in 1994. He would have been aged 110. Well, he nearly made it.

What about the Aldwych farces? How good were they and how well do they stand up today, compared to, say, Pinero? I've discussed *Tons of Money* and given the genesis of *It Pays to Advertise*. The latter play poked fun at the American methods of advertising, so would seem pretty light-weight stuff today even in this country, for we long ago dropped our prissy attitude to this form of selling, whilst commercials on television have ensured that any remaining hang-ups have been banished to the back of our minds together, on some occasions, with our good taste, even though the Advertising Standards Authority does its best.

Ben Travers' plays, on the other hand, still pop up from time to time and are generally received with critical approbation. When I presented them on television, there was always a part of each play which went extremely well – the bedroom scenes in *A Cuckoo in the Nest* and *Thark*, for instance, and the Scotland Yard scene in *Plunder* – but there were other scenes which were very hard work indeed. That's probably because not enough time had elapsed since their original production and ours on television (about thirty years) so they had not yet received the status of being period pieces, like the works of Pinero, Feydeau and Labiche and many of the social mores on view were at odds with the post-war social scene which existed in Britain. The original plays contained many a class-conscious snigger, at the expense of the 'lower-orders', which might well get a laugh of disbelief now, but in the late fifties these politically incorrect jokes caused much embarrassed easing of the collar and uneasy squirming in the seat. A well-known example is from *Thark* when a 'sporty' baronet (Tom Walls) is thanking his maid-servant for some act of domestic diplomacy:

'You're a good girl.' (He pauses briefly and appraises her.) 'I suppose? Are you a good girl?'
'Yes, sir.'
'Then don't waste my time.'

We cut as many of them as possible but dropped h's and malapropisms still appeared in profusion – although Mary Brough's delivery of that famous line in *Rookery Nook*, 'I will come at eight-thirty in the morning; earlier than that I cannot be', ensured that the quotation was chuckled over for many a long year, by all political persuasions.

When Ben Travers fastened onto a pun, he hung on like a bulldog and shook it to the bitter end. He gave the butler in *Thark* – a creepy, sepulchral creature gliding around the haunted house – the splendid name of 'Death'. No tombstone was left unturned: 'Would you care for me to come along to you tonight?'; 'It's only the last post'; 'What time would you like your call?' echoed around the candle-lit hall of

'Thark' with eerie exactitude, the lines written by a playwright who knew just how far he could stretch a joke.

Ben illustrated the importance of the feed line in a farce rather neatly. In *A Cup of Kindness* an actor who appeared in several of the plays, Kenneth Kove, was taking his leave with Tom Walls shouting after him that he could 'go to hell'. 'Right-ho' said Kove, 'then I'll see you later' which was always greeted with a loud laugh.

One night, Walls overheard Kenneth Kove complaining off-stage that he was the one who got the loudest laugh in the show, but no one appreciated that fact. When it came to Kove's exit, Walls changed his line from 'go to hell' to 'go away'. Kove's 'Right-ho; then I'll see you later' was received in deathly silence. When the scene was over, Tom Walls sought out Kove: 'Now who gets the bloody laughs in this show?'

But I was meant to be discussing the merits of the plays themselves. *A Cuckoo in the Nest* was a jaunty comment on the state of the divorce laws at the time – a well-worn theme for a playwright – but given new light and lustre by Travers. In the twenties it was taken for granted that any couple who shared a room in a hotel must be guilty of adultery, although some tangible evidence or identification did help matters along in the courts. In *Cuckoo*, Ben placed Ralph Lynn and Yvonne Arnaud in this position, and although the Lord Chamberlain's Office had some difficulty over the scene, Yvonne Arnaud's delightful 'innocence' and Ralph Lynn's vacuous fatuity won the day, even though they were aware of the perils ahead:

'My husband hasn't got a nasty mind. Has your wife got a nasty mind?'
'No, but she's got a nasty mother.'
'To any decent-minded person there's nothing wrong in your sleeping on the floor of my bedroom, is there?'
'No. But where's the decent-minded person?'

A winning treble there. The classic mother-in-law joke, a comment on the prurience of the average punter and, to add spice to the whole thing, Yvonne Arnaud was *French*! What more could an audience ask?

Rookery Nook became famous for the introduction of Winifred Shotter as the juvenile lead, and the character of Poppy Dickey selling flags for the life-boat. The play had all the classic farce ingredients: rented house, two male cousins (Walls and Lynn) staying there, pyjama-clad girl running away from her irascible

German step-father who, in turn, was a funny foreigner; hen-pecked husband who is bullied to keep quiet about the goings-on, deception as flag-selling girl takes the place of the pyjama-clad girl, final jumbled explanation and all ends happily ever after. The farce was a resounding success and for over thirty years was toured, acted in repertory and amateur companies and a sheet-anchor as far as the Dominions (Ben's description – not mine!) were concerned. When I came to do it on television in the late fifties it was already somewhat long in the tooth, and when the Theatre of Comedy presented it in 1986, even the combined talents of Tom Courtenay, Ian Ogilvy, Nicola McAuliffe, Geoffrey Sumner and Lionel Jeffries couldn't breathe life into what was now a corpse.

I have mentioned *Thark* so often that you must have an idea of its storyline. It was Tom Walls' brainwave to do a ghost story, for he commanded Ben in these somewhat brusque terms: 'The next one has got to be about a haunted house; so get on with it.' Ben did just that and produced one of his funniest farces, which still stands up today. He describes his starting point thus: 'A haunted house – all right – where? Somewhere in cold windswept isolation. Norfolk? Yes, Norfolk seemed to supply the right blend of the civilised and the remote. A bleak old Norfolk manor then – bleak – stark. It must have a name implying bleak, stark, weird bogyness. Got it – Thark Manor. *Thark*. As in the case of *Rookery Nook*, the first line I wrote of *Thark* was its title.'

The last scene of *Thark* was in the haunted bedroom. Tom Walls, as an irascible uncle, agrees to share a small double bed with his nephew, Ralph Lynn. The old boy is armed with a duck gun, which brings forth a plaintive complaint from his nephew that the trouble isn't caused by ducks. In spite of acute discomfort, the uncle falls asleep, which brings a further complaint that he has been giving 'a nasal organ recital'. It's a very funny scene, one which produced a 'longer and louder sequence of laughs than any other scene between Walls and Lynn in the history of Aldwych farce', according to its author, Ben Travers. It certainly went down a storm when Leo Franklyn and I did it on television in 1958, and will continue to do so, for it is a classic mixture of knockabout and verbal comedy, only seen now in somewhat wilder haunted bedroom scenes in pantomime.

After *Thark* came *Plunder*, which received an ecstatic reception from the press and public alike, and continued to do so when we did it on television in 1957, and when the National Theatre presented it

ALDWYCH THEATRE

Proprietor - . . . . A. E. ABRAHAMS
Licensees and Managers - - TOM WALLS & LESLIE HENSON

General Manager - - { For Tom Walls and Leslie Henson, Ltd. } REGINALD HIGHLEY

EVERY EVENING at 8.15

Matinees: Wednesday and Friday at 2.30

TOM WALLS & LESLIE HENSON, Ltd.

present

Rookery Nook

By BEN TRAVERS
Author of "*A Cuckoo in the Nest*"

Characters in the order of their appearance :

Gertrude Twine	ETHEL COLERIDGE
Mrs. Leverett	MARY BROUGH
Harold Twine	J. ROBERTSON HARE
Clive Popkiss	TOM WALLS
Gerald Popkiss	RALPH LYNN
Rhoda Marley	WINIFRED SHOTTER
Putz	GRIFFITH HUMPHREYS
Admiral Juddy...	GORDON JAMES
Poppy Dickey	ENA MASON
Clara Popkiss	STELLA BONHEUR
Mrs. Possett	VERA GERALD

Programme from Ben Travers' second Aldwych farce, *Rookery Nook*.

119

twenty years after that. It has a storyline which is pure drama, not farce at all. Indeed, I always thought it was an amoral play, for the two leading men – Walls and Lynn – actually commit the perfect murder, but are never charged, and although the man they accidentally knock off a ladder is a nasty piece of work, they are taking part in a robbery – so murder it must be. I never ceased to be amazed that the Lord Chamberlain let them get away with it, never mind the fictional Scotland Yard detectives. But nobody said a dicky and the play went on to be a huge box office success – so much so that Ben sloped off to Australia, at the end of 1928, to watch the Test matches, in those good old days when A P F Chapman's England team trounced Australia.

To his horror and amazement, Ben was summoned back to England to write a replacement for *Plunder*, which he had left playing to capacity. When he returned, he found it was still making a sizeable weekly profit, but not enough for Tom Walls, who was losing a fortune *at* the Fortune, in Drury Lane, which he had leased. He instructed Ben to write 'the cheapest production we've ever had. Just one set throughout and a pretty simple one. The smallest cast you can manage.' Ben was nonplussed, as they say. He fully expected the audience to want something elaborate, after the four complicated settings in *Plunder*, but Tom was adamant, for he needed to make as much money as possible at the gold mine of the Aldwych, to pour down the open drain of the Fortune. 'Go for contrast. Something domestic,' he said.

So Ben did just that. *A Cup of Kindness* was a 'Romeo and Juliet story of the suburbs'. The Montagues were Tom Walls and Mary Brough, with their two sons, Ralph Lynn and Kenneth Kove, whilst the Capulets were Robertson Hare, Marie Wright and Winifred Shotter. The warring families had come together for the wedding of Ralph Lynn to Winifred Shotter, when Ralph is arrested for an unintentional breach of the law, just as the families are posing for the wedding photos. You can imagine the chaos which ensues, before all is solved, leaving the cast joining hands and singing 'Auld Lang Syne' – hence the title of the play. Like *Plunder*, it was different but, also like *Plunder*, it was very successful.

About this time (1929), *Rookery Nook* was made into one of the first British 'talkies'. Ben was horrified with the result, but it was hugely successful and all thoughts of continuing frugality were forgotten at the Aldwych. *A Night Like This*, which followed *A Cup of Kindness*, had a large cast and no less than six sets. One of these represented a London street in a pea-souper (very common in those days) with an old-fashioned cab and real-live cab-horse on show. Unfortunately, even the thick gauze front cloth (to simulate the fog) allowed the audience to see, all too clearly, the goings-on on stage, which, at most performances, included the horse misbehaving as only horses can misbehave. Ralph Lynn's ad-libs would certainly have closed the show, if the Lord Chamberlain's officials had been in front, as would the embarrassed audience reaction to the event. A model horse had to be found, which behaved in a model way, but in spite of removing a possible cause for an early termination of the run, the play achieved a mere 267 performances and the writing was on the wall. The five remaining Aldwych farces ran for only another twenty-seven months, with Tom Walls opting out of the last year altogether and Ben breaking his long-held belief in basic reality in *A Bit of a Test*, by making 'Bunny' Hare the captain of the England Test team on an Australian tour, with Ralph Lynn as the leading batsman. Being kidnapped by Aussie bushrangers didn't help matters either, and really the whole farrago was no more than an elongated music-hall sketch. A long way from those halcyon days of *Cuckoo* and the Famous Five . . .

So ended the Aldwych Farces – but Ben Travers was anything but finished. In 1936 he wrote a piece called *O Mistress Mine* (originally – *very* originally – entitled *Nun's Veiling*), but as it was all about a royal family and the abdication of a king, and as the play opened on the night King Edward VIII abdicated in reality, it was *not* a resounding success. Ben returned to something like his old form with his next play though, a farce called *Banana Ridge*, with a new farce team (and a new management, O'Bryen, Linnit and Dunfee, who became the main presenters of farce until I came along twelve years later), led by Alfred Drayton and Robertson Hare. It was Ben's favourite play, for he believed he had written the perfect merging of comedy with farce. He certainly hit upon a novel idea, based upon his own days in the Far East, where Mr Pound (the domineering Drayton boss) and Mr Pink (the pompous but brow-beaten Hare employee) are jointly and severally accused of fathering a son, along with three other possibles, Mr Butcher, Mr Corker and Mr Tope who have paid for the boy's upbringing. Now it is up to Mr Pound and Mr Pink to provide the lad's adult employment. Mr Pound ships his possible offspring off to a rubber estate, Bukit Pisang (Banana Ridge), under the tutelage of the manager, Mr Pink. The proper ration of Travers' farcical hilarity

Robertson 'Bunny' Hare and Alfred Drayton.

ensues, until the boy's real father turns up who, of course, is neither Mr Pound nor Mr Pink – nor Mr Butcher, Mr Corker, nor even Mr Tope. Olga Lindo played the boy's mother, whilst the boy himself was portrayed by no less an actor than Robert Flemyng. All highly diverting stuff – the more so, because Ben Travers himself played the part of the Chinese servant, simply to prove that he, too, could go on every night at the Strand Theatre for 291 performances, but also because he was the only available person around who could actually speak the lingo. Alfred Drayton bet him that he wouldn't last the run. Well, he did and collected £5 from Drayton on the last night. That alone was something of a miracle, for Drayton was not exactly known for his liberality.

In 1976, Ray Cooney revived the play at the Savoy Theatre, with Robert Morley and George Cole playing the original Drayton and Hare parts. It was a resounding success, for both players were consummate farceurs, although it is doubtful if either would ever put such an accomplishment at the top of their credits. When George Cole left the cast, Ray Cooney took over with indecent haste and to astonished acclaim, which pleased him greatly for his greatest ambition is to be known as a consummate farceur, not only as an author but also upon the stage. He actually *likes* going on night after night after night. There's no accounting for taste.

Ben Travers followed *Banana Ridge* at the Strand Theatre with another farce for Drayton and Hare, *Spotted Dick*, which achieved the impossible – for Ben anyway. It ran for nine performances! I must be fair, though, and explain it was presented just before the outbreak of World War II, when all London theatres were automatically closed, and it came back later in 1939 to achieve a further few months before finally sinking in the West End.

After that came *She Follows Me About* in 1943, with Robertson Hare, Basil Radford, Catherine Lacey and Joyce Heron in the cast, but to no real avail, for it was mauled by the critics and only lasted a few months. Prior to that, though, it had been mauled by the Lord Chamberlain, who insisted that more than a dozen of the play's best lines had to go. Ben used to tell of one ridiculous interview with the Chamberlain's representative who insisted that he would not accept Robertson Hare being suspected of 'what he calls hi-tiddly-i-ti whilst wearing a clerical collar'. Now you know why the Lord Chamberlain's censors also had to go . . .

Ralph Lynn came back to join 'Bunny' Hare for Travers' next

piece, *Outrageous Fortune*, which achieved a modest success at the Winter Garden in 1947, with 250 performances. But runs were getting longer, for the war had introduced a huge audience to 'popular' theatre, so 250 performances might have been respectable in the good old Aldwych days, but seemed very small beer some decade-and-a-half later. Ralph and Bunny came together again, for the last time, in 1952, for *Wild Horses*, which returned them to their old home at the Aldwych, but to no avail. It was a great disappointment, made all the worse by audience nostalgia being faced by the fact that playwright and actors had passed their apogee as an invincible laughter-making team. It was sad really. I know. I saw them. I don't think I laughed once and I never had the courage to own up. But can you blame me? After all, a few years later I was doing the Aldwych farces on television, and dear Ben was signing my copy of his autobiography, *Vale of Laughter*, in these words:

To Brian Rix, on the 5th June 1965.

To celebrate this happy date,
(The TV show of *Rookery*)
To you I bring this token thing,
Myself as seen in bookery.
That farce of mine contains a line
– I hope your favourite cue –
'Your kind of friendship never ends'
That goes from me to you.

SLOW CURTAIN

ACT III

Scene ii: A street close to the Palace of Westminster

Laugh, and the world laughs with you;
Weep, and you weep alone,
For the sad old earth must borrow its mirth,
But has trouble enough of its own.

Ella Wheeler Wilcox.

WITH THE END of the Aldwych Farces, the genre went into hibernation, only waking up, fit and well, around the end of the Second World War and then continuing in various guises, more or less without a break, until the early 1990s. Of course, there were the occasional stirrings before and during the war, but these were the green shoots of recovery (a phrase we came to know and dread *in* the 1990s) which promised well but then slipped once more into a torpor. There were three authors really, apart from Ben Travers – Austin Melford, Vernon Sylvaine and Philip King – who kept their noses twitching above the surface during that time and, of those, Austin Melford specialised in musical comedy and Philip King only showed his promise in *Without the Prince*, which was produced at the Whitehall in 1940. The rest, including that most prolific writer of successful modern farce, Ray Cooney, came later, and of those five, only Ben Travers was the non-actor (apart from his unique appearance in *Banana Ridge*), which serves to underline the fact that over ninety per cent of all successful farces have been written throughout history by those who trod the boards. Until you have experienced the rhythm and timing necessary to get a laugh on stage, the need to believe in the character you are acting – outrageous as it might be – and the ability to play your audience like an expert fly-fisherman, you are short of the necessary expertise,

125

Ben being an honourable exception. Even Pinero had been an actor for a number of years before putting pen to paper, as had Shakespeare and, according to legend, Plautus.

Austin Melford (1884 – 1971) was a man of many talents, not only as an actor but as a playwright, a play doctor and a director, both in the theatre and in films. His main writing credits seem to be more involved with musical farce, rather than the less melodious kind, and he had a penchant for adapting plays from the German. His greatest success in this regard was *It's A Boy*, a non-musical farce from the German of Franz Arnold and Ernst Bach, which starred Leslie Henson and Sydney Howard (with Melford himself getting some good notices as the rather obviously-named Dudley Leake). It ran for 366 performances at the Strand Theatre from 2 October 1930. He followed this with his own original farce, *It's A Girl* but this was not a particular success. His writing spanned many years, beginning in 1921 with a revue, *Ring Up*, which he wrote in conjunction with Inglis Allen and that marvellously irascible, camp old English butler in many a Hollywood film, Eric Blore. His final works were *Bob's Your Uncle*, with music by Noel Gay, presented at the Saville Theatre on 5 May 1948, and another adaptation, *Blue for*

Austin Melford.

Programme for the 1948 production of *Bob's Your Uncle*.

a Boy, which was produced at His Majesty's on 30 November 1950. His obituary in the *Times* on 19 August 1971 sums it up rather neatly (but then, that's what obituaries are for): 'Austin Melford's return to the stage with Mr Leslie Henson in 1948 in the cheerful musical farce *Bob's Your Uncle* was warmly welcomed. Two years later he provided excellent material for two other leading comedians Mr Fred Emney and Mr Richard Hearne in *Blue for a Boy*, in which he contributed a delightful performance as a prim, precise and essentially innocent husband. In 1953 he and Mr Emney jointly wrote and played in *Happy as a King* at the Princes Theatre, and he appeared in the short-lived production of *Happy Holiday* at the same theatre in the next year.' There we go again. Yet another career ending on anything but a grace note. Old Ben Travers with his *Bed Before Yesterday* at the age of eighty-nine was, quite simply, a remarkable exception to the rule that age *can*, and does, wither. Bloody awful, really.

Vernon Sylvaine (1897 – 1957) should be there amongst the better-known farce writers, for he had a remarkable string of successes in the late-1930s, right up to the early 1950s but, somehow, he is always forgotten. I must try and put the record straight, for I believe I owe him that, at least, as I presented most of his farces twice on television, either as full-length or cut-down versions, and also achieved my best critical notices ever with one of his plays, *Nap Hand* (which he wrote with Guy Bolton before the Second World War) and which was transmogrified by Michael Pertwee, in 1969, into *She's Done It Again*. The idea of the play was based on the birth of the famous Dionne Quins but in discussing it here I am being somewhat premature – if you'll pardon the pun – so would ask you to bear with me until we reach full term.

Like so many other farceurs, Vernon always wanted to write a 'serious' work, and began his theatrical life as a 'serious' actor, likened by the critics to Henry Ainley. Indeed, his first play, *The Road of Poplars* was a First World War one-act drama, presented at the Coliseum for a Sunday try-out, whilst his second, *. . . and a Woman Passed By* enjoyed (if that is the right word) a short run at the Duke of York's Theatre, but was eventually turned from a drama into a farce by Sylvaine, ending up as his first real success, *Aren't Men Beasts*, which ran for 283 performances at the Strand Theatre from 13 May 1936. In this, Vernon was inspired to team together the bullying, bald, Alfred Drayton with the bullied, bald, Robertson Hare. It was a happy mixture he was to repeat in *A Spot of Bother* (1937), *Women*

Aren't Angels (1940), *Madame Louise* (1945), *One Wild Oat* (1948) and *Will Any Gentleman?* (1950), and which Ben Travers was to steal with his *Banana Ridge* in 1938. During the run of *Will Any Gentleman?* Alfred Drayton died and his part was taken over by Arthur Riscoe. He, in turn, joined Drayton in the Elysian Fields, leaving Brian Reece to finish the run. But the magical combination of those two boiled eggheads, Drayton and Hare, was no more and Vernon had to turn to pastures new. His was a happy choice, both in regard to the play's title, *As Long As They're Happy*, but also with his choice of leading man – Jack Buchanan. The play (an early skit on pop-stars) ran for 369 performances at Buchanan's own theatre, the Garrick. After that came *Three Times a Day* (re-titled *What the Dr Ordered*, and written with Lawrence Huntington), which only came into the West End for one night when I presented it for a television performance from the Whitehall and, subsequently, in an hour's version adapted by Michael Pertwee when I did *Six of Rix* – half-a-dozen Sylvaine farces cut down and re-written as one-hour plays by Michael, recorded by BBC Television at various theatres out on tour as double bills, but presented by the Beeb singly for six weeks in 1972. Unhappily, Vernon Sylvaine was not around to see them, for he had died from cancer in November 1957.

Vernon was the first English farce writer of the last hundred years who indicated quite clearly that the Alfred Drayton character enjoyed sex with his mistresses – and got away with it, in spite of the Lord Chamberlain sitting in judgement. Ben Travers always contented himself with innuendo and pinched bottoms; Vernon actually conjured up visions of sexual intercourse taking place and somehow the Chamberlain's Men allowed it to go through. Amazing, really, but, of course, the bawdy grotesques played by Drayton contrasted superbly with the puritanical grotesques play by Hare, and the latter's sepulchral disapproval removed any lingering doubt that hanky-panky was most definitely going on. The plots were quite simple, too. Domineering wives to threaten; nubile, scantily-clad mistresses to conceal; Drayton forced to reveal all to Hare; Hare forced to take all the blame; both forced to dress up in drag and Hare forced to lose his trousers. Sylvaine's web of deceit was woven both skilfully and certainly and he never put a foot wrong in the six plays he wrote for his leading comics. 'Oh, calamity' never happened to them in reality, even though it threatened 'Bunny' Hare in every play.

Vernon Sylvaine, with Guy Bolton, did write one play for that other great farceur, Ralph Lynn, but unfortunately its production coincided with the Battle of Britain and it was bombed off. I have already mentioned it, for it was *Nap Hand*, when the wives of two cousins each present their husbands with twins. The Ralph Lynn character, Freddie Quibble, suggests that they pool the twins, borrow another baby and present them to the world as quins. Remember, this was in the days before fertility drugs and in vitro fertilisation, and the Dionne Quintuplets, born just before the war in Canada, had made a fortune – so the plot was both topical and possible. As I say, Marshall Goering's Luftwaffe put an end to the first West End run, but eventually I did it for a one-night BBC television production. It went extremely well, but it went even better several years later when I presented it in a completely new version by Michael Pertwee as *She's Done It Again* at the Garrick Theatre on 5 October 1969.

Philip King (1903 – 79) was a fellow East Riding man, having been born in Beverley very close to my birthplace at Cottingham, and always displayed a paternalistic concern for my work in farce over the years. He was a kind, gentle chap, hiding his good fortune as a playwright behind a bluff, pipe-smoking exterior. He could easily have been mistaken for a farmer rather than a hugely successful farce writer and a rather less successful actor. But it was acting which always attracted him (rather like Ray Cooney) and he sallied forth as the Bishop of Lax in his greatest farce, *See How They Run*, at the drop of a mitre. But then, he had been an actor since he left school, touring with a fit-up company round the Durham mining villages, followed by a season at the Bristol Little Theatre, before settling into a seven-year stint with the White Rose Players in Harrogate which saw the première of his very first play, *Without the Prince* in 1940, coming to the Whitehall Theatre for a short run in the same year, when it was blitzed into near oblivion.

It was *Without the Prince* which helped me get my first job in the theatre. Here's how I described the occasion in the first part of my autobiography, *My Farce From My Elbow* in 1974:

> In the spring of 1942, I was appearing in Hornsea for my mum as the Stranger in Philip King's *Without the Prince*. This was a very funny farce but the Stranger had to be played straight, for he was supposed to be a famous actor (I was far too young for the part) suffering from amnesia, who becomes involved in a Parish Hall production of *Hamlet*. At one time I had to speak the whole of the 'O, what a rogue and peasant slave am I'

soliloquy, which was greeted with unbridled laughter as various members of the cast reacted to it. As we were *actually* playing in a Parish Hall I don't know how we had the nerve . . .

Donald Wolfit was once more on tour in a piece called *David Garrick* and I plucked up courage to ask if I could audition for him.

'Have you got an audition piece?' he asked.

'Well, I know Robert Service's "Bessie's Boil" . . . and "O, what a rogue and peasant slave am I",' I said casually. Wolfit was suitably impressed . . . 'Come and see me after the matinée this Thursday and I'll hear you.'

So, I went, auditioned and landed the job in his autumn tour of *King Lear, Hamlet, Twelfth Night* and *A Midsummer Night's Dream*. It shows how desperate he must have been to find young actors, for my version of Hamlet's soliloquy was quite dreadful! 'Bessie's Boil' was better.

Philip King's next farce, *See How They Run* was probably his greatest – it even stood up to close scrutiny some forty years after its original production by Harry Hanson's company in Peterborough in 1944, transferring to the Comedy Theatre a few months later when the Theatre of Comedy presented it at the Shaftesbury Theatre with a marvellous cast: Maureen Lipman as the village busybody, Miss Skillon; Michael Denison as the Bishop of Lax; Derek Nimmo as the visiting curate, Mr Humphrey; Liza Goddard as Penny Toop; Royce Mills as her husband, the Reverend Lionel Toop, and Christopher Timothy playing Clive, the soldier sneaking out of camp and the cause of all the trouble. When I presented it on television in 1962, Fabia Drake was Miss Skillon, Henry Kendall was the Bishop, my wife Elspet Gray was Penny and I played Clive. On all occasions the play went wonderfully well, and I am sure it always will, for it is an historic piece, showing wartime restrictions in all their farcical absurdity, village communities at their worst and the wonderful spectacle of five members of the clergy (two of them false), all in dog-collars and all trying to persuade the local Home Guard of their authenticity, with a drunken Miss Skillon popping in and out of the cupboard under the stairs. Even describing it brings a smile to my face, for the complexities of the plot are woven into a faultless farcical fabric.

Philip King tried to re-create the characters again, in the same village, Merton-cum-Middlewick, in a 1961 farce, *Pool's Paradise*, but it didn't work. Never mind. He had plenty of other successes,

Brian Rix in rehearsal for the television production of *See How They Run*.

mainly written with a Harrogate doctor, Falkland L Cary, but *On Monday Next* . . . was a solo work and was the successful forerunner to Michael Frayn's *Noises Off* – in other words, a farce about actors backstage. I was never very keen on either. Not because they failed to amuse the average theatre-goer, but because I slightly resented actors being shown in such a jokey light. Oh dear, I am probably being pompous. I apologise to the shade of Philip and to the more substantial Michael.

Actually I presented and played in *On Monday Next* . . . on television and it almost stopped my small-screen career in its tracks. The then Controller of BBC Television, Cecil McGivern, was a stern guardian of the Sabbath day and he resisted presenting any farce on a Sunday until *Sunday Night at the Palladium* pinched all his viewers and we were then invited to compete, from time to time. Anyway, he found one gag in the play unacceptable. In the light of today's liberal thinking, it seems incomprehensible that such a harmless little joke should cause so much trouble, but attitudes in 1958 were very different, as you will see.

On Monday Next . . . was about a struggling repertory company presenting a ghastly new melodrama. I played the old Henry Kendall part of the frustrated director, and Harry himself directed the television production. Just before the transmission he remembered a gag he'd put in the original 1949 Comedy Theatre presentation and suggested I try it. I did. The juvenile, Ray Cooney (playing the original Leslie Phillips part), had a line which went something like, 'He's never been able to look Milady in the face ever since he caught her hiding the Ace of Spades in her fan.'

THE DIRECTOR (me):	'In her what?'
BEMUSED JUVENILE:	'In her fan.'
THE DIRECTOR (pause):	'Well, I suppose it's all right if the Lord Chamberlain passed it.'

Of course, there was one dirty-minded bloke in front who got it. He guffawed loudly and the rest of the house followed suit. Cecil McGivern was watching the play with his family at home and, according to the angry letter he wrote me, they all reacted violently against the line, and he regretted that it had been 'perpetrated on a family audience, especially as it had been on a Sunday.'

I can only re-read that story in amazement and realise how the world has changed. Broadcasting Standards, Mrs Whitehouse, violence watershed after 9pm, video nasties, Red Hot Dutch, pornographic films in hotels – my goodness, I'd hate to think it all started with me . . .

It was also a Philip King farce which began my television career with the BBC, way back in 1952. After the enormous success of the televised first-act excerpt from *Reluctant Heroes* in the May of that year, the BBC and I decided to present a new farce for one full-length performance in the October. The play chosen was Philip King's *Postman's Knock* – not a particularly good farce, but more than satisfactory when cut down to ninety minutes. The audience sitting in the theatre, warmed up by the late, lamented Brian Johnston, loved it, as did the audience at home. Thus was born *Laughter from the Whitehall* (and later, *Laughter from the Garrick*), which filled the screen with five farces a year on Sundays and Bank Holidays until 1972. That's why there is hardly a farce, good, bad or indifferent, which I have not read or performed or tried out or rejected, dating from the beginning of the current era of British farce, the 1880s to the present day. Yes, I know I retired from active actor-management in 1977, but I've seen pretty well everything else since then and, quite frankly, nothing has changed very much. Of course Joe Orton has been visited upon us and many a high-falutin' writer has deigned to use farce as a useful writing tool or as an insert in a play to illustrate some point in a somewhat different way but, truthfully, little has changed since Pinero and Travers or, earlier, Labiche and Feydeau. Perhaps that is why the current crop of farce writing is pretty thin on the ground. Philip King would have been very disappointed but not in the least surprised, for he knew what a hard task it was to write a successful piece.

His last successes were all written with Falkland Cary, who was very strong on plot-lines, leaving much of the dialogue and business to Philip. They were a formidable couple, writing the *Sailor* series, the first being *Sailor, Beware!*, introducing Peggy Mount to an astonished and delighted public as the virago, Emma Hornett, and which ran for 1,231 performances at the Strand Theatre from 16 February 1955. This was followed by *Watch It, Sailor!* in 1960 and *Rock-a-Bye Sailor!* in 1962. Finally, the two writers collaborated to bring forth *Big Bad Mouse*, which began in 1964 with Jimmy Edwards and Eric Sykes taking unbelievable liberties with the script. It was hugely popular and if ever King or Cary felt any resentment as to what was happening to their precious words, they kept it to themselves, for the royalty cheques came rolling in, come hell or high water, and both men were realists in a profession not overburdened with such pragmatic attitudes.

Ray Cooney once wrote this programme note to accompany a Churchill Theatre, Bromley production of *See How They Run*. I think it worthy of reproduction, for it says it all about farce in general and Philip King in particular:

> Most theatre folk will say that Ben Travers' plays are the 'Daddy' of the modern British farce. I don't agree. It seems to me that Ben's wonderful Aldwych pieces are basically light comedies which were given farcical overtones by Tom Walls, Ralph Lynn and Robertson Hare. Also, the Travers comedies nearly all retained the established 1920s thread of the juvenile love interest. *See How They Run* was probably the first comedy to eliminate the juveniles and, at the same time, although Philip King continued with the verbal tomfoolery of Ben Travers, he established a much purer farcical line in *See How They Run* than any of the Aldwych farces. Indeed, I can see how much influence this beautifully constructed play has had on my own writing. I am afraid there are even lines of dialogue from my plays in which one can detect the derivation:

> *See How They Run*
> CLIVE: Of course we've got a lily-pond. Everyone's got a lily-pond. Come on Bishop, we'll investigate.
> BISHOP: But I'm not dressed for the lily-pond.
> CLIVE: Lily won't mind.

> *One For The Pot*
> HARDCASTLE: What's he doing in the garden?
> CHARLIE: Planting berries.
> HARDCASTLE: But it's pitch black.
> BILLY: Aye. They're blackberries.

> *Chase Me Comrade!*
> GERRY: Very sad. Hoskins fell down the well.
> RIMMINGTON: What well?
> GERRY: The well in the garden.
> RIMMINGTON: I didn't know there was a well in the garden.
> GERRY: Neither did Hoskins. That's how he came to fall down it.

> I won't go on! However, it's in the construction of the plays that I can appreciate, today, how much I learnt from Philip King's classic piece.

The importance of creating believable characters and relationships and how vital it is to start off as totally normal and only gradually (and feasibly!) develop into the complications of the middle Act and then the absolute chaos of the third Act: ordinary people in situations that come to be outside their control; the simple white lie that has to be elaborated upon – again and then again.

Well, there you have it – straight from the horse's mouth, and who will say him neigh! You see, it's catching! If a pun's worth doing, it's worth doing well, that's what I always say – and so do the majority of farce writers. They also say much the same about good farce construction as does Ray above. Many have written to me along those lines, and their words will follow in the pages ahead. Which all goes to prove Dorothy Parker was right: 'You can't teach an old dogma new tricks.'

As we are approaching the middle of the twentieth century, Whitehall farce, solipsism and narcissism may be words which spring to your mind, for I fear that I now enter the farcical scene in quite a big way. As indicated in the Prologue, I have no desire to rehearse yet again my previous writings on the subject and, indeed, quite a number of references have been made already to various authors, plays and televisions with which I was connected, but I think I should give you a little background about the Whitehall Theatre itself, and how I came to be there.

The theatre was built on the site of Ye Old Ship Tavern, which was first 'licensed' in 1650, transferring its name to a pub across the road when it was demolished in the late 1920s. The theatre, with architecture by Edward Stone and interior design by Marc-Henri and Laverdet (described as 'a dream in black and silver') opened in 1930 with a play which transferred from the Duke of York's Theatre, *The Way to Treat a Woman* by Walter Hackett. It then had a mixed bag of success and failure until the war, when it fell on hard times and was eventually bought at a knock-down price by an entrepreneur, Louis Cooper. He was in luck, for not only did he acquire the property cheaply, but also had as his 'sitting' tenant Phyllis Dixey in her *Peek-a-Boo* Revue, which enjoyed such an enormous success with the troops during World War II. This was followed by Ronnie Shiner in H J Barlow's presentation of R F Delderfield's famous, long-running play about a ghastly RAF North Country billet, *Worm's Eye View*, which opened in 1945. I came on the scene some five years later, when Barlow had fallen out with Cooper, his lease expired and he took his play to the Comedy Theatre. Louis Cooper put in a disaster of a farce called *The Dish Ran Away* and in desperation sent for me when I was in my umpteenth week of touring Colin Morris's army farce, *Reluctant Heroes*. The rest is history – well, theatrical history, anyway, and the term 'Whitehall Farce' is still used freely by lobby correspondents to this very day – as is the term, *Reluctant Heroes*. Incidentally, when I was made a Life Peer, I chose for my title 'Lord Rix of Whitehall in the City of Westminster and Hornsea in Yorkshire.' Rather long-winded, I know, but at least mine is an affectionate non-bureaucratic use of the term 'Whitehall', whilst I was determined to place my home town, Hornsea, back where it belonged – in Yorkshire, not the dreaded North Humberside.

That is the background to the various writings which follow, not only from me, but Colin Morris, John Chapman and Ray Cooney, who were the authors of the five hugely-successful Whitehall farces which ran from 1950 to 1966. Then it was over to the Garrick, and various contributions follow from there, as well.

You will notice that so far I have omitted any mention of the films in which I appeared because, quite frankly, I am a little like Ben Travers in this matter. He was horrified by the way his farces translated from the stage to the big screen and I must admit to a similar reaction. Only one film still appeals to me and that was written especially by John Chapman with the cinema in mind, *The Night We Dropped A Clanger*. The rest, mostly transported from stage to screen, seemed to miss the intimacy of a small theatre and the cheerful goodwill and raucous reaction of an audience. That's why I preferred the television productions, for they were transmitted from the theatre and the audience responded to them in a truly theatrical way, not like your carefully edited sit-com, with laughter tracks dubbed on. Another problem with filming is that you see yourself as others see you and you have to be *very* thick-skinned to overcome that masochism. No, self-criticism is a weakness with the great majority of actors (if you consider that a weakness, of course; some might call it a strength) but in allowing yourself that indulgence, you fight like hell if anyone else dares to pick holes in your work. Nevertheless, I was a little surprised at the longevity of Colin Morris' memory, which follows. I would have thought any remembrance of the foot-in-the-bucket routine would have been long sicklied o'er with the pale cast of thought – but I was wrong. For the record, Colin was an actor in

Songsheet for the music from the film *The Night We Dropped a Clanger*.

138

the Hull Rep. before the war and I remember seeing him as Macbeth when he was a mere juvenile. What's more, the battlements collapsed during his final fight with Macduff which got a huge laugh – from me, anyway. He then went into the army, serving as an officer and then a military observer with the 8th Army, writing dispatches for the Ministry of Information, resulting in his first serious army play, *Desert Rats*, presented at the Adelphi after the war by Henry Sherek. This was followed by *Reluctant Heroes*, an army farce – except that Colin would never admit to that description, as you will see if you just read on. His words, not mine . . .

THE WHITEHALL FARCES
Reluctant Heroes by Colin Morris
1,610 performances at the Whitehall Theatre
from 12 September 1950

I have never written a farce wittingly. Farce is unreal people in unreal situations; comedy, real people in real situations. There is a dividing line but it is frequently crossed and respective authors don't care, or hope purists won't notice.

My own comedy *Reluctant Heroes*, billed for commercial reasons as a farce, fits the above definition, although non-soldiers who saw and remember it may find the situations hard to credit.

The exaggerations arose from the Army Establishment camouflaging normal life with military eccentricities in the hope of turning civilians into soldiers. What possible reason could there be for painting snow white the curbs of garrison roads except to help drunken soldiers find their way in darkness to their own hut?

Another example of military folly was the creation of a machine gun post to defend the 55th Training Regiment in the expectation of a German invasion. First, a hole was selected which meant building a tall pyramid of sandbags to give the machine gun a commanding view of the approaching Hun. A dozen soldiers, including myself, laboured during a heatwave, filling and positioning sandbags without being instructed in the sound Egyptian principle of filling in the middle. Soldiers passed each morning marvelling at the magnificent pyramid which eventually reached a height of eighty feet. Then the rain fell and the whole collapsed, as if struck by lightning, which had the overall benefit of filling in the original hole and cancelling the invasion.

This was comedy because it was honest endeavour, enacted according to Army planning, although the effect would be held by all to be farcical.

I have never succeeded in writing farce – only comedies which failed.

Programme cover for *Reluctant Heroes*.

Comedy is from the heart, concerned with feelings; farce is from the head, a matter of the intellect. If the definition of an intellectual is one who spins out thought to infinity in order to postpone action indefinitely, intellectuals have a natural outlet in farce. They can sit at home gazing at a word processor.

The line between comedy and farce is crossed not only by writers but directors and actors. Sometimes it slips into burlesque. Brian Rix (a recruit, Gregory), during the kit handout (Act I, scene ii) accidentally kicked a bucket lying about the hut and got a laugh. Next night and every night he kicked it again, finally managing to get his foot in it, and out, and in it again, and we all stood around until the audience stopped laughing, which proved to me that some audiences have no taste whatsoever. At that point we went from comedy through farce, pantomime and music-hall to the end of the pier. Later in the same scene he got into trouble with an excessively large pullover which developed over the weeks into what we called 'The Dance of the Seven Veils'. One of his innumerable gifts is the capacity to be forgiven for almost anything!

Well . . . I'm not going to argue, but Colin's memory *is* a tinge sicklied o'er. The bucket routine (which I admit, quite freely, was my invention) actually came in Act II; 'The Dance of the Seven Veils' (also my invention) *was* Act I, scene ii – and if I now quote you the script, perhaps you can see why I was tempted to go over the top. 'Never written a farce wittingly' indeed!

(Enter Sergeant)

SERGEANT: (speaking offstage in a very posh voice.) Squad! Squad, 'shun! Right wheel, forward, left wheel, forward.

(Enter two very pretty members of the WRAC. The first, PAT THOMP-SON, is twenty-three, Cockney and companionable. The other is a lovely blonde of nineteen, elegant, but not highly intelligent, named PENELOPE RAYMOND. PAT marches onto the end of the male line, and when she reaches almost to this point the SERGEANT says: 'Alt!' This is executed smartly. He then says: 'Right turn!' which is also smartly done. He then says: 'Stand at ease,' whereon the GIRLS stand at ease and GREGORY comes to attention, dropping his rifle. He hastily picks it up. The SERGEANT hurtles across to C.)

SERGEANT: (dropping downstage to view the juxtaposition.) The men stand fast. (Sweetly) The ladies, shun! Four paces sideways, march!

(PAT and PENNY move sideways in step R. GREGORY moves off D.L.)

Are you going far, Gregory?

(Unable to take four paces owing to the left wall, GREGORY is endeavouring to show his willingness by a kind of marking time.)

Say something, son, if it's only goodbye!

(Realising his error, GREGORY resumes his position, dropping his rifle butt on MORGAN's toe.)

Can you wonder I put my foot in the bucket? It happened when I was marking time. Personally, I thought I was a model of restraint.

The notices were wonderful, completely contradicting Colin's view of his own play. Or were we responsible for *Heroes* being popped into the wrong category?

Left: Basil Lord in *Worm's Eye View*; *centre:* Brian Rix, Larry Noble and John Slater in *Reluctant Heroes; Right:* John Chapman and Wally Patch in *Reluctant Heroes.*

'A rollicking anthology of music-hall jokes about the Army . . .'

Sunday Pictorial

'*Reluctant Heroes* at the Whitehall Theatre is a roaring farce of military life, and it is bound to be successful, because its conscripts, NCO's and officers are very real people running wildly loose in a panorama of improbabilities. The laughter is continuous.'

Jewish Chronicle

Sounds like a very witting farce to me, God wot, but there we are. Colin never wrote another one – or a comedy, for that matter. He found his true métier simply by becoming the most successful-ever writer of documentaries for BBC Television, winning many awards, and was the progenitor of *Z-Cars* with a short semi-documentary series called *Jacks and Knaves*. At no time did he try his hand with the true story of Salome and the 'Dance of the Seven Veils', though. Somehow I don't think he'd have cast me in the part if he had . . .

DRY ROT by John Chapman
1,475 performances at the Whitehall Theatre
from 31 August 1954

During the first two years of the run of *Heroes*, my understudy – who also played a small part of a Scots commando in Act III and fell on with our kit in Act I – was an actor called John Chapman. A bright lad, fresh out of drama school, he realised he had a great deal of time on his hands during each performance and started to write. He then asked if he could be released from his contract (it was 'run of the play' in those days) so as to gain some more experience in rep. at Folkestone. I released him and off he went to play in the staple diet of those days: Agatha Christie, *See How They Run* and similar thrillers and farces. He considered many works to be so inept that he was sure he could do better and was encouraged to finish the play he had started in his long waits at the Whitehall. Further encouraged by others he showed it to me and I knew that my search for a successor to *Heroes* was over – with suitable re-writing, of course, for there was no part for me! The result was *Dry Rot*, which was the second Whitehall farce, beginning on the hottest night of the year, 31 August 1954 and running for over three-and-a-half years. Apart from Kenneth Tynan's dismissive notice (quoted in the Prologue), it was generally well received by the critics, but by now we just presented the first act on television and the audiences poured in:

'*Dry Rot* nearly brought the house down. It careered madly on with the dialogue half-drowned by joyful shrieks from the audience.'

Daily Mirror

'John Chapman, author of this romp, for that is the best term to apply to it, clearly believes that there is no joke like an old joke in his fast and furious tale . . . about the machinations of several questionable characters intent on "switching" two racehorses, who use for their purpose a country inn run by an exasperated ex-Indian Army Colonel and his family. John Slater projects his nonsense with immense gusto and attack . . . As his partner in perfidy, Brian Rix, that frozen moon-calf whose Broad-Acred gormlessness never fails to register, is again very funny and far superior to his material. So much so, in fact, that one looks forward to seeing him in some of the great broad comedy parts of Shakespeare, Ben Jonson and the Restoration dramatists. What a delightful Abel Drugger he would make!'

The Stage

The snag is, no one ever asked!

Anyhow, now you know something about the play, you had better know more about its author. Here is John Chapman's story, written in his own fair hand, together with his definition of farce. You will by now have some idea of the panoply of opinions available:

It's a curious fact that nowadays less than two per cent of the population go to the theatre, and probably sixty per cent read books and periodicals, yet two hundred and fifty years ago it was the other way round. What caused this reversal? Quite simply, the arrival of the novel, and with it an increase in literacy. During the previous two-and-a-half thousand years drama had reigned supreme. If you wanted to tell the story, to communicate, you had to write a play. There was no option.

Life in those days was a good deal grimmer than it is now, so the populace enjoyed a regular catharsis through watching a tragedy. Then one day, quite by chance, from tears of grief came tears of laughter.

I rather suspect it was caused by that ingenious piece of stage-craft, the *deus ex machina*. The ancient Greeks had a saying: 'Never act with children, animals or a dodgy *deus ex machina*.'

It's a very dramatic and uplifting moment when the deus finally arrives in his machina. But after a long run the ropes suspending the machina get a bit frayed. So one Saturday night, second house, the deus parted company from his machina and plummeted onto the stage, knocking six bells out of Agamemnon who deviated from the script slightly and was heard to mutter: 'Sod this for a game of soldiers.' A titter spread through

144

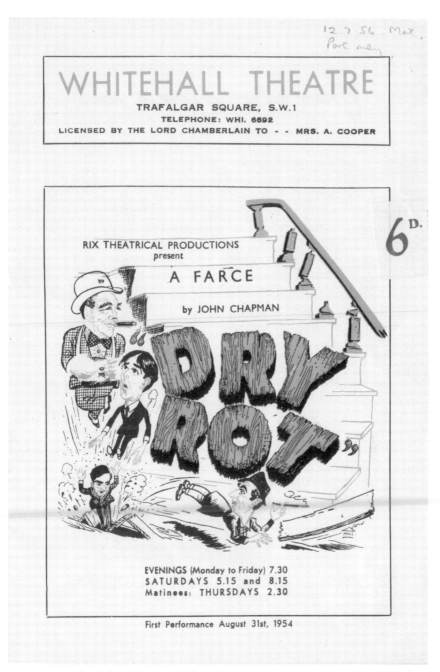

Programme for John Chapman's farce *Dry Rot* – after Leo Franklyn had taken over the part of Alf Tubbe, the bookie, from John Slater.

the audience, the actors got the giggles and then gradually laughter spread like a forest fire throughout the arena. A new kind of catharsis had emerged and a new kind of playwright was urgently needed.

Aristophanes, who'd been churning out comedies for years and had an urn full of rejection slips, was suddenly deluged with offers. Laughter became respectable. Thus out of tragedy, comedy and farce were born.

My definition of farce is simply this – a desperate struggle by basically likeable people to avert disaster. Now you may say that tragedy could be described in the same way. True. But in farce the characters succeed in their endeavours, and in tragedy they don't.

The borderline between farce and comedy is sometimes difficult to define, but broadly speaking comedy is cerebral and farce is physical. Imagine *Hamlet* being played by a touring company one wet matinée. There's hardly anyone in the audience, but they've paid their money, so the show must go on. At one point the actor playing Polonius is seized by an irresistible desire to get a laugh and hand in his notice. The moment comes when Hamlet enters his mother's bedroom where Polonius has just hidden himself behind the arras. Hamlet assumes the bulge to be Claudius, and lunges through the curtain with his sword, yelling, 'How now! A rat! Dead for a ducat! Dead.' Instead of dying, Polonius pops his head out and says, 'Ha-ha, missed.'

That's a fair example of farce, but only an isolated moment. The trick is to construct two hours of that sort of thing and make it reasonably plausible to intelligent people. Strange to say it's a trick one only discovers by chance. No eight-year-old ever says, 'When I grow up I'm going to write a farce.' Or if he does he's hastily put into a darkened room with a doctor and two trained nurses.

My own route to writing farce was purely accidental. I had just one ambition in life, to be an actor, and to that end I auditioned for the Royal Academy of Dramatic Art in 1948 and was accepted. During my first year at the Academy I learnt how to walk, breathe, sit down, open a door and light a cigarette. I also found out that although I had an aptitude for modern comedy I showed a distinct inadequacy when it came to Shakespeare. My fencing was also suspect. 'Don't you realise, young man,' said our instructor, 'that in Shakespearean duels there is always a winner as well as a loser. You can't guarantee to be cast every time in the losing role.' My fervent hope was that I wouldn't be cast in either.

I had a further problem. 'Voice production'. This I studied under a teacher of great renown who had helped King George VI to overcome his stammer. One day in my second year he told me my voice was 'tweedy'. I was somewhat nonplussed, and asked him to explain what he meant by 'tweedy'. 'Well,' he paused and sought inspiration from the ceiling, 'just tweedy.' It was obviously high-time to re-think my future career. At the end of each year RADA was turning out brilliant swordsmen with clear ringing voices. What possible chance would I stand, who could only walk, breathe, open a door and light a cigarette?

I went to see the Principal, Sir Kenneth Barnes and asked him if I could leave. 'That would be a great pity,' he said, 'you won't be here at the end of the course to receive your Diploma.' 'Well,' I said, 'perhaps you could post it on.' 'I mean,' he replied politely, 'you won't receive one at all.' 'Oh,' I said, somewhat tweedily. 'And moreover,' he went on, 'you will deny yourself the chance of winning any medals.' 'Ah. Am I in the running for any?' He paused. 'Er – no.'

We parted amicably, and as I left he wished me the best of luck for the future and added that in our profession there was room for all types of acting – even mine.

On the day I left RADA I walked into a theatrical agent's office in St Martin's Lane, and on the spot I was sent along to an audition for understudy in a pre-London tour of what was then an unknown play called *Reluctant Heroes*. I stood nervously in front of the author, the director and a budding young actor-manager named Brian Rix. Mr Rix asked me politely what I'd done recently. I said, 'Well if you mean today, I left RADA.'

Nobody asked to see my Diploma or my fencing, and by a stroke of luck I got a job in what turned out to be the first of the Whitehall Farces, two of which I subsequently wrote.

After forty years of writing farce it's pleasing to think that probably the two most famous plays throughout the entire world are *Hamlet* and *Charley's Aunt*.

One or two of John's are pretty well known, too. Here's his second farce:

SIMPLE SPYMEN by John Chapman
1,404 performances at the Whitehall Theatre
from 19 March 1958

I always think John Chapman's second farce, *Simple Spymen*, to be greatly superior to his first attempt, *Dry Rot*, but that is probably with hindsight for, at the time, both plays seemed absolutely splendid to me as they enjoyed their respective long-run tenure at the Whitehall. *Spymen* had a manic quality about it, though, which lifted it above the rather complicated, largely offstage, plot of *Dry Rot*, and this surreal quality was evident right from the opening scene – a heavily guarded room at the War Office:

It is morning and there is no one in the room when the CURTAIN RISES.

After a few seconds a voice is heard off left. It is the sentry, CORPORAL FLIGHT.

CORPORAL:	Halt! Who goes there?
VOICE:	Friend.
CORPORAL:	Advance friend and be recognised.

(Door opens and the CORPORAL takes up his position smartly just inside the room. He puts his rifle down to his side.)

CORPORAL:	Name?
VOICE:	Lieutenant Fosgrove.
CORPORAL:	Employment?
VOICE:	P.A. to the D.E.A.D. S.L.O.W.
CORPORAL:	Number?
VOICE:	A stroke C237884 stroke P.
CORPORAL:	Password?
VOICE:	Strike a light.
CORPORAL:	Your pass.

(LIEUTENANT FOSGROVE'S hand appears with the pass. He gives it to the CORPORAL who tries to open it with one hand but can't, so he puts the rifle in between his knees, then opens the pass. His rifle drops to the floor.)

Would you mind?

(FOSGROVE'S hand appears again and picks up the rifle. He gives it to the CORPORAL.)

Ta.

(Returns the pass and then comes smartly to attention.)

Advance.

(Enter LIEUTENANT FOSGROVE with hat, stick, gloves and the *Daily Telegraph*. He is about thirty and very 'Army', but not very bright. He salutes vaguely as he enters. The official preliminaries are now over.)

FOSGROVE:	Morning, Flighty. (Crosses to hat-stand, hangs hat on peg.)
CORPORAL:	Morning, Fussy. (Closes door, leans rifle against it.)
FOSGROVE:	Any tea yet?
CORPORAL:	No.

FOSGROVE:	Bad show. (Moves C. Looks at COLONEL'S desk.) Colonel in yet? (Moves back L.)
CORPORAL:	No.
FOSGROVE:	Good show. (Crosses to his desk, puts down stick and gloves.) Any orders?
CORPORAL:	Couple of top secret priority.
FOSGROVE:	Read them?
CORPORAL:	Yeah.
FOSGROVE:	Important?
CORPORAL:	No. (Crosses R. to L. of FOSGROVE.)
FOSGROVE:	Good show. Done the crossword? (Getting out his *Daily Telegraph*.)
CORPORAL:	All except three down.
FOSGROVE:	Oh. I shall have to get to work. All except three down, eh? (Reads the clue.) 'Rubbish in the Far East.'
CORPORAL:	Yes, it's a difficult one. (Moves L. a pace.) How's the wife, all right?
FOSGROVE:	Yes, except for this awful cold. Sniff, sniff all day and cough, cough all night. It's very wearing.
CORPORAL:	Yes, monotonous.
FOSGROVE:	If she could only vary it a bit.
CORPORAL:	Cough, cough all day and sniff, sniff all night?
FOSGROVE:	Yes, or sniff cough, sniff cough.
CORPORAL:	Yes, that would do it. (Crosses to door L., picks up rifle. About to exit, opens door.)
FOSGROVE:	How's your wife?
CORPORAL:	All right.
FOSGROVE:	Good.
CORPORAL:	Well, I say all right, but she 'ad 'er appendix out last night.
FOSGROVE:	Really, what was the trouble?
CORPORAL:	Appendicitis. (Exits.)

There it is. The opening lines in a fifties farce, with all that zany quality we remember from the best of the Marx Brothers' films, as well as the much-praised *Monty Python* television series

149

Toby Perkins, Larry Noble and Charles Cameron in John Chapman's *Simple Spymen*.

which followed. Furthermore, this zaniness did not stop there. The quality and quantity improved as the play moved on, and if I remind you that eventually two street musicians (Leo Franklyn and me in the original production) are mistaken for MI5 agents, in disguise, and are ordered to hunt down a nuclear pile restorer being imported by a certain Mr Grobchick (Andrew Sachs, who eventually became Manuel in those superb mini-farces on television, *Fawlty Towers*) and that the nuclear pile restorer turns out to be the New Clear Pile Restorer – a carpet cleaner – you will see how far down the truly farcical road we travelled. It was a joyous play in which to appear – Leo and I changed character and costume at the drop of a hat – and it called on us all to indulge in absurdities which are the dreams of childhood, but never possible except in our imaginations. I loved it. My only regret is that when John Chapman suggested that I return to the stage for a short season at the Lyric Theatre in Shaftesbury Avenue, after my retirement from MENCAP in 1988, the play chosen was his *Dry Rot* rather than *Simple Spymen*. In my opinion, there is no doubt which of the two will stand up to scrutiny as the years go by but, by then, I shall be too old to care. Well, I am now, really, I suppose . . .

How many others of his works will stand the test of time, I wonder? Take your pick: *Dry Rot*, *Simple Spymen*, *The Brides of March*, *Diplomatic Baggage* (adapted from a *Dial Rix* television production by John, then entitled *Between the Balance Sheets*), *Oh Clarence!* (a comedy, adapted from the P G Wodehouse story), *Not Now Darling* (with Ray Cooney), *My Giddy Aunt* (a comedy-thriller, with Ray Cooney), *Move Over Mrs Markham* (with Ray Cooney),

Leo Franklyn and his grand-daughter Sabina Franklyn.

151

There Goes the Bride (with Ray Cooney), *It Happened in Harrods* (a comedy), *Shut Your Eyes and Think of England* (a comedy, with Anthony Marriott), *Keeping Down With the Joneses* (with Jeremy Lloyd), *Key For Two* (a comedy, with Dave Freeman), *Look No Hans* (with Michael Pertwee), *Holiday Snap* (with Michael Pertwee). Add to that little lot God knows how many television productions, and a tweedy voice and no RADA Diploma seem of little consequence.

Appearing in the small part of the Corporal in *Spymen* was a certain Raymond Cooney, who had already toured for me as Flash Harry in *Dry Rot*. Like John Chapman in *Reluctant Heroes*, he also had time on his hands and used it to good effect by writing (and performing), along with Tony Hilton (another of my *Dry Rot* touring cast), short black-out sketches for John Slater in his television advertising magazine programme, *Slater's Bazaar*. John had left *Dry Rot* at the Whitehall after two years and taken the play on tour. That's where he got to know these two young putative writers. Anyway, Ray (he changed to the shorter Christian name after his first writing success – it was more matey for farce) and Tony put their heads together and eventually presented me with their first play.

ONE FOR THE POT by Ray Cooney and Tony Hilton
1,221 performances at the Whitehall Theatre
from 2 August 1961

This was a magical farce, fooling the audience from start to finish, and the more they were fooled, the more they laughed. And the magic? Quite simply I played quads in the play – four brothers who had been parted at birth and brought up separately in Yorkshire, France, Ireland and at a very laid-back public school somewhere in the south of England. The brothers were all after the same thing, money, so you can imagine the quadruple-dealing which went on to take the prize – and the bewilderment of the audience as four Brian Rixes kept popping up from every part of the stage. It was hard work, I can tell you, but worth every drop of sweat.

The critics were unanimous in their praise:

'So good – so very, very good.'

Harold Hobson, *Sunday Times*

The company of Ben Travers' farce, *The Bed Before Yesterday. Back row:* Gabrielle Daye, Leonard Fenton, Frank Grimes, Helen Mirren; *Centre:* John Moffatt, Joan Plowright, Royce Mills; *Front row:* Patsy Rowlands, Lindsay Anderson, Ben Travers, Sebastian Abineri.

Production of *Rookery Nook* by Ben Travers.

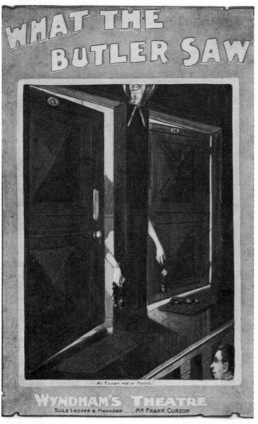

What the Butler Saw by Joe Orton.

Above: Robertson ('Bunny') Hare and Alfred Drayton.

Above right: Programme for *Blue For A Boy* by Austin Melford.

Right: Programme for Philip King's *On Monday Next*.

THE STRAND THEATRE

A FUNNY THING
HAPPENED ON THE WAY TO THE FORUM

Opposite page: Frankie Howerd and company in Sondheim's musical farce, *A Funny Thing Happened On the Way to the Forum.*

Right: Poster for the first Whitehall Farce, *Reluctant Heroes* by Colin Morris.

Below: Old and new members of the cast of *Reluctant Heroes* celebrating the 1000th performance. *Left to right:* Brian Rix, Larry Noble, John Slater, Wally Patch, Pamela Abbott, Elspet Gray, Viera (Colin Morris' wife and a well-known cabaret artiste), Dermot Walsh, Darcy Conyers, Colin Morris.

WYNDHAM'S
THEATRE   CHARING CROSS ROAD

Licensed by the Lord Chamberlain to Sir Bronson Albery
Lessees: The Wyndham Theatres Ltd.   Managing Director: Donald Albery

BRIAN RIX AND **DONALD ALBERY**
(for BRIAN RIX ENTERPRISES LTD.) (for CALABASH PRODUCTIONS LTD.)

present

CHARLES HESLOP
JOHN CHAPMAN
ELSPET GRAY

In a new Farce
JOHN CHAPMAN

THE DIPLOMATIC BAGGAGE

PROGRAMME

with

ROGER DELGADO
and
JOHN BARRON

Directed by
WALLACE DOUGLAS
Settings by RHODA GRAY

Left: Programme for *Diplomatic Baggage* by John Chapman.

Below: Programme for *One For the Pot* by Ray Cooney and Tony Hilton.

Opposite page above: Poster for *Chase Me Comrade!* by Ray Cooney.

Opposite page below: Dry Rot by John Chapman.

RIX THEATRICAL
PRODUCTIONS
present

BRIAN RIX
LEO **FRANKLYN**   BASIL **LORD**
in

"ONE FOR THE POT"

and TERRY **SCOTT**   *with* LARRY **NOBLE**

Brewed by RAY COONEY and TONY HILTON
Stirred by HENRY KENDALL
SOUVENIR 1/- PROGRAMME

WHITEHALL THEATRE
CORNER OF TRAFALGAR SQUARE

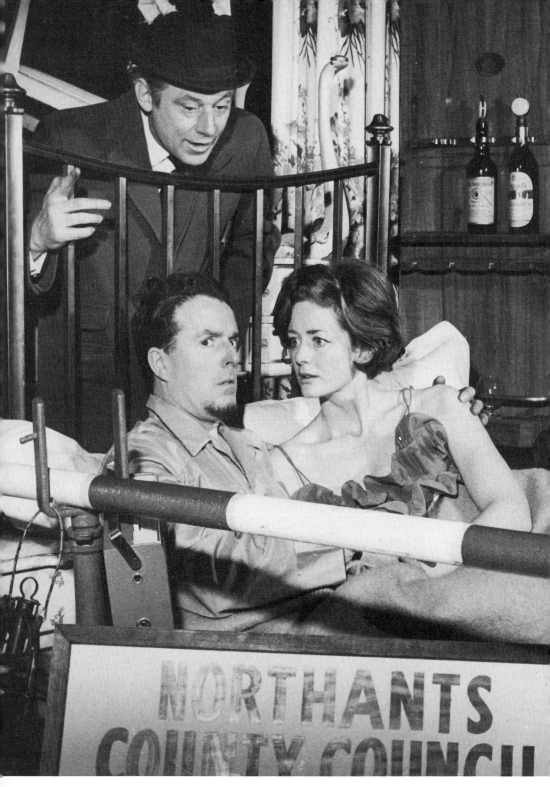

Brian Rix, Elspet Gray and Patrick Cargill in a *Dial Rix* television production.

'Fine art in farce, well up to the Whitehall standard, gets funnier as it goes on and will no doubt run for years.'

W A Darlington, *Daily Telegraph*

and on and on – not a dissenting voice anywhere.

And so began the writing career of the most productive and, arguably, the most successful of all modern English farce writers, Ray Cooney – although John Chapman and Ben Travers are hard on his heels. Tony Hilton only collaborated with Ray on one other play and then dropped out of contention and, eventually, died somewhat prematurely. Ray went on from strength to strength, so let's have a look at the plays he has written to date, before asking him to give his views on farce: *One For The Pot* (with Tony Hilton), *Chase Me Comrade!*, *Bang Bang Beirut* (with Tony Hilton), *Charlie Girl* (with Hugh and Margaret Williams), *Not Now Darling* (with John Chapman), *Move Over Mrs Markham* (with John Chapman), *Why Not Stay For Breakfast?* (with Gene Stone), *My Giddy Aunt* (with John Chapman), *There Goes the Bride* (with John Chapman), *Her Royal Highness* (with Royce Ryton), *Run For Your Wife*, *Wife Begins at Forty*, *Two Into One*, *Out of Order*, *It Runs In the Family*, *Funny Money* and *Elvis* (with Jack Good).

The Rules of Farce
by Ray Cooney

Being asked to write the Rules of Farce is akin to being asked to describe the Rules of Life – where do you start and what do you leave out? Also, it implies that farce, or any other kind of theatrical endeavour, can be learnt by studying some kind of manual. However, having written in this particular genre for over thirty years, a certain amount of introspection is inevitable, so I will attempt (for the very first time!) to unravel what goes into my work – and why.

However, before laying bare my formula, I should say that 'farce' covers a wide area. There would seem to be a point at which 'comedy' becomes 'farce' and, having become 'farce', it then flows into several farcical tributaries. Therefore, you, the reader, could well be presented with a totally different set of rules by, say, Alan Ayckbourn, Michael Frayn or Neil Simon – if I may allow myself to be placed alongside my three colleagues.

I believe I can see the roots of my kind of farce in Shakespeare's comedies, through Feydeau, Pinero, Ben Travers, Vernon Sylvaine, Philip King and, finally, John Chapman's Whitehall farces. This is not

153

Poster for the Cooney/Hilton farce, *One for the Pot*.

surprising as I was a young actor who had the benefit of spending his early years in various Repertory companies appearing in the comedies of these Masters and without realising it, soaking up the wealth of theatrical experience handed down over the years by these writers and the artistes who appeared in their plays. After all, I was acting with actors who had, in their youth, acted with actors who had acted with actors who had acted with actors who had appeared in the original productions of *The Comedy of Errors* and *A Midsummer Night's Dream*.

Over these thirty years what seems to have developed into a 'Ray Cooney' comedy is, I hope, a well-structured piece of drama that would have satisfied those early craftsmen with the addition of my own convoluted yet chess-like, almost algebraic, development of plot.

And so, to my Rules – for *my* kind of farce:

1. In the beginning there is THE PLOT. I'm not searching for a 'comedy' plot or a 'funny' storyline. I'm searching for a tragedy. Farce, more than comedy, is akin to tragedy.

In *Run For Your Wife* the 'hero' is a bigamist: this situation in real life is an absolute tragedy for those involved. My play doesn't dwell on the tragedy (a farce is intended to get laughs), but the audience instinctively understands what is at stake.

In *Out of Order*, a Cabinet Minister's illicit evening in a London hotel is brought to an abrupt halt when he and the young lady discover a dead body in the bedroom. The Government could fall ('one more scandal for the Conservatives etc. etc.'), and so he embarks on a cover-up which risks both his marriage and his political future.

In real life – as politicians know – this situation brings tragedy. In *Out of Order* it also brings laughter, because the audience knows what's at stake for the characters in the play.

2. THE CHARACTERS must be truthful and recognisable. Again, this is why the audience laughs. The characters are believable – it is the situations that are slightly out of the ordinary; ordinary people who are out of their depth in a predicament which is beyond their control and they are unable to contain – tragedy again.

3. The ability to RE-WRITE is essential. My farces are pure concoctions. I never get it exactly right the first time. The original script is comparable to a middle-of-the-range Ford motor car. By the time it appears on the West End stage it must have acquired the precision, the elegance and the comfort of a Rolls Royce.

I attempt to achieve this by, initially, having a play-reading of the first draft of the script to a small invited audience. Then, having learnt if the basic premise holds good and how the various comedic ramifications have amused them, I take the play back to the drawing board.

Huge areas are then restructured, re-written and generally re-shaped before the next step, which is a 'try-out' production in a regional repertory theatre. Characters may be added or removed in order to serve the requirements of the play. Once I know from the initial response that the basis of the play is sound, no amount of time and effort is spared to get the play right for its regional try-out.

And after the try-out, more re-writing. Every single moment has to work. A West End production is not mounted until I know for sure that the play is as perfect as I can get it to be.

4. CASTING is vital. Because of the laughter my kind of play invokes, it is sometimes thought that 'comedians' serve farce well. Invariably, disaster! Farce needs actors and actresses who can play tragedy, but also they must have the technique, the stamina, the precision and the dexterity that farce demands. And, almost above all, they must have generosity of spirit. Farce is teamwork. You can't have selfish actors pulling attention at the wrong moment.

Focus is vital. It all looks so easy when you're in the audience – and so it should – but many an established actor has come unstuck playing farce. There are no beautiful, poetic monologues to hide behind. It's mundane language. The characters are not standing centre-stage, spot-lit, intellectualising about their predicament. They're rushing around dealing with it.

5. A rule personal to me is REAL TIME. The two hours spent in the theatre by the audience is two hours in the existence of the characters in the play. No fade-outs. No passage of time between Acts I and II. When the curtain rises on the second act the characters are exactly how we left them at the end of Act I, and the action is continuous.

This imposes huge demands on the playwright. Only one setting and two hours of continuous drama/laughter – but the rewards are worth it. And the conjuror has done everything 'before your very eyes'.

6. Finally, never underestimate the intelligence of THE AUDIENCE. Several people who first read *Run For Your Wife* (including my own wife) said, 'It's very funny but the complications become so convoluted that I had to keep going back to the script to check what was what, who was who and who'd said what to whom.' That, of course, was reading the play. Farces have to performed, not read.

The audience is always the missing ingredient; this is who farces are written for. As it turned out, the audience never missed a trick in *Run For Your Wife*. They remember everything. Moments that are set up in Act I and pay off in Act II are taken up by the audience without a pause.

I believe that the audience likes to work. Anybody who has paid upwards of £20 for a ticket, suffered the slings and arrows of British Rail or been reduced to penury by parking in a West End garage, deserves respect. The audience has had the intelligence to leave their television sets, and the least the playwright can do is set before them the very best that can be mustered. Long may they live – and laugh.

Here endeth the lesson according to Ray Cooney . . .

CHASE ME COMRADE! by Ray Cooney
773 performances at the Whitehall Theatre
from 16 July 1964

Ray Cooney's first solo farce, inspired by Rudolf Nureyev's then recent defection to the West, was *Chase Me Comrade!*, which followed *One For The Pot*. At first glance, it looks as though we had lost our touch and the magic had gone, for the play ran for less than a thousand performances. Let me disabuse you – for this farce received splendid notices, with the still-to-be-knighted Harold Hobson of the *Sunday Times* leading the fray:

> The truth is that farce, with its multiple changes, seems to satisfy some need in Mr Rix's nature, a need which in some measure we share with him. There are moments when we would all like to be something other than we are, and these moments are isolated, enriched and fulfilled for us by Mr Rix.
>
> In his latest venture, Ray Cooney's *Chase Me Comrade!*, Mr Rix, with an extraordinarily suave yet at the same time desperate aplomb, turns himself into a naval commander, a tiger, a ballet dancer, and a man ten feet tall. He is Protean, multiform, plural and innumerable, free of the limitations of personality and character. Fresh, eager, greatly talented in speed, timing, and exactness and clarity of speech, Mr Rix comes up to each transformation, each new, insuperable difficulty, with the confident enthusiasm of an innocently clever pupil about to receive the headmaster's prize. His joy is communicated, and we go fifty-fifty in the satisfaction of his accomplishment.

No – the reason the play came off was largely personal and down to a decision which I made in the January of 1966, the year I left the Whitehall.

For a long time I had been trying to buy the lease of the theatre but always came unstuck over last-minute problems with the, then, selling management. In the January of 1966 I received an offer to

Whitehall Theatre
Corner of Trafalgar Sq. Tel. WHItehall 6692
EVGS. 7-30. MATS. WEDS. 2-30. SATS. 5-15 & 8-15.

BRIAN
RIX

and the
FAMOUS WHITEHALL
LAUGHTER TEAM
in

CHASE ME
COMRADE!

"COMRADE RIX DOES IT AGAIN—SEE FOR YOURSELF"
Evening News

"AGONIES OF HELPLESS LAUGHTER"
The Guardian

"BRIAN RIX GIVES THE PUBLIC WHAT IT WANTS—HIS JOY IS COMMUNICATED"
Sunday Times

"CONSTANT ROAR OF LAUGHTER"
Daily Mirror

"GUARANTEED—A LOAD OF LAUGHS"
Daily Sketch

"A STORM OF LAUGHTER"
Financial Times

"NEW SUCCESS FOR THE BRIAN RIX TEAM"
News of the World

"HONOUR BRIAN RIX— MASTER OF FARCE. FAMILY ENTERTAIN- MENT DE LUXE. A RIOTOUS TIME. THE GREATEST FARCE FACTORY IN THE WORLD"
Yorkshire Post

All Seats bookable, no extra charge
STALLS 17/6, 12/6; DRESS CIRCLE 15/-;
UPPER CIRCLE 7/6.

Poster for Ray Cooney's *Chase Me Comrade!*

take *Chase Me Comrade!* out-of-town for a summer season and a lengthy tour. The offer was so good it gave me the chance to stamp my foot, as our protracted negotiations once more ground to a halt, and flounce out of the theatre to teach everyone a lesson. Mind you, I took the precaution of presenting another show to take my place, with Peter Bridge, and had the option to return to the theatre at the end of the year, refreshed by a lot of money and with my appetite for long runs once more restored.

That was the theory, anyway. I reckoned without the vagaries of the theatre. The musical farce I chose to take my place was Danny La Rue and Barbara Windsor in *Come Spy With Me*, with book, lyrics and music by Bryan Blackburn and directed by Ned Sherrin. With a team like that – in those days – you would think we would have had an unbeatable combination. Well – we hadn't. The musical never really enjoyed a packed house at every performance and, with the overheads it carried, such capacity business was necessary. It ran along merrily enough, but not rewarding enough for me to be able to return at the end of the year, as we had to keep *Come Spy With Me* on in the hope of recovering our investment. I had to find another home!

Well, I found one: the Garrick Theatre across Trafalgar Square, which was big enough backstage for me to try out a long-held ambition of mine – a repertoire of farce. I tried – and I failed. But I stayed at the Garrick, nevertheless, for several years, returning to the Whitehall for one last fling, in 1976, with *Fringe Benefits*.

After that, I gave it all up . . .

SLOW FADE TO BLACK
CURTAIN

ACT III

Scene iii: Various playhouses in London's Theatreland

Dear Madam, you have seen this play;
I never saw it till today
You know the details of the plot,
But, let me tell you, I do not.
The actors in their funny way
Have several funny things to say,
But they do not amuse me more
If you have said them just before . . .

A P Herbert.

R AY COONEY was right, audiences deserve to get value for money, but Sir Alan Herbert was also right – audiences can be very odd. They certainly need to be spoon-fed information about forthcoming attractions, but once they've cottoned on to a play or an actor they turn up in shoals. They did that without let or hindrance for sixteen years at the Whitehall, but when the venue changed to the Garrick, they became confused; not so much by the move across Trafalgar Square but because I changed my policy and hadn't enough money to publicise the fact. This meant that when I put on a repertoire of plays – *Stand By Your Bedouin*, *Uproar in the House* and *Let Sleeping Wives Lie* – they read the notices (which were pretty good), then watched the television excerpts and were convinced that each successive play was on for a short run only. In other words, they packed the house when a play opened, but when it came back again in the repertoire they appeared to have lost interest and stayed away. It was all very frustrating, and after six months I abandoned the idea, transferred *Uproar in the House* to another management (who promptly moved the play to the Whitehall), failed

160

to stand by *Stand By Your Bedouin* and concentrated on *Let Sleeping Wives Lie*, which filled the Garrick for a further two years.

All very disappointing, especially as the Sunday 'heavies' were giving me great support. Here is an example, from the pen of Harold Hobson of the *Sunday Times*:

> Mr Hall [the future Sir Peter] speaks of forming a permanent company as a matter of immense travail, towards which a Treasury grant of £80,000 is derisory. Hearing his eloquent and despairing words, one would imagine that setting up a permanent company was as rare and difficult a crusade as seeking the Holy Grail. Yet for years Mr Brian Rix has had a permanent company at the Whitehall Theatre (now at the Garrick) without, so far as I know, any encouragement from the Arts Council. It is a company that has developed its own style of production and acting, and created its own audience.
>
> Why has Mr Rix been able to accomplish, without any fuss, what comes so hard to our leading avant-garde organisation, fortified as it is by journalist approval, Government assistance, the colossal talents of Peter Brook and Michael Saint-Denis, and its quiet sense of performing a social service? One must in justice remark that the scale of the two ventures is quite different; and creating a style which finds its culmination in the removal of a pair of trousers is not the same thing as reaching out towards Beckett and Pinter and Shakespeare. Nevertheless, the reason for Mr Rix's success is one which more pompous enterprises should ponder.

Whilst Ronald Bryden of the *New Statesman* and the *Observer* wrote:

> There they are: the most robust survivors of a great tradition, the most successful British theatrical enterprise of our time. Curious that no one can be found to speak up wholeheartedly for them – no one, that is, outside enthusiastic millions who have packed every British theatre where they have played.
>
> It's particularly curious considering the current intellectual agitation for a theatre of the masses, a true working-class drama. Everything, apparently, for which Joan Littlewood has struggled – the boisterous, extrovert playing, the integrated teamwork, the Cockney irreverence of any unself-conscious, unacademic audience bent purely on pleasure – exists, patently and profitably at the Whitehall (and now, the Garrick). Yet how many devout pilgrims to Stratford East have hazarded the shorter journey to Trafalgar Square to worship at the effortless shrine of the thing itself? How many Arts Council grants have sustained Mr Rix's company? How many *Evening Standard* awards went to *Dry Rot*? How many theses have been written on the art of Colin Morris, John Chapman or Ray Cooney? The time has come, surely, to fill the gap.

Unhappily, the gap was never filled. Grant-aid on a pretty massive scale is necessary if you are to create an effective repertoire company, such as the Royal National Theatre or the Royal Shakespeare Company, and such aid was never on offer to me, in spite of the welcome intervention of Messrs Hobson, Bryden and the like. If support on a comparable scale had been forthcoming, it would have been possible to present a variety of farcical productions, from Molière to Ayckbourn, from Shakespeare to Cooney, but it was not to be. We just ground on for another eleven years, until I became bored, the audience became increasingly elderly and the music stopped. That's why, in 1977, I gave it all up.

All that was a long time ago and, frankly, leaving farce behind had an almost liberating effect on me, allowing me to take up another career and view the theatre with a more dispassionate eye, generally as a member of the audience. I love it, still, but – oddly enough – visit farce nowadays almost out of curiosity, rather than for pleasure. I am, truly, a poacher turned gamekeeper.

But first, the repertoire. *Stand By Your Bedouin*, the second play to be written by Ray Cooney and Tony Hilton, was originally entitled *Bang Bang Beirut*, but we changed the title for an even more obvious joke. At one time we even considered calling it *Florence of Arabia* (for the leading character was a variety pro. called Fred Florence), but we got cold feet about that one, too. I can't think why.

I suppose the play was remarkably prescient, really, for the Middle Eastern troubles were soon to increase – and the play was about troubles in the Middle East. However, the piece hardly treated the matter seriously and had originally been toured by my management, splitting the week with *Chase Me Comrade!*, in which I continued to play my original part of Gerry Buss, with Dickie Henderson playing the part of Fred Florence in *Bang Bang Beirut*, as it was then called. Later, when the play came to the Garrick, I alternated in the role with Leslie Crowther. That added to the audience confusion, too. Which of us was playing in what play? My grand design to give the Great British Public a variety of actors and authors came apart at the seams almost before it was conceived.

After *Bedouin* came *Uproar in the House*, the first play by Anthony Marriott and Alastair Foot. Their second, *No Sex Please – We're British!* is rather better known and will shortly be described in some

Uproar in the House, showing Rhoda Gray's set. On the top floor, left to right: Elspet Gray, Brian Rix, Derek Farr, Helen Jessop, and on the ground floor, left to right: Dennis Ramsden, Sheila Mercier, Alan Tilvern, Leo Franklyn and Wendy Padbury.

detail by its highly-successful producer, John Gale, but their first was funny enough. It concerned a Conservative parliamentary candidate who becomes involved in all manner of shenanigans in an Ideal Home show-house. My designer and my sister-in-law, Rhoda Gray, created a very witty set; the cast, with my wife, Elspet Gray, my sister Sheila Mercier, and me, ensured that nepotism still flourished in the theatre, and a good time was had by all. When the play was transferred to the Whitehall, Nicholas Parsons took over my part, Sheila went with him and nepotism became somewhat dispersed. Elspet stayed with me and Rhoda designed my new set for *Let Sleeping Wives Lie* at the Garrick, whilst *Uproar* ran on for another eighteen months in its *new* home, which was my *old* home – if you know what I mean. By way of compensation, we received a weekly royalty for the rights, as well as a lump sum for the set, so the bank manager was well satisfied. I wasn't, though. I'd rather have been back at the Whitehall.

The third play in the repertoire, *Let Sleeping Wives Lie* by Harold Brooke and Kay Bannerman (whose earlier farce, *All For Mary*, with David Tomlinson, Michael Shepley and Kathleen Harrison had been presented at the Duke of York's Theatre in 1954), was probably the funniest of the trio, as it poked fun at American business methods being transplanted onto British business. As the American tycoon, Mr Wymark, Derek Farr was absolutely splendid, whilst the rest of the cast, too, gave of their best: Bill Treacher (of *EastEnders* fame), Carmel Cryan, Leo Franklyn, Andrew Sachs, Dennis Ramsden, Anna Dawson, Elspet Gray, Leslie Crowther and me. I've listed them all, for they were, or are, extremely good farceurs and had been exercising their talents, with distinction, in the other two plays in the repertoire, as well. Now, they settled down for the obligatory long run in *Wives* of over 700 performances. It's difficult to be absolutely accurate about numbers, for there were some performances in the repertoire before the long, unbroken, run and *Who's Who in the Theatre* doesn't count those. Even *Worm's Eye View* had its performances separated, for it had to leave the Whitehall for a short time in 1947 and was deemed to have given 500 performances in the first part of the run, and 1,745 in the 'revival' a few weeks later. H J Barlow, who presented the play, was furious; if the two runs had been added together it would have made *Worm's Eye View* the, then, longest run on the London stage, beating *Chu Chin Chow* by seven performances. But John Parker, the editor of *Who's Who in the Theatre* decided otherwise, and H J Barlow and author, R F Delderfield, never held their record and never forgave John Parker his pedantry. I think Barlow would have taken the play off a year earlier if he'd known he was to be denied his moment of triumph, for that was when Ronnie Shiner left the production and it transferred from the Whitehall to the Comedy. I'm glad he didn't, though. It gave me time to tour *Reluctant Heroes* and be around when the Whitehall management were hunting for another service comedy. But for Barlow's stubbornness, Whitehall Farce might never have come into being. What's more, it was his mentioning the play (which he'd seen in Birmingham) to the owners of the Whitehall which made them aware of our existence, and by that somewhat tortuous route we finally arrived at our West End home. Such are the vagaries and the successes due to chance in the theatrical world.

Towards the end of the run of *Let Sleeping Wives Lie* at the Garrick, the *Sunday Times* carried an interview with me by Robert Lacey, under the title of the 'Beauty of the Well-Timed Gag'. I think it's worth re-printing in full, for it reflects pretty accurately my views then on farce – views which I still largely hold to this day, although time has dated some of them, and which compare in many ways to those expressed by others in this book, particularly the more recent authors.

My plays are total escapism and are meant to be. But in order to escape, the farce has to be founded on some aspect of everyday life. The secret is to take something that is fairly recognisable to everyone – life in the army, tax problems, American methods in British business – establish it firmly as a context people will believe in, and then push the situation to its extreme.

Reluctant Heroes and *Sailor Beware!* were both very popular when a lot of people had recent experiences of service life. Nowadays you could use the same jokes, but you'd probably have to put them in a more modern context.

Chase Me Comrade!, for example, started off as a terribly antiquated play called *How's Your Father?*, all about a man who escaped from prison. Now, fifty years ago old lags were funny. Put a convict in broad arrows with a ball and chain round his ankle and you had them convulsed. But nowadays it doesn't get a titter, so we changed the plot to one about a Russian ballet dancer who defects to the West. It's exactly the same situation. There's a man you've got to hide. And we kept six hysterically funny scenes from the original play.

It's funny how habits in laughter change. Civil Servants are 1969 figures of fun. And policemen don't get laughs as they did before *Z-Cars*.

For some time I was interested in a play about petty officialdom. It's called *Collapse of Stout Party*, all about a woman who's so fat she can't get out of a room that's been let to new tenants, and how bureaucracy runs riot trying to get her out. Hysterically funny, though I suppose when I recount the plot like that it sounds rather tasteless.

But I think there's a strong vein of cruelty in all humour. People laugh at other people's discomfiture, because they're damn glad not to be in that predicament themselves. That is why the adulterer, or the man who wishes he were – and don't most people wish that at some time or another? – will fall about when he sees an adulterer getting caught on the stage. But you've got to be very careful how you draw the line. British audiences will laugh at homosexuality and deafness, even though neither is really comic at all. But they won't laugh at blindness, even though it could be argued that being deaf, being cut off from communication with other people, is the more tragic situation.

It is a terribly difficult line to draw, but if a particular character

165

rings true to the plot, and if you aren't just exploiting his weakness for cheap laughs, then he is a legitimate figure of fun. I have a mentally handicapped daughter, and I'd feel very strongly if I saw such a person being ridiculed on the stage. But I did not object to the portrayal of the child in the *Joe Egg* comedy even though it made me laugh. I thought that was a splendid attempt to present a tragic problem in a theatrically acceptable form.

The whole point of good farce is that it teeters on the edge of tragedy. It always threatens ultimate catastrophe, and that is what sustains the dramatic tension. But by a slight twist it makes people roll about with laughter. It is tragedy with its trousers down.

Some people criticise my farces for being ludicrous and unbelievable. Well usually they are people who never come to see them, and really their objection applies to any play. The essence of drama is the suspension of reality.

This is why all my company at the Garrick are actors first and comedians second. A comedian, a stand-up music-hall comic, is just himself, he is inclined to be the same whatever role he plays, he finds it difficult to create real drama. But any good actor should be able to play farce, because he can adapt – he can become somebody else – and he must convince the audience completely. But he must also have a meticulous sense of timing.

I really do savour the pleasure of timing a line perfectly. It's rather like changing gear properly or playing a classic off-drive at cricket, and of course there's the sexual element. It's like making love really well, it's a deeply physical feeling. But then laughter itself is deeply physical; it involves an extraordinary explosion of energy that can hit you like a sledgehammer in the theatre. A responsive audience whips you on so it hurts, like a horse under a jockey. And it's so physical, you know, that on a humid day you actually get fewer laughs – the closeness makes laughing physically more difficult.

A critic once said that my farces are vulgar in the truest sense of the word – of the people, and that is something of which I am very proud. I am proud that my audiences contain so many coach parties, and I resent the implication that coach parties are some sort of sub-human species. Thank God for them, because without them the West End theatre just could not keep going.

I know we're not highbrow in the conventional Arts Council sense, but I'd claim a lot on behalf of our entertainment, less possibly for what it contains, than for the effect it has on people. Take the opposite extreme – something like a bullfight. It's a tatty, blood-soaked, third-rate entertainment, with tired seedy old uniforms and sawdust. It is the reaction that the spectacle elicits from the crowd that is the truly crucial part of the business, the degrading expressions on the faces of the crowd. The animal is brought low, but the spectators are brought lower still.

I'd claim that my farces produce a totally opposite reaction. If you can get an audience to roll about with laughter, and it's open honest laughter, then you've achieved some sort of precious liberation, a release from tension and violence, a release that even football matches seem no longer able to sustain. I think our farces achieve a rare suspension of time, people completely forget their everyday troubles and worries and I think the effect of this release on people's everyday behaviour to be both healthy and positive.

You can see this was written in 1969, before football hooliganism had become such a problem – and when we still had a house in Spain, otherwise there would have been no reference to bull-fighting! Even so, a quarter of a century later, I think it still makes some kind of sense. It certainly did at the time, especially after two years of laughter in London with *Let Sleeping Wives Lie*, followed by a short tour and summer season, opening the delightful little Playhouse at Weston-Super-Mare. Then I was ready to present the next farce at the Garrick Theatre – and my first one in the West End from the pen of Michael Pertwee.

Michael had established a particularly successful career as a film writer, often in cahoots with Jack Davies and Mario Zampi (*Laughter in Paradise* being their first, with those superb farceurs, Alistair Sim, George Cole, Joyce Grenfell and A E Matthews in the cast) or, later, with Mel Frank (*A Funny Thing Happened on the Way to the Forum* being *their* second, with those equally superb American farceurs, Zero Mostel, Phil Silvers and Buster Keaton in that cast) – but three funny plays came about through his association with me, *She's Done It Again, Don't Just Lie There, Say Something!* and *A Bit Between the Teeth*.

As I have already mentioned, Michael had taken the bare bones of an earlier farce, *Nap Hand*, by Vernon Sylvaine and Guy Bolton (which I had presented in its original form on television), and transformed it into *She's Done It Again*. It was the beginning of a working partnership which lasted for seven years, spanning three plays, a film of the play *Don't Just Lie There, Say Something!*, with Leslie Phillips and Joanna Lumley, and a television series, *Men of Affairs*, also based on *Don't Just Lie There, Say Something!*, with Warren Mitchell playing the adulterous Minister, created in the play by Alfred Marks.

Brian Rix and Warren Mitchell in the television production *Men of Affairs*.

Shortly after those seven years I 'retired' as an actor-manager, but my friendship with Michael, away from the professional arena of the theatre, continued as strongly as before and, of course, he went on writing most successfully, on his own with *Sextet*, which starred Leslie Phillips and had a two-year run at the Criterion Theatre, and occasionally with John Chapman, with whom he wrote *Holiday Snap* for Keith Barron and *Look, No Hans!* especially for David Jason. Michael was absolutely splendid company, constantly amusing and informative, as well as being a dear friend to both my wife, Elspet, and myself. He was very brave in the face of death, actually attending the first night of his re-write of Ivor Novello's *King's Rhapsody* wearing a surgical mask to combat any diseases flying about, for he was in the middle of chemotherapy – which didn't work – as he finally succumbed to a rare form of leukaemia, on top of massive heart attacks and major heart surgery. In spite of all these trials and tribulations, his sense of humour was as acute in his last days, a week before his seventy-sixth birthday, as it had ever been in his halcyon ones. He left behind one autobiography, *Name Dropping*, published by Leslie Frewin some seventeen years before his death in 1991, which is a very funny read, but not completely up-to-date. A great deal happened to Michael between 1974 and 1991 – alas, never to be recorded by him in his dry, inimitable style, but touched upon above.

Michael would certainly have followed Colin Morris, John Chapman and Ray Cooney in contributing to this book, had he been able. However, I have done the next best thing and obtained permission from his widow, the delightful Maya (My-My) to re-publish here some of his writing. I only wish he was around for it to be freshly minted . . .

Looking back I am astonished at the amount of words I turned out in 1953. I wrote two stage plays. The first, *Death and Brown Windsor*, based on the Haigh murders, has never done more than reps and amateurs. The second, *Tell the Marines!* was another collaboration with my father, Roland, in which we decided we had found the key to a fortune.

At the time a young actor named Brian Rix, who had not been noticeably successful in provincial repertory, had suddenly burst into the West End and was packing them in at the Whitehall Theatre in an army farce by Colin Morris, *Reluctant Heroes*. Roland and I went to see it. When we came out we decided it was all too easy. Harmless slapstick, discreet lavatory humour, no subtlety, a series of mechanically, although cleverly worked out 'routines', and yet the public lapped it up and the author raked it in.

So we sat down and wrote a sequel. All went according to plan. Brian read it, liked it and optioned it. Too easy, as we had thought. [Forgive me for jogging Michael's memory, but it was not 'too easy'. As I mentioned earlier, the play was originally banned by the Lord Chamberlain.] He decided to send it out on tour to test its strength. Wally Patch starred as a bullying sergeant major. Brian directed the play himself. On its opening week it did better business than had *Reluctant Heroes*, at the same provincial theatre. We started to work out how we would spend our fortune. Then, as the tour progressed, business dropped and, with the drop in business, so Brian's enthusiasm waned. At the end of the tour he decided not to go ahead with it.

I learned a valuable lesson from this. It is *not* easy to write farce – successful farce. It is probably more difficult than any other type of play. It is absolutely fatal to approach farce writing in a cynical frame of mind which says: 'Anything for a laugh.' Farce has to combine the incredible with being credible. Nothing fails like excess. Laughter dies the moment audiences cease to believe what they are seeing. A man losing his trousers can only be funny if there is a good reason for him to lose them. If it is done for the sake of a cheap laugh, it will not raise a titter. You cannot afford to let up in farce. A pleasant verbal love scene, which would be quite acceptable in a play by William Douglas-Home, would kill a farce stone dead. Thus the farce author has a constant, desperate search for action which moves from one high spot to the next, giving the audience the minimum of time to think and dissect. You cannot write anyone really unpleasant into a farce. Even the 'heavy' must be funny and reasonably sympathetic. You cannot be too near the knuckle, because the farce audience is a family audience. Thus a fine balance must be struck between good honest vulgarity and a deeper exploration of sexual problems. A study of the majority of farces will show that however evil the intentions of any character he very rarely makes it with a woman. Most of the fun of farce is found in the *failure* to score. A farce is not so much written as constructed, piece by piece, to form a whole. I would advise nobody to try their hand at it who is not prepared for months of hard, and sometimes soul-destroying, work.

The débâcle of *Tell the Marines* had one positive result in that it laid the foundations of an abiding friendship between myself, Brian and his wife, Elspet. However, this was not enough for me. I hate to be defeated and I swore that I would one day write him a farce which he would not only option, but also present in the West End. I had to wait sixteen years to achieve this.

Those sixteen years went by all too quickly. When Michael finally made it with *She's Done It Again*, the piece was greeted with wondrous notices, none better than this from Harold Hobson in the *Sunday Times*: 'I have no doubt at all about what has been the principal theatrical event this week. The Master is back again and London can once more be gay. Michael Pertwee's farce is the funniest in which the great Brian Rix has ever appeared. There are difficulties in the way of communicating a proper sense of its delicious and delirious qualities. But what looks feeble and hackneyed on the page glows with glorious life in the Garrick Theatre . . . Several times during the evening I was on the point of rising from my seat and demanding: "Where's your Georgie Feydeau now?" '

Yes, it *was* a very funny play, with a glorious sub-plot, grafted onto the original idea of putting a bunch of newly-born babies together to make up a fivesome, which entailed my character, Hubert, a vicar, taking the church fête funds, packed in a briefcase, by mistake and the Bishop receiving Hubert's personal briefcase instead. Unfortunately this contained a cheese sandwich and a dirty book, which Hubert had confiscated off a choirboy. As you can imagine, this provoked much fear and trembling on Hubert's part, much censorious disapproval from the Bishop and much laughter from the audience. Add to that a doddery old gynaecologist (superbly played by Derek Royle) who muddled up mothers and babies with reckless abandon, a venal tax-inspector staying in the hotel where the play was set, with his dumb blonde girlfriend quite incapable of remembering her nom de guerre, and discovered in her underwear clasping on to Hubert, without his trousers, by the Bishop on one of his ill-timed entrances, and you can perhaps see why Harold Hobson was moved to compare the play with one of those by the great Georges Feydeau. Michael deserved his accolade, for he had re-written the play no less than five times before the director, Wallace Douglas, and I were satisfied. He deserved an award for stamina alone.

Mention of Wallace Douglas reminds me that I have not yet paid tribute to the work of that much-maligned breed – the directors of farce. In the late thirties, up to the early seventies, there were a hand-ful of them who directed West End productions. Wally Douglas, of course, who also directed many of my television presentations, Henry Kendall, Richard Bird, Charles Hickman and 'Jolly' Jack Minster. There were others, too, but those were the names you would gen-erally see on a playbill. Sometimes I popped in with the odd spot of directing, although, unlike Tom Walls, I believed a third party was better out front master-minding operations. Ray Cooney, on the other hand, is of the Tom Walls persuasion, for he not only directs his farces, he writes and presents them as well, and often plays the lead. He didn't do that in my day, though, when he was writing for me.

Whichever way you go about it, the director is a vital cog in the machinery of farce. Actors are, by their very nature, inclined to be over-enthusiastic and a wildly over-the-top performance can stifle laughter just as effectively as an underplayed and inaudible one. Furthermore, the slightest hint of staleness in a long run dampens an audience's enthusiasm and that is why a director needs to pop in and view his (or her) handiwork on a pretty regular basis – and why he (or she) is paid an ongoing percentage from the weekly box office takings, just to keep up his (or her) enthusiasm. Authors, too, need to get on with their directors and respect their judgement, otherwise a slight spot of dichotomy takes place and the actors are distinctly confused. Feydeau always directed his own plays, having written down the most detailed stage directions for the actors first; Ray Cooney, as mentioned above, does the same, whilst Alan Ayckbourn almost invariably follows a similar, singular role of writing and directing. Some authors take their work so seriously they not only include the detailed stage directions but the inflections for the actors as well, so there is no possibility of an incorrect interpretation. Kenneth Horne (not the broadcaster) was one such author. I presented six of his excellent comedies or farces on television (*Love in a Mist*, *Jane Steps Out*, *Sleeping Partnership*, *Wolf's Clothing*, *Trial and Error* and *A Public Mischief*) and the scripts were like trying to follow a railway time-table – all underlines and squiggles and footnotes. But worth it, mind you, for Kenneth was the forerunner of Alan Ayckbourn, without the underlying seriousness, and his small cast plays were tremendously successful.

Michael Pertwee was one who always took notice of his director, and he and Wally Douglas had a very good relationship, which was just as well, for Wally could be very brusque when he tried. He directed both of Michael's next two farces, which kept me busily engaged for the following four years, *Don't Just Lie There, Say Something!* and *A Bit Between the Teeth*. *Don't Just Lie There* was the first of the political farces where the Minister concerned is seen behaving in a way we have come to believe Minister's behave in extra-

Poster for Michael Pertwee's *She's Done It Again!*

marital matters. Ray Cooney has subsequently written two more of a similar nature, *Two into One* and *Out of Order*, whilst Tom Stoppard descended from his Olympian heights to write *Dirty Linen*. All four plays were immediately successful – which is quite understandable, for the public love to see their political masters portrayed with feet of clay. It is often nearer the truth than any eulogy.

I am happy to say that my name appeared on the credits of both of Michael's next two plays written for me, as I was involved in their creation and their construction. In fact, *A Bit Between the Teeth* was loosely based on the adulterous activities of a friend of mine, who recognised the similarity when he came to see the play. Luckily, he was in no position to do anything about it.

My last Whitehall farce, ending on 8 January 1977, was *Fringe Benefits*, by Peter Yeldham and Donald Churchill – with considerable contributions from Ray Cooney. It ran for barely twelve months – my shortest run ever. I took the hint and decided to retire as an actor-manager and let someone else have a go. I had employed myself for no less than thirty years. And that's how I eventually left the theatre altogether and went to MENCAP. It's amazing how resourceful you become if you drop your trousers for a living . . .

So what else was going on in the farcical world outside the Whitehall and Garrick Theatres, or away from the writings of John Chapman, Ray Cooney and Michael Pertwee? Well, two record-breaking productions, for one thing, both presented by a one-time President of the, then, Society of West End Theatre (known as SWET), John Gale OBE. Let him tell his own story:

> In my career I presented over a hundred productions worldwide but I think it would be fair to say that I was best known as a producer of comedy and farce, although this is despite the fact that in my career I only produced about five farces. Two of these were *Boeing-Boeing* and *No Sex Please – We're British!* which both had world-record runs in the West End of London. *Boeing-Boeing* opened in 1962 and ran for over 2,000 performances at the Apollo and Duchess Theatres. The previous record (discounting *Worm's Eye View* because of its broken run) for a comedy or a farce was held by Noël Coward's *Blithe Spirit* which ran for 1,997 performances. *Boeing, Boeing* was directed by Jack Minster and starred (originally) David Tomlinson, Patrick Cargill and Carmel McSharry. I think it would be hard to find more accomplished performers in the art of playing farce. The dexterity and skill they brought to the play under Jack

Poster for Michael Pertwee's *A Bit Between the Teeth*.

Minster's brilliant direction found no equal in anything I have personally seen before or since.

The play was an almost literal translation by Beverley Cross from the French of Marc Camoletti. It had opened in Paris in 1959 and is still running there some thirty-five years and 14,000 performances later. I well remember going to see the play in its original home, the Comédie Caumartin, with Beverley Cross and David Tomlinson and although we found the physical production very poor, the French audiences were obviously delighted by the play.

The plot was very simple: a bachelor living in Paris had three girlfriends who worked for different International Airlines and each in turn spent two days with him. Brilliantly assisted in his time-tabling by his maid, all proceeds smoothly until the arrival of his friend from the country. With seven doors on the stage the fun was fast and furious while the two men tried to prevent the girls from meeting.

As always with a brilliant idea the critics thought it was a one-joke play. They thought the same of *Private Lives* some thirty years earlier! The play was an instant smash hit in London and despite the fact that the theatre owner had promised the theatre to another producer five weeks later, the Apollo did not become available for nearly five years.

Some nine years later, in 1971, I presented *No Sex Please – We're British!* at the Strand Theatre starring Michael Crawford and Evelyn Laye, which was to run a total of nearly seventeen years. It easily broke all longevity records for farce and comedy and became the world's longest running comedy when it passed the 3,213 performances of *Life With Father* on Broadway.

Again, the plot was simplicity itself. A young married couple just back from their honeymoon and living in a flat over the bank, where the husband works, are inundated with different types of pornographic material. Their frantic efforts to hide this material from their mother, boss, bank inspector and policeman are clumsily assisted by a friend from the bank. This young man, with the glorious name of Runnicles, was superbly played by Michael Crawford. It would be difficult to exaggerate his contribution to the play as he combined athleticism and gymnastic ability with the deadpan face of a young Stan Laurel or Buster Keaton. The play was written by Anthony Marriott and Alastair Foot and directed by Allan Davis, in a setting by Hutchison Scott.

Many people, critics included, thought the play's phenomenal success was due to its title; it was not. It was a classic farce in the mould of the Aldwych and Whitehall farces, which, first and foremost, audiences find hilarious but, underpinning the funny basic idea was the first-class construction which is necessary for any play to succeed. Quite simply, I believe the critics – in their ignorance – misjudged the qualities of the play and saw no further than what they regarded as a cheap title. As the years rolled by and the play ran and ran, I was often accused of presenting it solely to entice tourists into the theatre. Even if true (which it wasn't) is that such a heinous crime?

It would be a man of some genius who could read a script and think that in the years to come 'this will be a tourist best-seller'. I produced the play because I thought it was an amusing piece which, if well cast, would have a reasonable chance of success in London. Even when it had been running two years it never crossed my mind that the play would still be running fourteen years later.

Well, it was – and only Ray Cooney's *Run For Your Wife* approached *No Sex* in its West End lifespan. Times have changed, though. In my day, I had to replace the plays every three or four years to stop myself from going mad. John Gale and Ray Cooney simply replaced the casts, and the plays could run and run for as long as there was an audience to see them. They didn't even have to play to full houses every night, for the production costs had long been repaid and the running losses and profits could be amortised over a year, with the troughs of hot or cold weather and West End bombs smoothed out by the peaks of the tourist season. The really hard decision was when finally to call it a day and take the plays off. I believe both John and Ray found that the most difficult task of all.

Now let us turn to some other authors, extant, who have toyed with farce as a genre – or certainly used farcical overtones in their plays, from time to time.

The most obvious example is the greatest living author of English comedy, Alan Ayckbourn. Mind you, he has written farces in his time, apart from comedies – or maybe it was because they were played by farceurs they came over as such. For instance, *How the Other Half Loves* was originally led by Robert Morley, and there is no way he would have played that script as a comedy. Years later, when the play was revived in London at the Duke of York's, with Christopher Benjamin playing the Morley part (and my daughter, Louisa, in the cast as well), it still came over as a farce, for you cannot ask an actor to gallop on for his first entrance in a pair of running shorts concealing a certain amount of avoirdupois without inviting an audience to react accordingly. Farce or comedy, it was a very funny play. Then there was that unforgettable scene in *Absurd*

Person Singular, when the distraught woman is trying to top herself, whilst all around her are preparing for dinner, totally oblivious to her desperate attempts to commit suicide. Black farce, indeed, and both moving and funny in fairly equal proportions. His first-ever play in London, *Relatively Speaking*, with Michael Hordern, Celia Johnson and Richard Briers in the cast, was described thus by critic Milton Shulman: 'The mistaken identity joke has been the backbone of farce from Aristophanes to Brian Rix. But not since Shakespeare's *Comedy of Errors* has any play relied upon this revered gag so heavily as does Alan Ayckbourn's *Relatively Speaking* at the Duke of York's Theatre.

The author was confused:

When I started writing I had no idea what to call my plays – though I suspect they were farces. Or embryo ones. How can anyone of nineteen write a farce? Anyway, when my first play (*Relatively Speaking*) was bought by Peter Bridge for the West End he advised me to call it a Comedy as that sounded 'classier'. Being still green and innocent, I complied. Later on, certain critics with nothing better to do began to doubt whether the plays were Comedies at all but maybe they were Farces. This became very boring so I called my next play 'a Farce' in the vain hope of shutting them up. One of them then wrote a very long piece saying that my play certainly wasn't a Farce it was indeed a Comedy and how dare I?

These days I don't call my plays anything at all. That way I am free to claim, should the audience laugh uproariously, that of course it was a farce. Should they smile pleasantly that it was, obviously, a light comedy all along. And in the event of glum silence that it was a serious social documentary reflecting the times we live in. I think it's known as hedging your bets.

There are two things (I've just remembered) about farce. One: there's no such thing as an 'interesting' one – unlike so-called straight plays. Farce is either good or bad. And the fact is that everyone knows which is which. The good ones you laugh at, the bad ones you leave. And two: because its job is to persuade people not just to suspend their disbelief but often their entire logical centre, farce requires the most consummate of artists – writers, actors, directors – everyone – technicians, designers, stage-managers. Yet because the aim of farce is merely (merely!) to create laughter it is the most misunderstood and often the most underrated form of theatre there is. Often overlooked by scholars and the so-called theatrical establishment – if not the public, thank God. But then, Brian, you don't need me to tell you all that.

We tend, as a nation, to take our comic artists seriously only long after they're dead and preferably long after their jokes are no longer relevant or funny. Mind you, in our trade, who the hell wants to be taken seriously? You finish up in that graveyard of all creative talent, the English Set Book.

I believe that is the most charming and self-effacing self-analysis I have ever read. And look at some of the plays he has written, apart from the three mentioned above. I will make no attempt to list them all, for I would be out-of-date before this chapter was finished. Alan Ayckbourn's output and high standard is astonishing: *Absent Friends*, *Bedroom Farce*, *Chorus of Disapproval*, *Confusions*, *Intimate Exchanges*, *Joking Apart*, *Just Between Ourselves*, *Man of the Moment*, *Season's Greetings*, *Sisterly Feelings*, *Small Family Business* (with one of the funniest opening scenes I can remember), *Taking Steps*, *Time and Time Again*, *Time of my Life*, *Ten Times Table*, *Way Upstream* (I had to wait nearly an hour for the curtain to go up on this one at the National. The boat had stuck!), *Wildest Dreams*, *Woman in Mind* and on and on – not forgetting that amazing trilogy, *The Norman Conquests*. Q.E.D., I think you will agree.

We now come to an author who is perhaps best known for one farce above all his other writings, which have been numerous, in the mixed world of literature, the theatre and the newspapers. I am referring to *Noises Off* and the playwright is Michael Frayn. Yet he has been responsible for some splendid comedies in the theatre, including *Alphabetical Order*, *Clouds* and *Donkey's Years*, with more dramatic works such as *Benefactors* and *Make and Break*, plus a whole host of translations of the plays and stories of Anton Chekhov. *The Cherry Orchard*, *The Seagull*, *Three Sisters* and *Wild Honey* have all been adapted by Michael Frayn, whilst his translation and adaptation of four Chekhovian 'vaudevilles' (shades of Feydeau) and four short stories, under the generic title *The Sneeze*, were presented at the Aldwych Theatre in 1988 with Rowan Atkinson, Cheryl Kennedy and Timothy West in the cast. Room for a few farcical moments there, I would imagine.

In his introduction to *The Sneeze* (published by Methuen and, for the theatre, by Samuel French), Michael wrote the following:

The Bear and *The Proposal* are classics of the comic theatre, full of

179

energy, invention, and actors' opportunities. They are larger than life, certainly, but splendid in their magnification. Chekhov's designation for them both, 'joke', is usually translated into English as 'farce'. The term is of course as capacious as 'Chekhovian', but there is a considerable difference between these plays and most French or English farces. As we know, the form usually depends upon panic, and the panic is usually generated by guilt and the prospect of some kind of social disgrace. The panic leads in its turn to deceit, which produces further and yet more alarming prospects of disgrace, from which grows ever greater panic, in a spiral known to scientists as positive feedback. There is no panic in *The Bear* or *The Proposal*, no deceit or threatened disgrace. What drives these characters is a sense of outrage – of anger at the failure of others to recognise their claims, whether to money or to land or to a certain status. In their anger, it is true, they lose the ability to control their destinies or even to recognise their own best interests, just as the characters of traditional farce do in their panic. This is what these plays have in common with English and French farces – that their characters are reduced by their passions to the level of blind and inflexible machines; though this reduction is precisely what Bergson thought (implausibly, to my mind) was the common factor in all comedy.*

In his letter to me, Michael Frayn writes: 'One of the funny things about farce is that it seems to defy definition . . . farce is wonderful when it works and dreadful when it doesn't, and that it's incredibly hard to do. Hard to set up, and harder still to sustain.'

Well, Michael certainly set up *Noises Off* with great aplomb and, what is more, sustained it to the end. It won numerous awards after it opened in 1982 and is still mentioned with bated breath by many a play-goer. Indeed, Peter Kemp, writing in the *Times Literary Supplement*, described this tale about a tatty touring company producing a piece called 'Nothing On' as 'a farce about a farce taking the clichés of the genre, and shaking them inventively through a series of kaleidoscope patterns . . . a farce that makes you think as well as laugh.'

It certainly made me think when I saw it – think on the fact that I was rather glad that I had given up so much frenetic activity five years before. To think I had rushed around like that for more than

---

*Henri Bergson, the French philosopher, was actually naturalised. He was born in Paris of Irish-Jewish parents. They should have known about comedy, even if Henri apparently didn't.

half my life in search of laughs and a living. Phew! It doesn't bear thinking about . . .

There may seem little point in dwelling for too long on the works of our next playwright, for he only wrote three plays of note, he has been dead for over twenty-five years and Harold Hobson dismissed him as an agent of the Devil. Yes, you've guessed it – Joe Orton. Furthermore, Harold went on: 'Gradually, Orton's terrible obsession with perversion, which is regarded as having brought life to an end and choked his very high talent, poisons the atmosphere of the play [*What the Butler Saw*]. And what should have been a piece of gaily irresponsible nonsense becomes impregnated with evil.'

In that pretty condemnatory piece in the *Christian Science Monitor* Hobson was merely expressing the widely held opinion of Orton's work at the time. Very few critics stepped forward to defend his last play, *What the Butler Saw*, but then, who can blame them? Orton had already been dead for nearly two years, killed by his lover, Kenneth Halliwell, so wasn't around during rehearsals, as any author of a farce should be, to point out the obvious mistakes in casting, performance, direction or the script. In this case, casting (or, rather, miscasting) was the main cause of a major theatrical disaster, for Sir Ralph Richardson played the lead (supported by Coral Browne and Stanley Baxter), and did not appear to understand the text or the form of the play, and was heartily booed for his pains on the First Night, 5 March 1969, at the Queen's Theatre.* Furthermore, he was advised by a member of the gallery to give back his knighthood. Fortunately, he didn't have to suffer that indignity, as the play only lasted for 101 performances, and he was soon able to return to more suitable roles. Mind you, it was a close run thing, such was Orton's unpopularity with certain members of the theatre-going public – even stretching back to his first play, *Entertaining Mr Sloane* which opened at Wyndhams Theatre in 1964, followed by *Loot* at the Criterion Theatre two years later.

In *Entertaining Mr Sloane*, Mr Sloane is a young man looking for a room in a slum boarding-house. He finds one, complete with amorous landlady who seduces him (shades of many a theatrical touring story), followed by her brother, who also seduces Mr Sloane. Dad now enters the scene, accuses Mr Sloane of a neighbourhood murder and is kicked to death for his pains. Sister and brother are now completely happy

---

*Richard Wilson of television's renowned *One Foot in the Grave* (a series of mini-farces on a par with *Fawlty Towers*), was cheered for his performance at the Royal National Theatre in the 1995 revival.

for they can enjoy Mr Sloane's favours, each for six months of the year.†

On the night of Mrs McLeavy's death in *Loot*, her son, Hal, and his friend, Dennis, have just robbed a bank, which is next-door to the undertakers where Dennis works and where Mrs McLeavy lies waiting to be embalmed. The two young criminals first hide the money in the house, but when the police get suspicious, pop it into Mrs McLeavy's coffin and shove the body into a cupboard. Meanwhile the late Mrs McLeavy's nurse is trying to marry the widower, Mr McLeavy ('the leading Catholic layman within a radius of forty miles') for his money, but finds out what the lads are up to, demanding her share of the loot. Inspector Truscott, disguised as a Water Board official arrives to question the suspects and becomes involved in some dubious corruption. The coffin is burned, but not destroyed, at the crematorium, the nurse is accused of poisoning Mrs McLeavy – which she did – but all ends happily for the miscreants, with Mr McLeavy arrested for the robbery and Inspector Truscott sharing in the proceeds, along with the actual robbers and the poisonous nurse.

Finally, *What the Butler Saw*. Dr Prentice is a psychiatrist who has worked out that the best way to interview a girl for a job is to seduce her. Mrs Prentice has similar theories and brings home a page boy from a hotel to continue with her seduction. A 'state inspector' calls and the rest of the play is mayhem, as disguises, discoveries and disappearances abound.

All three plots sound pretty banal, I must admit, recounted like that. But some splendid dialogue, inventive business and an anarchical approach ensured that all three were very funny plays, if you were prepared to give them a chance. In their early days, many didn't. Now, well, to quote Alan Ayckbourn out of context, they have almost reached the dread status of the English Set Book.

---

†Incidentally, *Entertaining Mr Sloane* was succeeded in September 1964 (three months after its opening at Wyndhams) by a production of mine, in conjunction with Donald Albery, called *Diplomatic Baggage*. Originally written by John Chapman as *Between the Balance Sheets* for a *Dial Rix* television, it had now been lengthened, with author John Chapman playing my original role, my wife Elspet continuing where she had left off and Charles Heslop introduced into the cast, playing the part created by Leo Franklyn. Both old actors were marvellous, the one on television, the other on stage. I hasten to add that John and Elspet were pretty good, too, with Derek Royle giving one of his funniest 'falling-down' performances, almost all in dumb-show, as a French waiter with a recalcitrant trolley. It was physical clowning of the highest order.

Of course, the first two had to twist and turn to avoid the depredations of the Lord Chamberlain, whereas *What the Butler Saw* was unshackled and ran smack into the puritanical streak endemic in the British – particularly many of those who venture into the theatre or those who react at third-hand and 'tut-tut' at all the prurient details over which they can salivate when reading the average tabloid press. Old ladies tore up their programmes, jumped up and down and then marched out screaming abuse as they left. Old, and not-so-old, gentlemen did the same, bellowing 'Rubbish', 'Filth' and 'Take it off' as they struggled towards the exits. It was reported that even the House Manager had to leave town when the play 'enjoyed' its pre-London week at the Theatre Royal, Brighton. Mr Orton was not a popular playwright.

Extraordinary, really, for he was only exploring in a slightly different way the panic stations which face all characters in good farce. Furthermore, he went back to the olden days of Greek and Roman comedy, with his phalli, his dead bodies, his incest, but few seemed to recognise that fact. Orton himself said that 'a lot of farces today are still based on the preconceptions of a century ago, particularly the preconceptions about sex . . . originally farce was very close to tragedy and differed only in the treatment of its themes.' He concluded with the factual statement that 'the Greeks were prepared to treat any subject farcically.'

Now, of course, Orton is seen as a symbol of theatrical freedom and perception, a writer of beautifully-crafted dialogue and situation who is greatly missed. His plays are still regularly staged – *What the Butler Saw*, starring Richard Wilson, John Alderton and Nicola Pagett, was revived by the Royal National Theatre in March 1995, to glowing notices. What would have happened to his work, had he lived, or how might his continuing influence have moulded the writing talents of burgeoning playwrights? We shall never know – but we do know that other 'serious' playwrights have become interested in the world of farce because of his influence and that his free-ranging, anarchic style has many imitators, though few have yet dared to go so far in their pursuit of irony and laughter.

Which seems as good a time as any to mention one or two 'new' authors who are floating around today before dealing with the rest of the Establishment. Patrick Prior is one of the emerging farceurs, with three satirical farces under his belt, all produced at Stratford

East. They are *Blackboard Bungle* (obviously about schools and clearly highlighting all the problems inherent in our education system today), then there is another punning title, in the best tradition of farce, *Revolting Peasants*, about the poll tax and, finally, a very obvious target, the National Health Service, and a pretty obvious title, too, *Cut and Trust*. So let's see what he has to say about us oldies. If he repeats anything I, or my contemporaries, have written already, then it proves we're good tutors, doesn't it? With or without the English Set Book.

In the beginning Farce was a seditious form. The works of Aristophanes, Plautus etc. developed from the Greek knockabout Satyr plays, allowing the writers, through low comedy, to satirise the state of things. *Lysistrata* may be a comedy of erections and sexual frustration, but at its heart it sends up a macho ruling ethos. The form then developed, taking on other influences, the broad humour of the mediaeval religious drama, elements of the *commedia dell'arte*. Playwrights like Molière and the Restoration writers adapted and used the form to produce comic, populist farces. But always there was at the heart of these works the acid tongue of sedition. This was because the form is in itself inately anarchic.

But I'd like to suggest that the British farce lost its satiric function sometime in the nineteenth century. This was in part due to the Boulevardier farceurs like Feydeau, who replaced satire with bedroom farce. Infidelity became the primum mobile. In Britain, Arthur Wing Pinero became associated with what we would today recognise as the present form of mainstream farce. By the time we get to the Ben Travers Aldwych farces and later the Whitehall farces the metamorphosis is complete. Mainstream British farce is essentially comic-whimsy/bedroom farce, with little or no political dimension.

The obvious strength of British farce is in the technical perfection the form achieves. The actors are masters of the raised eyebrows, the bewildered look, the timing which takes the perfect beat to get the laugh . . . the synchronised glances of panic. Writers like Ray Cooney and Michael Pertwee are superb technicians, plots click with wondrous precision. As one who has written farces I can appreciate the sheer symmetrical beauty of the exercise.

But it took an Italian writer, Dario Fo, to show the British that farce was worth more than a canter across the stage and dropped trousers. In the 1970s *Accidental Death of an Anarchist* and later *Can't Pay?, Won't Pay* had 'em rolling in the aisles in the West End. Only Fo was saying serious things, hilariously. This was farce with a genuine edge, farce that owed its roots to Aristophanes, not Feydeau.

Of course, there's no rule that says writers have to have anything to say, or that farce is for anything but a laugh. But the problem, I would suggest, is that British mainstream farce has become an empty exercise in stage gymnastics. It reminds me of those beautiful town hall clocks seen in Germany and Switzerland. The hour strikes and the little figures trundle out in a perfect clockwork ballet. Gongs are struck, cows are milked, the little man and woman bow to each other. Charming. But in another hour they'll be back doing the same things, with the same beautiful precision. I don't suggest that farce should be a polemical form, or a piece of agitprop, but surely such a dynamic form should be utilised to provoke thought as well as make people laugh.

Farce, and elements of farce, will continue to be used by playwrights. But at the moment British mainstream farce's *raison d'être* is the form. The form serves the form not the content. The plays are not *about any-thing*. Certainly the iron law of 'bums on seats' will be used to illustrate that if it ain't broke, don't fix it. All I'd like to suggest is that farce has a noble lineage and perhaps deserves more respect than we give it. Clockwork ballets can get tedious after a while.

Well, I think Patrick Prior's got a point. Several points, in fact. I must admit to being a tinge bored with bedroom farce myself – especially with rather elderly actors and actresses holding in their tummies as they try to recreate love's young dream. The trouble is, I think I would become rather bored with a diet of political farce, too, as I would with omnipotent Orton or constant Cooney. I mean, look how quickly *Spitting Image* deteriorated after its initial impact on television. Even Hogarth or Rowlandson might have lost their appeal if their work had been trotted out week after week in front of more than half the population. Variety is all – provided plays, performances and productions are first-class and, as far as possible, original. But, as I say, Mr Prior has a point . . .

As does Sandi Toksvig, well known to the tele-viewing public as one of the original stars – and talents – of *Whose Line Is It Anyway?*, but less well known to the theatre-going public as a budding author of farce. Not so budding, either, for she has already had one West End production, *The Pocket Dream*, which began life at the Nottingham Playhouse and came into the Albery Theatre in 1992, where it enjoyed a modest run. My daughter Louisa played a second-rate, over-acting and over-sexed leading lady in a tatty touring production of *A Midsummer Night's Dream* which has to be extemporised (shades of *Whose Line Is It Anyway?*), for the majority of the cast have walked out on Louisa's overbearing character and are in the pub next-door. The stage-manager (Sandi Toksvig herself) and the theatre manager (Mike McShane) are called in to play a variety of roles, as are others, and a very disorganised performance takes place. Actually, it was all great fun, and brought many young people into the theatre, especially at the Nottingham Playhouse, who then proceeded to enjoy Sandi's short-cut version of Shakespeare. I must confess that I enjoyed it, too, although there were a number of holes in the production, but that's only to be expected in a tyro's first farce. The fact that a new farceur had appeared – and was being produced – could only to be welcomed. A second farce, *Big Night Out at the Little Sands Picture Palace*, began, and ended, at the Nottingham Playhouse. But let Sandi tell the story herself:

> If you ask an audience for a 'style of theatre' during an evening of improvisation, almost inevitably someone will shout 'farce'. The improviser, whether involved in a scene in future space, a submarine or a greengrocers, is then guaranteed a laugh if someone on stage drops their trousers and shouts 'Oh, oh the vicar's coming'. Any mad running about on stage and miming opening and closing doors will usually build on the laugh. There are those who would claim that farce is an old-fashioned comic medium yet parts of its make-up are so ingrained in British culture that even the trendiest audience can recognise it instantly. More importantly, they also appreciate it instantly. However, if you asked the bright young things whether they would ever go and see a traditional farce they would probably frown behind their dark glasses and plug in a personal stereo.
>
> Farce just isn't fashionable any more and I think it's a great shame because all comic writers have a great deal to learn from it, even if they don't want to write full-blown Whitehall, drop-your-pants-and-run examples of it. The first farce I ever saw was *A Flea in Her Ear* at the Yvonne Arnaud Theatre while I was still at school. That has a lot of door banging in it and I remember being mainly focused on the shakiness of the set which meant that naughty husbands were more likely to be found out by a wall collapsing than by their wives appearing in a doorway at an inopportune moment. It wasn't the best introduction. It was Michael Frayn's *Noises Off* which provided a great light above my fledgling comedy-writing brain. In his play we see both the on-stage action and backstage. It is the juxtaposition of the two which makes the play so funny.
>
> It seemed to me that the great writers of farce hold this 'bigger picture' of the action in their minds the whole time. Even if we can only see a portion of what is going on (because of the limits of the stage), each time someone runs out of sight, the audience has to imagine where

186

they are going and what effect this will have on the situation. Because farce is done at high speed this is a great effort for the writer. I wrote a play for the Nottingham Playhouse called *Big Night Out at the Little Sands Picture Palace*. The second half involved the concealment of a dead body from his brother, a missionary. In order to bring up the speed of the action, the body was placed on a tea trolley and spent much of the act whizzing backwards and forwards just being missed by the religious brother. I found it incredibly difficult during the writing process to recall exactly where everyone was and what they knew from the last scene in order to build the action and 'get the laughs'. I could have done with some advice from the great exponents of the Whitehall farce.

But why a vicar? What is the British obsession with this character? I thought I chose a religious man to contrast with his unpleasant, boorish brother in the first half (the parts were played by the same actor) but in fact I was tapping into a British comic stereotype. The vicar represents instant respectability and suppressed sexuality. We all want to know what lies behind the dog collar and the pious statements. It was somehow funnier to have a vicar spouting about his missionary work while an usherette whizzed past on a tea trolley with a dead body.

Writing farce or even a play with farcical elements is fantastically difficult and I take my hat off to anyone who can come up with one of the 'oops, there goes my wife's trousers' type which are so often decried by modern critics. There are so many elements which the writer and then the director and the actors have to put together to get a perfectly timed piece. It only takes one hiccup in the build-up and the entire effort is lost. In rehearsal for *Big Night Out* Anita Dobson and I spent a whole day working with director Pip Broughton on a single thirty second sequence.

In the end my play did not quite function (despite the fantastic work of director, designer and cast) because it is an art form to which I am a complete newcomer. I shall certainly try again. I often hear modern comics relegate farce to the vaults of theatrical history and critics denigrate it as 'unworthy'. My advice to them would be twofold – either try and write one yourself or go and see a classic farce. Maybe then their lofty attitude would be tempered by experience. It's a great sound hearing people laughing.

It is indeed.

Other, 'serious', playwrights have thought this, too. Indeed during the last twenty-or-so years, farce had become a staple ingredient in many a play – if only on display for a short time. For instance, I recently went to see a Royal National Theatre production of Harold Pinter's first play, *The Birthday Party*. In the opening, disastrous, production of this seminal work at the Lyric, Hammersmith in 1958, the part of the seaside landlady, Meg, was played by Beatrix Lehmann, but in the National production, nearly forty years later, Meg was portrayed by Dora Bryan. I never saw Miss Lehmann, but imagine she was splendid, offering a sinister undercurrent to the play which must have been in keeping with the unspecified menace of the piece. Dora, on the other hand, was gloriously funny (and moving) – winning a Lawrence Olivier award for her performance – in a manner and a setting which would have done credit to one of Leslie Sands' three seaside farces, *Beside the Seaside*, *Basinful of the Briny* and *Good Old Summertime*, when the tyrannical landlady, Mrs Austin, terrorises her lodgers with her bread and butter pudding. I presented all three plays on television, with Mrs Austin played, successively (and successfully), by Thora Hird, Marjorie Rhodes and Joan Sanderson. Dora could easily have joined the throng – and yet her performance was quite in keeping with Pinter's play and served to illumine the author's professional theatrical background: digs, tatty weekly rep., box sets and an endless diet of farces, thrillers and light comedies. *The Birthday Party* could have turned into any of Leslie Sands' plays, Walter Greenwood's or R F Delderfield's – but it didn't. It turned into quintessential Pinter, but used totally recognisable stock characters and a setting which became all the more menacing due to its very ordinariness. Remarkable, really.

Pinter continued his flirting with the theatre of his past in a number of his plays: *The Caretaker*, with its music-hall monologues and cross-talk acts which then went on in *The Homecoming*, but much greater erudition has been expended on these works than I could possibly bring to bear, so I will merely pass on to other writers who are credited with farcical flirtations from time to time: Edward Bond in *Early Morning*, *Narrow Road to the Deep North* and *Lear*, whilst Caryl Churchill in *Cloud Nine* is described by C W Thomsen in a pamphlet 'Three Socialist Playwrights' as 'using techniques which may seem experimental but are in fact firmly rooted in the tradition of farce.' Certainly I found nothing farcical about a subsequent play, *Serious Money* – but I must report that many of the audience fell about with laughter, whilst many of the audience left in the interval.

Tom Stoppard has more than flirted with farce, partially in

Travesties, with its Wildean pastiche of *The Importance of Being Earnest*, definitely in *On the Razzle*, to which I have already referred, and *Dirty Linen*, with the activities of the parliamentary committee's secretary, Maddie Gotobed, described thus: 'We face the possibility that a sexual swathe has passed through Westminster claiming the reputations of, to put no finer point upon it, one hundred and nineteen Members. Someone is going through the ranks like a lawn-mower in knickers.' I wish I'd had the opportunity to speak such lines from time to time. I suppose I did, really. I just didn't notice at the time. I was too busy running away from the lawn-mower. . .

Finally, Peter Shaffer with *Black Comedy*. I think most people quote this play as his one great farce but, in fact, it was really an elongated afterpiece, with Strindberg's *Miss Julie* as a curtain-raiser – the whole being conceived and produced for the, then, National Theatre Company's 1965 summer season at Chichester. Shaffer had seen two men fight a duel in the dark (with all the stage lights on, of course) in Peking and this inspired him to believe that the same ruse could be used in a modern setting, given a power-cut or the main fuse blowing. Laurence Olivier, directing at Chichester, accepted the idea, with the enthusastic prompting of Ken Tynan (by then, the National's literary manager) and John Dexter (the director). Peter Shaffer whisked through a first draft and then left for New York and the writing of a film script. His initial work was not appreciated and he had to have a second bash at the script – with the Chichester double-bill already sold out. Shaffer complained that he was having nightmares about an audience in front for his latest work, being faced by an empty stage. Actually, this is but an extension of the actor's nightmare – being onstage, and not knowing a word of the play you have to perform. I've suffered it many a time. Just like the bad dreams of being back at school or in the services.

Luckily for Shaffer, his second attempt was accepted and rehearsals began, with re-writes going on to the bitter end. Nothing new for old farce hands like Ben Travers, Michael Pertwee, Ray Cooney, John Chapman or me, but a totally strange world to the great and the good in this profession. As Olivier remarked: 'This is farce written under farce conditions.' Tom Walls would have fallen about with ribald laughter. He didn't even rehearse the last act until the final days of rehearsal, never mind stirring his stumps to begin rehearsing himself. Peter Shaffer would have been locked in the lavatory and told to get on with it . . .

Eventually, on 27 July 1965 the play opened at Chichester to an enthusiastic press. Indeed, on his second visit to the play Milton Shulman in the *Evening Standard* commented: '*Black Comedy* by Peter Shaffer at the National Theatre [it had moved there from Chichester] is basically a single-joke revue sketch which has been stretched by devilish invention and a glorious cast into an hilarious one-act play . . . Derek Jacobi as the frantic young sculptor trying to impress his girlfriend's military-type father, hide a former fiancée and prevent his homosexual neighbour from knowing that he has borrowed his precious furniture for a night, gives a beautifully-timed comic performance. Albert Finney, hand on hip and licking his forelock into place, gets some explosive laughs as the queer neighbour . . .'

Interesting! Today's 'politically correct' author wouldn't dream of writing about a 'queer neighbour' in a farce and would certainly be verbally mugged for his pains if he did. Mind you, Ray Cooney got away with 'gay' jokes right up to the end of the West End presentation of *Run For Your Wife* and nobody seemed to mind. I do think things are different nowadays, but I may be wrong. Certainly, in 1965, Joe Orton – not exactly unknown for his homosexuality – commented: 'I think that the portrait of the queer in Peter Shaffer's *Black Comedy* is very funny, but it's an awfully conventional portrait . . . audiences love it of course . . . but one shouldn't pander to audiences.'

That's pretty mild criticism, by any standard, as I'm sure you will agree.

EPILOGUE

Laughter is not at all a bad beginning for a friendship,
and it is far the best ending for one.

Oscar Wilde, *The Picture of Dorian Gray*

I BEGAN THIS BOOK with a Prologue which hazarded a guess that my work would be more anecdotal than academic, and I hope you have found it thus and that we are still friends. But I would certainly lose a number of mates if I omitted some of your favourite farces or farceurs, and I will now hasten to fill the gap. Not over the centuries, of course, for that would be a fruitless exercise, merely listing thousands of farce titles just to cover my back. Better that I concentrate on a few famous farces over the last fifty years or so, which any keen theatre-goer will notice have not been mentioned in the text. It will also give me the opportunity to pop in the odd actor or two, also missing by default.

Dame Margaret Rutherford, for example. Dame Margaret was built for farce. A wonderful St Bernard face, with jowls shaking with righteous indignation and a plummy voice which was in total keeping with her other physical attributes, she, like Alistair Sim, Robert Morley or Robertson Hare, had only to walk onto a stage for an audience to start bubbling with gleeful, anticipated laughter to come. Madame Arcati in Noël Coward's *Blithe Spirit* (with that other great comic actor, Cecil Parker, as Charles Condomine), Miss Prism in *The Importance of Being Earnest* and Miss Evelyn Whitchurch in John Dighton's one-off successful farce *The Happiest Days of Your Life*, all delighted theatre-goers year in and year out. Add to that her numerous film performances and you can see why film-goers, too, were just as entertained over the years. Incidentally, Dame Margaret

191

also appeared with Joyce Grenfell on a number of occasions – another fine comic lady – whilst John Dighton did write a second farce, *Man Alive*, which saw its title in the lights of the West End, but which was soon extinguished and never emulated *Happiest Days* as a smash-hit.

Alan Bennett ventured into another country with his farce, *Habeas Corpus* – a penetrating prod (if you will forgive the expression) at the sexual excesses of the permissive society of the sixties and early seventies. Possibly a little old-fashioned today (if sex can ever be considered thus), but a very funny play, nevertheless. Michael Billington in the *Guardian* compared it to the works of Joe Orton and described it as 'a gorgeously vulgar but densely plotted farce that is a downright celebration of sex and the human body. The effect is rather like seeing an animated McGill postcard in which the captions have been written by an elegant verbal stylist.' Perhaps rather surprisingly, the lead of the sex-mad doctor was played by Alec Guinness, although those who only think of him in *Star Wars* or as George Smiley in the John le Carré thrillers should remember his very funny performances as Boniface in *Hotel Paradiso* at the Winter Garden Theatre in 1956 or in the earlier Ealing film comedies.

J B Priestley created an archetypal North Country farce with *When We Are Married*, and superb North Country monsters with the Helliwells, the Parkers and the Soppitts. The drunken photographer, Henry Ormonroyd, sent to photograph the three ghastly couples on their silver wedding anniversary, is a comic gift of a part which any character actor would give his eye teeth to play. Many other plays have followed in the footsteps of *When We Are Married* but I do not think any are as flawless. I last saw a Theatre of Comedy production at my old stamping ground, the Whitehall Theatre, with Timothy West, Prunella Scales, Elizabeth Spriggs, Brian Murphy, Patricia Routledge, James Grout, and Bill Fraser as Ormonroyd. Absolutely fabulous. Superb actors – comic or straight – to a man or a woman.

I'm not sure if Terence Frisby would care to be mentioned here, for *There's a Girl in My Soup* had a highly successful West End run but is classed as a comedy. Nevertheless, its storyline – a food and wine newspaper columnist falling for a rather common, down-to-earth young thing who finally leaves him for a pop musician – has definite farcical ingredients. Farce or comedy, Terence Frisby is still waiting to emulate his first play's huge success.

Then there is Derek Benfield. Derek who? All right, all right, I'll explain. Derek – who was once an actor with me when I first began

Peter Glenville's translation of *Hotel Paradiso* by George Feydeau and Maurice Desvallières.

as an actor-manager – has probably written more farces than either Ray Cooney or John Chapman but, as far as I know, not one has ever played in the West End. Derek writes, perhaps intentionally, for a very lucrative market indeed – the old rep. stand-by and the inveterate amateur favourite. At least fourteen of his plays have been published by Samuel French, and I wouldn't be surprised if they have been reprinted more than any other. And yet, as I say, you may well have never heard of him. Remember though, there are thousands of amateur groups up and down the country and around the world, too. Often complicated settings and incomprehensible BUS put them off better-known farces. Derek Benfield's plays fill the gap perfectly. Simple plots, simple settings, simple royalties and the local parish hall is filled to expectant capacity. Let me explain a little more . . .

Many will instantly recognise the name of playwright Richard Harris with his two most famous plays, *Outside Edge* and *Stepping Out*. Indeed, the former has been turned into a very successful television series and the latter into a Hollywood film. However, those are comedies but he has written two farces with Leslie Darbon, rejoicing in the rather obvious titles of *Two and Two Make Sex* and *Who Goes Bare*. I fear the plays are as obvious as the titles – but somewhere in the world they will almost certainly be being performed this week.

As will Robin Hawdon's *The Mating Game*, which has been the staple diet of many a summer season and many an amateur production for more years than I care to remember. Titles like that titillate, even though the scantily-clad ladies rushing round the stage are probably pillars of the local church, the Women's Institute and the Townswomen's Guild. Lest this rather simple explanation of a play's success should prove an incentive to any putative farceur – be warned. A title alone does *not* guarantee success. Nor does a famous name for a playwright. But it helps.

For instance, the highly-respected Irish playwright, Hugh Leonard, has written one farce, *Patrick Pearce Motel*, which was a great success in Ireland but fell on its face when presented in the West End at the Queen's Theatre. I'm not quite sure why, for it was an expertly crafted piece, in the tradition of true French farce. Just one more example of the difficulties of picking winners; that's why critics often appear so smug. Being wise after the event is hardly a creative exercise.

How about Ray Dyer? Now you've heard of *him* – but probably under his posh play's first name, *Charles* Dyer. But it was *Ray* when I presented his splendidly old-fashioned, but very funny, farcical thriller on television back in the early sixties. Indeed, he has always had fond memories of *Wanted, One Body*, even calling his house 'Old Wob' as the royalties rolled in. But then, as I say, he became posh, changed his name to Charles and wrote *Rattle of a Simple Man*, *Staircase*, *Lovers Dancing* and others. His one contribution to the world of farce is worth a quick glance, though, even now.

I must mention Mike Harding for the title of his North Country farce alone: *Fur Coat and No Knickers* – which *is* an expression in fairly common use, describing, as I'm sure you know, a female who is all show and no substance. In this play, most of the characters seem to spend their time either blind drunk before the wedding of Deirdre and Mark, or equally paralytic after it. Add to that a Grandad pulling on a vast pair of hired Moss Bros trousers and commenting that they have 'more bloody ballroom than Blackpool Tower' plus a pissed parson in his underwear, clutching a nubile blow-up doll, and you get some idea of the play's content – and final curtain. As far as I know, the play has never come further south than Oldham. More's the pity.

Mike Harding also wrote another piece which owed much to *Lysistrata*: *Not With a Bang* is its title and pokes fun at male members [sic] of the Territorial Army, whose wives eventually withhold their sexual favours to persuade their partners to ban the bomb. Aristophanes might not have recognised the North Country accents or the question of nuclear disarmament, but he would certainly have recognised the plot.

Hull Truck (the company which began life, as you might expect, in my home town, Hull) have presented numerous works by John Godber, who has had one or two nifty comedies on display which stray from time to time into the realms of farce – *On the Piste* and *Bouncers* being prime examples. Often very funny, very cruel, very earthy and very modern. Terry Johnson, on the other hand, is just as funny, cruel, earthy and modern – but his works, too, especially *Hysteria* and *Dead Funny*, are only garnished with farce. The serious side of the writing is there for all to see (especially in *Dead Funny*) when the sadness and the loneliness of the characters are so movingly, and yet so amusingly, illustrated by a writer who is in danger of being compared to Alan Ayckbourn. Another playwright who falls into this category is Tim Firth, whose *Neville's Island* at the Apollo Theatre began as hilarious farce and ended on a more profound note of human degeneration, when faced with adversity.

I must also mention Dave Freeman, for I was once part of the management presenting his only solus farce, *A Bedfull of Foreigners*, at the Duke of York's Theatre in the late seventies. His other farce, *Key For Two* was written with John Chapman. *Bedfull*, though, starred Terry Scott and June Whitfield and got many a belly-laugh. Set during a Festival in a French village near the German border, it has a naked girl lowered out of a window, attached by a rope to a radiator which is pulled up to the ceiling by her weight, characters dressed as nuns and monks rushing in and out and seductions by the score. June gave her usual, impeccable, cool performance, whilst Terry was at his frenetic best. His first farcical experience, incidentally, was with me at the Whitehall in *One For The Pot*. He was very funny, as he was in quite a number of the television productions we were presenting at the time. But the BBC called, off he went into *Hugh and I*, with Hugh Lloyd (another funny man) and written by John Chapman. He never looked back – until his last illness and untimely death in 1994.

Someone else who has never looked back since he took over from Terry in *A Bedfull of Foreigners* is David Jason. At that time his career was just beginning to burgeon, but he was not then popular enough to sustain the run. My goodness, things would be different today. It's 'get hold of David Jason and we'll think of a play later'. He is what is known as bankable.

In the olden days, many a play ended with a rhyming couplet or the title of the play spoken as dialogue, and almost certainly an Epilogue – followed, at the curtain call, by a tableau. Indeed, Ben Travers used that device in the Aldwych farces, being plural in his devising of tableaux, which followed on each Act, as well as the final curtain, continuing the story and enhancing the laughter and applause. We used a similar device in many a Whitehall farce; not so much a tableau, but a piece of business to stoke up the audience reaction at the end. For instance, in *Chase Me, Comrade!* there was I at the final curtain, still prancing around in my tights and tutu. The curtain rose for the first curtain call with me apparently being held aloft by the assembled cast in a plural lift. On a whispered 'go', they stepped back into their places, leaving me teetering unsteadily on the top of a rickety pair of steps. And that is farce . . .

I promised this would be no polemic. Of course, I have broken my promise on numerous occasions, for many an opinion has been ventured. Craving your indulgence, here's one more. If you are teetering unsteadily on the top of a pair of rickety steps and fall and break your neck – that's tragedy; leap athletically into space and perform a perfect pirouette – that's comedy; land on your backside, with your tights around your ankles – that's farce. But the drama, whatever its form, starts from the same premise. Its outcome merely depends on its development.

When François Rabelais died in 1553 his last words were 'bring down the curtain, the farce is played out.' In *A Day at the Races* in 1937 Groucho Marx said 'either he's dead or my watch has stopped.' Even though nearly four hundred years separate the feed from the gag, I think you can see why the great Russian actor and producer, Meyerhold, was right when he said 'the farce is eternal'. Proverbs, Chapter 17, verse 22 is even more specific: 'A merry heart doeth good like medicine.'

Just what the doctor ordered – life in the farce lane.

CURTAIN

BIBLIOGRAPHY

Bentley, Eric, *The Life of the Drama*, Methuen 1965.

Collection of the Most Esteemed Farces and Entertainments Performed on the British Stage, Volumes 1 and 2, Edinburgh 1782.

Davis, Jim, *John Liston, Comedian*, CUP 1985.

Encyclopaedia Britannica, Volume 7, London 1962.

Feydeau, Georges, (trans. Peter Meyer), *Three Farces*, BBC 1974.

Fitzgerald, Percy, *The Life of Mrs Catherine Clive*, A Reader 1888.

Frayn, Michael, *The Sneeze*, Methuen 1989.

Fyfe, Hamilton, *Arthur Wing Pinero*, Greening 1902.

    Sir Arthur Pinero's Plays and Players, E Benn 1930, reprinted Greenwood Press 1978.

Goodman, Walter, *The Keeleys*, R Bentley 1895.

Gore-Browne, Robert, *Gay Was the Pit*, Reinhardt 1957.

Hartnoll, Phyllis (ed.), *The Oxford Companion to the Theatre*, OUP 1957.

Hughes, Leo, *A Century of English Farce*, Princeton University Press 1956.

Mander & Mitchenson, *The Theatres of London*, Rupert Hart-Davis 1963.

Mathews, Mrs, *Anecdotes of Actors*, T C Newby 1844.

Nicoll, Allardyce, *The English Theatre*, Nelson 1936.

Parker, John (ed.), *Who's Who in the Theatre*, Pitman 1952, 1961.

Pertwee, Michael, *Name Dropping*, Leslie Frewin Publishers 1974.

Planché, J R, *Recollections and Reflections*, Tinsley 1872.

Richards, Kenneth & Thomson, Peter, *Nineteenth-Century British Theatre*, Methuen 1971.

Rix, Brian, *My Farce From My Elbow*, Secker & Warburg 1975.

    Farce About Face, Hodder & Stoughton 1989.

    Tour de Farce, Hodder & Stoughton 1992.

Rowell, George, *The Victorian Theatre*, OUP 1956.

Sands, Mollie, *Robson of the Olympic*, Society for Theatre Research 1979.

Smith, Leslie, *Modern British Farce*, Macmillan Press 1989.

Travers, Ben, *Vale of Laughter*, Geoffrey Bles 1957.

Scenes from:
Box and Cox by John Maddison Morton (1847).
The Magistrate by Arthur Wing Pinero (1885).
A Cuckoo in the Nest by Ben Travers (1925).
Thark by Ben Travers (1927).
Reluctant Heroes by Colin Morris (1950).
Simple Spymen by John Chapman (1958).

INDEX

201

INDEX OF PLAY TITLES

209